T0330223

Cross-Border Entrepreneurship and Economic Development in Europe's Border Regions

Cross-Border Entrepreneurship and Economic Development in Europe's Border Regions

Edited by

David Smallbone

Professor of Small Business and Entrepreneurship, Small Business Research Centre, Kingston University, UK

Friederike Welter

Jönköping International Business School, Sweden

Mirela Xheneti

University of Sussex, UK

Edward Elgar

Cheltenham, UK • Northampton, MA, USA

Published by
Edward Elgar Publishing Limited
The Lypiatts
15 Lansdown Road
Cheltenham
Glos GL50 2JA
UK

Edward Elgar Publishing, Inc.
William Pratt House
9 Dewey Court
Northampton
Massachusetts 01060
USA

A catalogue record for this book
is available from the British Library

Library of Congress Control Number: 2012939095

ISBN 978 1 84844 768 4

Typeset by Columns Design XML Ltd, Reading
Printed and bound by MPG Books Group, UK

Contents

Figures

Tables

Boxes

Contributors

Elena Aculai, Institute of Economy, Finance and Statistics (IEFS) of the Academy of Sciences of Moldova and the Ministry of Economy of the Republic of Moldova

Georgios Agelopoulos, University of Macedonia, Greece

Nadezhda Alex, formerly University of Siegen, Germany

Adela Bulgac, Institute of Economy, Finance and Statistics (IEFS) of the Academy of Sciences of Moldova and the Ministry of Economy of the Republic of Moldova

Vitalii Gryga, STEPS Centre, National Academy of Sciences of Ukraine, Kiev, Ukraine

Nina Isakova, STEPS Centre, National Academy of Sciences of Ukraine, Kiev, Ukraine

Kostadin Kolarov, University of National and World Economy, Bulgaria

Susanne Kolb, Siegerlandfonds, Germany

Olha Krasovska, STEPS Centre, National Academy of Sciences of Ukraine, Kiev, Ukraine

Lois Labrianidis, University of Macedonia, Greece

Olga Linchevskaya, Institute of Economics, the National Academy of Sciences of Belarus

Bogdan Piasecki, University of Lodz and Academy of Management, Lodz, Poland

Merle Pihlak, Tallinn University of Technology, Estonia

Anna Pobol, Belarusian State University, Belarus

Anna Rogut, University of Lodz and Academy of Management, Lodz, Poland

Marina Slonimska, Vitebsk State Technological University, Belarus

Anton Slonimski, Institute for Economic Research at the Ministry of Economy of Belarus

David Smallbone, Kingston University, UK

Kiril Todorov, University of National and World Economy, Bulgaria

Urve Venesaar, Tallinn University of Technology, Estonia

Nikos Vogiatzis, University of Thessaly, Greece

Efi Voutira, University of Macedonia, Greece

Friederike Welter, Jönköping International Business School, Sweden

Mirela Xheneti, University of Sussex, UK

Peter Zashev, Hanken & SSE Executive Education, Finland

1. Entrepreneurship in Europe's border regions

David Smallbone, Friederike Welter and Mirela Xheneti

INTRODUCING CROSS-BORDER ENTREPRENEURSHIP

This volume is concerned with entrepreneurship and economic development in Europe's border regions, focusing on the effects of EU enlargement, both within the EU and in neighbouring countries. Particular attention is paid to cross-border entrepreneurial activity, which we refer to as cross-border entrepreneurship. A wide range of types of entrepreneurial activity can take place across international borders, from informal shuttle or petty trading activity at one extreme to formalized joint ventures and strategic alliances between enterprises at the other. At a global level, the increasing internationalization of production systems inevitably leads to the development of cross-border operations, in forms that include partnerships of different types. These include subcontracting, joint ventures and franchise arrangements, which can operate at different spatial scales.

Although the existing evidence base is limited, there are examples of cross-border cooperation involving SMEs in different parts of the world, which demonstrates the potential contribution of this type of activity to regional development. For example, the economic success of the southern provinces of China from the 1980s onwards largely came about because of the highly efficient cross-border SME alliances and joint ventures involving mainland Chinese businesses and Hong Kong-based SMEs (Ze-wen et al., 1991). In Europe, a large number of cross-border partnerships have emerged, which involve German and Austrian SMEs working with SMEs in post-Communist economies, such as Poland, Hungary and the Czech Republic, as well as between Greek and Bulgarian SMEs (Huber, 2003; Krätke, 2002; Labrianidis, 1999).

In this context, faced with rapidly changing international market environments, cooperative inter-firm activity may be viewed as a rational strategy for SMEs seeking to respond to competitive pressures with limited internal resources. For entrepreneurs, such cooperation can offer an opportunity to access new markets and/or sources of supply, as well as possible access to sources of capital, labour and/or know-how. For firms located in border regions, which are often economically disadvantaged, cross-border cooperation may offer one of the few opportunities for business development. At the same time, the nature and extent of these opportunities will vary according to the nature of the border, the external environment for entrepreneurship, and characteristics of firms themselves. As a consequence, the nature and extent of this type of cross-border activity is affected by the heterogeneity of border regions, in terms of formal and social institutional structures, linguistics and ethnicity, all of which can influence economic processes long after the demise of formal and physical borders (Huber, 2003; Perkmann, 2005; 2003).

It is equally important to stress that cross-border partnerships must not be seen as a panacea for SMEs facing increasing internationalization forces. Some SMEs in transition and developing countries, in particular, have already experienced the negative effects of foreign companies seeking partners as a short-term expedient, faced with uncertain local market conditions. Such firms may also experience few of the learning benefits that are one of the prime justifications at the micro level for this type of strategy in the longer term.

Cross-border entrepreneurship can provide opportunities for regional development as well as for individual entrepreneurs. This particularly applies in the context of border regions, which are typically peripheral to the core of national economic activity, with few development assets. As a result, creating a policy environment to enable and facilitate productive forms of cross-border cooperation may be a necessary part of the regional development strategies for these border regions. However, the relationship between entrepreneurship development and cross-border cooperation is likely to be a reciprocal one. On the one hand, cross-border cooperation may act as a stimulus for entrepreneurship development in regions that in many respects appear disadvantaged and peripheral. On the other hand, the nature and extent of existing entrepreneurship in a region is likely to affect the level of interest in cross-border cooperation, because it will affect the number of individuals and businesses that seek the markets, suppliers, capital and know-how that cross-border enterprise cooperation potentially offers. Either way, there are implications for the environment for entrepreneurship, and thus for entrepreneurship policy.

Although cross-border cooperation may be viewed as a potential asset for regional development, with potential political, as well as economic benefits, the heterogeneity of border regions and the different levels of economic development, institutional settings and levels of entrepreneurship affect the processes of interaction across borders. These are important features to understand when designing relevant policies to assist in the development of these regions.

THE CONTEXT OF EU ENLARGEMENT

A key part of the context for this volume is the enlargement of the European Union. Without doubt, the process of EU enlargement has redrawn the political map of Europe, with particular implications for regions that are adjacent to the new borders of the EU. This presents entrepreneurs and businesses with new sources of threat and opportunity, which in turn have implications for regional development. The orientation of the new EU members towards the West combined with new regulations for cross-border movement of goods and people may significantly hamper existing cross-border cooperation of individuals and enterprises. On the other hand, cross-border cooperation offers a potential source of opportunity which can lead to enhanced competitiveness for entrepreneurs and businesses on both sides of a border. It may be argued that, unless special measures are taken, enlargement of the European Union will produce negative effects on the adjoining countries, such as Ukraine, Belarus and Moldova, and especially on their border regions.

For firms in the newly independent states (NIS), low domestic purchasing power can limit the scale and scope of domestic markets, encouraging those with ambitions to grow to look abroad to identify and develop new market opportunities. In such circumstances, subcontracting and other forms of collaborative arrangements with foreign firms offer certain advantages, compared with more independent strategies for penetrating foreign markets, since they can reduce market entry costs and barriers, with lower associated business risks. At a household level, cross-border cooperation can present opportunities for entrepreneurial people to engage in trading activities, which, although typically offering a means of survival, can also offer a stepping stone towards the development of more substantial enterprises, for those with substantial entrepreneurial drive. Additionally, institutional cooperation can be instrumental in facilitating sustainable cross-border partnerships between enterprises, contributing to enhanced competitiveness for participating regions.

In changing the shape of Europe, enlargement has resulted in some external borders moving, some internal borders being dissolved, old borders re-emerging, and new borders being established. The status of a number of previous EU border regions (such as in Austria and Germany) have changed from external to internal borders of the EU, and a number of new member states (for example Baltic countries, Czech Republic, Poland and the Former Yugoslav Republic of Macedonia (FYRoM)) have formed new external border regions/borders of the EU as a whole. EU integration has been accompanied by an increase in regional disparities as a result of the concentration of economic activities in capital cities or other core regions (Ezcurra et al., 2007; Petrakos, 2001; Dunford and Smith, 2000). The enlargement process favoured regions in proximity to the EU core, leaving many border regions in a vulnerable position (Monastiriotis, 2008; Hughes et al., 2003). As many border regions are among the more disadvantaged areas in Europe, their development prospects are an important aspect of the enlargement process, emphasizing the potential importance of cross-border interaction and cooperation for economic development purposes.

With the accession of ten new member states, the share of border regions in the total area of the EU increased from 22 per cent in the EU15 to more than 35 per cent in the EU25, while the percentage of the population living in border regions rose from 15 per cent to almost 25 per cent (Niebuhr, 2005). According to the European Commission (2001), regions along the former external EU border, in particular, may experience distinct integration effects because of their proximity to the new member states. In general, these internal border regions are expected to benefit from economic integration in the medium and long term, since increasing cross-border interaction, combined with a favourable location in the enlarged EU market may initiate dynamic growth processes in these areas, although the effects may be differentiated by the pre-existing level of economic development.

However, in the short run, internal border regions might face pronounced adjustment pressures due to increased competition in product and labour markets (Niebuhr, 2005). Regions with internal borders within the EU are not regarded by the European Commission as principally disadvantaged, whereas external border regions (that is, areas along the external EU borders), are assumed to be in a more difficult situation. This particularly applies to regions along the eastern borders of new member states. Hypothesized effects of recent and planned enlargement of the EU may be drawn from the experience of previous enlargements. In considering possible implications for border regions, it is important to note indirect influences through, for example, the effect of enlargement on national economies, as well as direct effects on border regions.

In the 1990s, Western European integration was strengthened by the creation of the Single Market in Europe, the EU accession of three EFTA member countries and by the introduction of the single currency (Fidrmuc et al., 2002, p. 46). The general view is that EU enlargements have changed the external business environment, offering new markets and challenges for entrepreneurs in all countries, but also threats (for example Lejour et al.,

2001; Brücker, 2001), particularly for weaker regions and weaker firms (for example Smallbone et al., 1999). Each of the previous enlargements has brought challenges, but it has been suggested that the nature and potential scale of Eastern enlargement is both the largest and most challenging to date (for example Lejour et al., 2001).

Eastern enlargement is also qualitatively different from earlier rounds, because it includes very different countries compared to existing members and occurred in a more integrated environment (Bellak, 2004). Brenton (2002, p. 1), for example, has noted that Eastern enlargement has four key differences compared with earlier enlargements: a broader dispersion of income levels; new members are transition countries on their way from centrally planned towards market economies; more EU legislation has to be adopted; and a substantial degree of pre-accession integration exists. In order for Central and Eastern European countries (CEECs) to join the EU, a number of conditions had to be met: the existence of a market economy; the capacity to withstand competitive pressures; and the capacity to take over and implement the *acquis communautaire* (EU law and regulations) (Grabbe and Hughes, 1998; Lavigne, 1998).

Although Eastern enlargement has expanded the population of the EU by about one-fifth, new member states only account for 4.6 per cent of the GDP of the enlarged EU (Trichet, 2004), reflecting the low per capita income levels in CEE countries. The process of catching-up assumes positive implications for economic growth and welfare, as well as fostering economic and financial integration. The enlarged EU represents the world's largest unified market, accounting for about one-quarter of total world trade and global income (Trichet, 2004). These changes create new conditions for enterprises, both in new member states (for example rapid trade expansion to the EU), and existing members (for example also new markets for goods; FDI to CEECs), but there are also threats.

THE PROJECTS

This volume is based on research undertaken in two related projects. These are briefly described below, although key findings are found throughout the book. The two projects had broadly similar objectives and common leadership, although the geographical focus was different, as was the level of funding. Project One focused on regions in the NIS that had borders with EU member states, whereas Project Two was concerned with border regions within EU member states. There was also some difference in timescale between the two projects. Nevertheless, the results are complementary as they focus on regions on different sides of the EU border. Both projects operated with local partners[1] in each country, who are responsible for the data collection within their country.

Project One: Cross-Border Cooperation in Belarus, Moldova and Ukraine and EU Enlargement (2005–07)

Funded under the INTAS[2] scheme, this project investigated the nature, extent and forms of cross-border cooperation in Ukraine, Belarus and Moldova in border regions with EU members and upcoming accession states, in order to assess its contribution to entrepreneurship, economic and social transformation. Key themes were the potential of cross-border entrepreneurial partnerships for economic development; the role of trust and learning in relation to cross-border cooperation; and the effects of EU enlargement. Interviews were conducted with representatives of households and enterprises in each of the case study regions. A total of 300 in-depth interviews were conducted face to face with representatives of institutions (10 per region), enterprises (20 per region) and households (10 per region) in Belarus, Moldova and the Ukraine.

Project Two: Cross-Border Cooperation and Entrepreneurship Development (CBCED) (2006–08)

Funded under the EU Framework VI programme, the CBCED project was concerned with entrepreneurship in EU border regions, focusing on cross-border cooperation. Through its focus on economic development, CBCED complemented previous projects (that is, EUDIMENSIONS, EXLINEA) which had investigated other aspects of cross-border cooperation. CBCED sought to contribute to evidence-based approaches to policy development with respect to cross-border entrepreneurship. The project has analysed the implications of EU enlargement on entrepreneurship development in different types of border regions and assessed the potential for cross-border entrepreneurship contributing to regional development, in EU border regions. A total of 510 in-depth interviews were conducted face to face with key institutional informants and business support organizations (15 per region), enterprises (15–20 per region) and households (10–15 per region).

Specific issues investigated include the effect of border changes on the perception of entrepreneurs and institutional actors, with respect to regional identity; the scope for the development of emerging clusters of economic activity in border regions; and assessing the role of individual and collective learning at the regional level, as well as personal and institutional trust, for fostering or impeding cross-border cooperation and its contribution to

economic development. A key element was to make practical recommendations to policy makers and practitioners in the fields of entrepreneurship and
economic development, concerning cross-border cooperation, which were
presented at a workshop in Brussels at the end of the project in the form of a
policy briefing.

In both projects, the methodology employed included a review of the
existing evidence base and relevant theoretical literature. It focused on eight
case studies of border regions in Project One and 12 case studies of border
regions in Project Two, each of which involved a combination of secondary
data and primary, empirical investigation. As well as interviewing the
owners and managers of businesses of different sizes that were, or had been,
involved in cross-border cooperation, in each case study region the
researchers investigated the experience of local actors, such as local authorities, business associations, business support organizations and informal
network groups, with respect to different forms of formal and informal
cooperation across borders. In order to capture a wide range of entrepreneurial activity, individual traders and households were included. In analysing the scope and nature of cross-border cooperation, the project
particularly focused on the role of trust, and on individual and collective
learning, assessed in relation to other factors, as influences on the success of
these cross-border relationships, in terms of their longevity and the benefits
that accrue to the respective partners.

INTRODUCING THE CASE STUDY REGIONS

Empirical investigation was conducted in a total of 20 regions: eight in
Project One and 12 in Project Two. The case study border regions were
located in Belarus, Finland, Germany, Moldova, Poland, Greece, Ukraine,
Bulgaria and Estonia. Each of the case study regions (CSRs) is briefly
described in the rest of this section. These summaries are intended to
provide a context for the detailed description of cross-border entrepreneurship in subsequent chapters.

Project One

In this project, empirical investigation was undertaken in three border
regions in Belarus and Ukraine and two regions in Moldova, which is a
much smaller country. In Belarus, the regions studied included Grodno,
which borders Poland and Lithuania; Brest, bordering Poland and Ukraine;
and Vitebsk, which borders Lithuania, Latvia and Russia. Official statistical
data for the number of small enterprises and individual entrepreneurs per

Notes:
CBCED regions: Tornio (1) and South Karelia (2) in Finland; Ida Viru (3) and South East
Estonia (4) in Estonia; Biała Podlaska (5) and Zgorzelec (6) in Poland; Gorlitz (6) and
Hochfranken (7) in Germany; Kyustendil (8) and Petrich (9) in Bulgaria; and Serres (9) and
Florina (10) in Greece.
INTAS regions: Western Ukraine (11) in Ukraine; Cahul district (12) and Edinet district (13)
in Moldova; Grodno (14), Brest (15) and Vitebsk (16) in Belarus.

Source: Adapted from http://www.nationsonline.org.

Figure 1.1   Map of the case study regions

1000 inhabitants reveals a higher level of entrepreneurial activity in the population in the regions containing Vitebsk and Grodno compared with Brest.

In Ukraine, the empirical investigation was undertaken in three border regions of western Ukraine: the Lviv, Volyn and Zakarpattya regions, which have common borders with Poland, Slovakia, Hungary and Romania. The three regions comprise 9 per cent of the total territory of Ukraine and 10 per cent of its population. The population density in the Lviv and Zakarpattya regions is above the Ukrainian average, whilst the Volyn region is less populated. The level of small business development in the Lviv and Zakarpattya regions (at 62 and 60 small enterprises per 10 000 inhabitants) is close to the Ukrainian average (60), but it is lower in the Volyn region (45 small enterprises per 10 000 inhabitants). All three of these regions in western Ukraine have suffered from a high level of emigration, related to a reduction of employment opportunities at home. Lviv and Zakarpattya belong to the Carpathian Euroregion territory and Volyn is part of the Bug Euroregion.

In Moldova, the case study regions included the Cahul district in the southern part of the country, and the Edinet district in the north. Both districts have a common border with Romania and are members of Euroregions. Cahul district is part of the Lower Danube Euroregion and Edinet district is part of the Upper Prut Euroregion.

Project Two

This project conducted empirical investigation in 12 case study regions (CSRs), two in each of the following countries: Finland, Germany, Poland, Greece, Bulgaria and Estonia.

Finland
Tornio is located in the Finnish Lapland bordering Sweden. It is a scarcely populated area, even in Finnish terms. This is why a medium-sized town such as Tornio has grown into an economically important centre. The economy of this CSR relies heavily on industry, particularly the paper and metal industries and IT. Proximity to Sweden has contributed to the growth of Tornio. Key issues for this CSR focus on employment, because of difficulties in attracting and retaining skilled labour, although the unemployment rate remains high. For the educated young people, southern Finland has a strong attraction. Unlike some other borders in the EU member states, the Finnish–Swedish border was never meant to truly keep people away from each other and thus was never perceived to be a true obstacle to cross-border cooperation. Furthermore, unlike other European

cross-border regions, the people living in Tornio–Haparanda and the surrounding regions always had a strong regional identity, which certainly helped to avoid the national rivalries and sometimes bitterness that exists in other regions due to a common history or different national cultures and values.

South Karelia borders the Finnish regions of Kymenlaakso, Southern Savonia, and North Karelia. It is an external border for Finland and for the EU with Russia. Soviet times were also of little help to local cross-border cooperation as the border was almost closed and all cooperation was settled in centralized talks between Moscow and Helsinki. In terms of economic development, South Karelia has a lower GDP than the average for Finland, although GDP per capita is higher than the average for EU27 countries. The region is heavily dependent on the forestry industry. There are a few large companies in the paper industry, which has traditionally provided stable employment; this has not encouraged the development of a culture of entrepreneurship. The number of SMEs in the region is somewhat smaller than in other regions, due to the dominance of large-scale industry in the region.

Germany
Görlitz is the easternmost town in Germany, situated on the river Neisse. After World War II, the Treaty of Potsdam divided Görlitz into a German part on the western side of the Neisse and a Polish part named Zgorzelec, making it a good example of a border artificially dividing what was previously a single functional unit. The impact of the political division was intensified by the displacement of Germans and Poles. The German inhabitants were forced to move behind the newly established border to Görlitz, while the eastern part of Görlitz was taken over by the Soviet military. The GDP per capita of Görlitz has continually been below the level for Germany as a whole, although in 2003 Görlitz showed the strongest economic development of the administrative district of Dresden, of which it is part. Historically, Görlitz has been an important location for the textile, optical, electronic and metal industries, as well as for vehicle construction and engineering. It is characterized by small enterprises and its main competencies are in the fields of machine construction, logistics and railway engineering. Enterprises in ICT and biotechnology have also settled in the region. However, the overall number of enterprises in the region is low.

Hochfranken is situated in North Bavaria, at the Bavarian–Czech border. Hochfranken is an old industrial region, with the main industrial resources in the fields of ceramics, glass and porcelain, as well as textiles. Hochfranken has a well developed transport infrastructure. The region is characterized by a prevalence of SMEs. The EU Eastern enlargement has aggravated the region's weaknesses, although some businesses shifted their production to the Czech Republic to take advantage of lower wage costs. Historically, the regions on both the German and Czech side of the border have a turbulent common history. After World War II, Sudeten Germans living in the border regions of Czechoslovakia were forced out of the country, and their property was confiscated by the Czechoslovakian state. At the same time Czech and Slovak people as well as other minorities were resettled in the border regions, thus probably impeding the creation of a consistent border identity on the Czech side. Hand in hand with the changing political and historical situation, long-standing relations were revived and new relations emerged. The main problems in developing cross-border activities in Hochfranken are the language barrier, differing mentalities and diverging socializations as well as the historical background of both nations.

Poland

Zgorzelec is located close to the borders with Germany and the Czech Republic, which is undoubtedly an advantage for economic development and cross-border activity. The accession of Poland and the Czech Republic to the EU in 2004 reinforced this by moving the region from the periphery to the centre of the EU. The economy is fairly diversified, covering manufacturing, construction, market and non-market services. The majority of enterprises in the area (about 40 per cent) operate in trade, with only 8.5 per cent in production and 8.8 per cent in construction. The rest provide services. After World War II, previously German populated areas such as Zgorzelec experienced the deportation of Germans and the settling in of people from eastern Poland. A number of Ukrainians, Lithuanians, Latvians and Belarusians, who had been sent there as forced labour, also inhabit Zgorzelec. Present-day inhabitants of Zgorzelec have acquired substantial openness to other nations, cultures and religions, as well as open mindedness to cooperation and international initiatives as a result of their history.

Biała Podlaska borders the Brest region of Belarus. Although Biała Podlaska is part of the Lublin region, the city of Biała Podlaska is closer to Brest than it is to Lublin. Economic changes and administrative reforms have meant that Biała Podlaska increasingly plays a subsidiary role in the Lublin region, with an increasing centralization of economic and political power in the city of Lublin. EU enlargement has led to a significant change in cross-border activity, which was substantial up to 2004 due to historic links and the fact that no visas were required. The economy of Biała Podlaska County is based on agriculture, which gives employment to over 60 per cent of the working population. Both private and public sector services are important employers in the county. The main difficulties in the development of cross-border cooperation are related to the consequences of the post-integration sealing of the border and more tense relations between Poland and Belarus at the national level. This has limited cross-border cooperation between SMEs, mainly due to the formal requirements related to crossing the border and problems with shipping goods.

Greece

Florina is located in the region of Western Macedonia in Greece, bordering FYRoM to the north and Albania to the east. The regional economy is small in size and faces extensive economic problems, including low levels of GDP, high unemployment and absence of investment activities. The region is mainly agricultural with only limited manufacturing activity in small units in the food and drinks industry and in the field of electric power production based on lignite. The business sector in Florina, as elsewhere in Greece, is characterized by small enterprises. Historical and cultural factors are an important part of the external environment alongside political and economic influences. In fact, commercial exchanges with the northern side of the border were common until 1994 when the Greek state imposed an embargo following the dispute over the use of the name 'Macedonia'. Another feature of Florina is the existence of an important Slav-speaking (bilingual) population, which is a result of population movements and exchanges during and after the dissolution of the Ottoman Empire (1912–14). This part of the population has kinship ties across the border in the FYRoM. The same applies to some Greek-speaking people on the FYRoM side of the border, who have links with the Greek side.

Serres is located in north-eastern Greek Macedonia, bordering the southeast region of FYRoM to the north-west and the Bulgarian district of Blagoevgrad to the north. Serres is mainly an agricultural region, particularly supporting livestock. The main economic problems are related to the agricultural sector: the small size of the agricultural units (and the high fixed costs), the low educational level of the farmers and the strong competition the area faces. Serres is also facing problems related to an ageing population and migration towards more developed areas in Greece. The borders were established after the Balkan Wars (1912–14). Despite hostilities between the Balkan states during the inter-war period, these borders were quite 'soft', due to the fact that people living on the two sides of the border shared common economic and social structures dating from the period of the Ottoman Empire. After World War II, the Greek–Bulgarian borders became 'hard' borders until the early 1990s. After Bulgaria's accession to the EU, the border has softened. There is a free movement of people and capital between the two countries, and border controls are gradually loosening.

Bulgaria

Petrich is situated in south-west Bulgaria, bordering Greece and the Former Yugoslav Republic of Macedonia (FYRoM). Petrich is one of the most fertile areas in Bulgaria, especially with regard to the growing of fruit and vegetables. It is also rich in mineral waters, which offers good opportunities for the development of recreational businesses. The E79 Sofia–Kulata–Greece road (connecting Sofia and Thessalonica) and the Zlatarevo–Strumica–Petrich–Sofia motorway pass through Petrich, both of which are important to the region in terms of its economic development and history of cross-border cooperation. Petrich has an industrial-agrarian economy and produces less than 5 per cent of the country's GDP. GDP per capita in Petrich is around 79 per cent of the national average, although Bulgaria as a whole has a GDP per capita averaging 43 per cent of EU27 GDP in 2008.[3] In terms of private sector development in the area, the leading sectors are light industries – clothing, wood processing, furniture, trade and repairing services, agriculture, warehousing and communications. Around 70 per cent of the industrial enterprises are joint-venture companies with foreign investors, mainly from Greece.

Kyustendil is situated in the south-western part of Bulgaria, bordering FYRoM and Serbia. Kyustendil has an industrial-agrarian economy, creating less than 5 per cent of the country's GDP. GDP per capita in Kyustendil has decreased, mainly because of large enterprise closures and restructuring and the out-migration of the region's population to the larger cities of the country. Both industry and services are dominated by SMEs – 90.1 per cent and 99.8 per cent respectively. Local entrepreneurship is weak as a result of a diminishing local market and low purchasing power of the local, ageing population. Many local firms operating in the production sector lack sufficient technological and financial capacity, resulting in low competitiveness. There is strong interest from Greek traders in Bulgarian foods produced in Kyustendil factories. However, the ordered quantities required by Greek customers are often too large for local producers, which restricts their ability to compete in the EU. The main (formal) barrier affecting the scope for cross-border cooperation (CBC) in the region is the visa regime for the citizens of Macedonia and Serbia introduced on 1 January 2007. There are no significant informal barriers to CBC, but there are prejudices, stereotypes or misunderstanding of the different cultural characteristics and customs across the border.

Estonia

The south-eastern region of Estonia borders Russia and Latvia. It is a former agricultural area that experienced sharp economic decline during the period of economic reforms. As a result it is now an economically weak region when compared to the Estonian average level of development. The region is characterized by an aged population and a large number of inactive working-age people. In south-east Estonia there is less capital and less foreign investment than in other regions in the country. The poor quality of infrastructure, low density of population and incoherent governmental regional policy do not favour foreign investments in this border region. The development of the region has been influenced by the re-marking of the Estonian–Russian border in 1991, which severely disrupted the local transport infrastructure.

Ida-Viru County is the second largest county by population in Estonia. A previously industrial region, the county is now economically weak compared with other counties in Estonia. GDP per capita in Ida-Viru County was 66.6 per cent of the Estonian average in 2005. Unemployment problems, due to the disappearance and restructuring of large industrial enterprises, together with the largest non-Estonian population in the country have created a situation where conditions for the development of the region are more complicated than in other parts of Estonia. In terms of cultural and economic relations between Ida-Viru county and Russia, more than 45 years of coexistence during the Soviet period have helped the regions to know each other well, and have facilitated the development of rich historical–cultural traditions. Estonia's independence caused relations between Estonia and Russia to worsen, and caused tensions and instability in the relationship. However, having population in both towns speaking the same language and sharing a close ethnic and cultural identity, helps to overcome the distrust and tensions, and to redevelop cross-border cooperation. A common language of communication is a good precondition for cooperation, but it also creates problems with integrating local people in the Estonian society and causes isolation of the region.

INTRODUCING THE CHAPTERS

The rest of the book consists of 10 chapters, which are divided into four main parts: conceptual issues; regional case studies from the EU; regional cases from the NIS; and finally policy perspectives.

In Chapter 2, Urve Venesaar and Merle Pihlak set the scene by identifying the consequences of EU enlargement for economic development in border regions. In assessing the enlargement-related effects, the authors stress the difference between soft, internal borders of two EU member states and hard external borders of the EU with non-member countries. Enlargement has removed many internal borders, such as those between Poland and Germany, thereby opening up new business opportunities. Alongside this, external borders have been strengthened to improve security, which in some cases makes cross-border cooperation more difficult.

Another important point stressed in Chapter 2 is the role of the regional context in enabling and/or constraining the development of entrepreneurship. Both the needs and potential of border regions depend on a number of social, cultural, economic, historical and institutional characteristics, which together create an external environment for entrepreneurship development. One of the emerging propositions is that the potential for regional economic development, including the development of entrepreneurship and cross-border cooperation, is likely to be affected by characteristics of the regions themselves.

Chapter 3 by Friederike Welter, Nadezhda Alex and Susanne Kolb consider the role of trust and learning in cross-border entrepreneurship. It is widely recognized that trust is an essential ingredient in successful networks, providing the glue which holds networks together. Similarly in a cross-border context, trust might be expected to play a particularly important role at the macro level because of the risks inherent in cross-border transactions. As a consequence, a priori, one would expect trust between cross-border partners to be high in the case of cooperation which is lasting and successful. Essentially, trust assists individuals in controlling risk and reducing the costs connected with each border crossing. Trust and learning are closely linked, although learning can happen independently of trust, but it can also be an outcome of trust and can influence trust building.

Two regional cases from the EU are presented in the second part of the book. The first is the case of Görlitz–Zgorzelec, which Anna Rogut and Friederike Welter present as an example of cross-border cooperation within an enlarged Europe (Chapter 4). There is a long history of cross-border cooperation in Görlitz–Zgorzelec, which includes institutional cooperation, in some cases funded through participation in EU programmes. Institutional cross-border cooperation has been accompanied by the development of spontaneous cooperation between companies and households, undertaken with or without the support of programmes and public resources. Prior to Poland's entry to the European Union, cross-border activity was stimulated by differences in prices, labour costs and regulations. However, in the post-accession period such differences have been gradually diminishing (European Commission, 2007; Rogut, 2008; Rokicki and Żołnowski, 2008), which in turn has led to a search for new sources of mutual benefit.

Chapter 5 is drawn from southern Europe. Lois Labrianidis, Kiril Todorov, Georgios Agelopoulos, Efi Voutira, Kostadin Kolarov and Nikos Vogiatzis describe the situation with respect to cross-border cooperation in the Bulgaria–Greece–FYRoM triangle. This case clearly demonstrates the role of context in shaping contemporary cross-border relationships better than any other in the book. This part of Europe is one of the most fragmented, based on small regional economies with competing historical memories of the past, conflicting notions of ownership and belonging, perpetuated by the presence of ethnic minorities that inhabit shared borders. Paradoxically, perhaps, substantial cross-border capital flows are occurring between the more and less developed areas in the Balkan region as a whole. The case also demonstrates how political disputes concerning use of the name 'Macedonia' have not prevented entrepreneurial people from developing significant cross-border cooperation on the ground.

The next part also contains regional case studies, but this time from the NIS: three from Ukraine and Belarus and two from Moldova. In Chapter 6, Elena Aculai and Adela Bulgac discuss the effects of EU enlargement on SME development in Moldova's border regions. For Moldova, the significant change came in 2007 when Romania joined the EU. Whilst there may be spillover benefits into Moldova in the longer term, a tightening of the visa and customs regimes has made cross-border entrepreneurial activity more difficult, which is a familiar story in countries located at the hard external borders of the EU. Moldovan entrepreneurs also complain that the Romanian market has become increasingly competitive as the number of foreign companies active in the market has increased.

Chapter 7 by Nina Isakova, Vitalii Gryga and Olha Krasovska focuses on innovative SMEs in western Ukraine. Ukraine remains a difficult environment for the development of entrepreneurship, with the regulatory environment for business remaining full of holes. SMEs seeking to innovate face all the problems that other SMEs face but with additional issues. As a consequence, it is not surprising that the level of innovation in Ukrainian SMEs is low due to the scarcity of internal capital and other resources, a lack of venture capital in the country and limited cooperative links with new knowledge producers. In this context, as some of the enterprise case studies demonstrate, SMEs in peripheral border regions can address some of these deficiencies by engaging in cross-border cooperation with Western business partners.

In Chapter 8, Anton Slonimski, Anna Pobol, Olga Linchevskaya, and Marina Slonimska describe household involvement in cross-border trading and entrepreneurship in Belarus. In this chapter, the focus shifts from cooperation between enterprises to a simpler form of cross-border trading activity involving households and individuals. However, as the research revealed, a simple concept can be complex in its organization. Moreover, the nature of shuttle trading presented a methodological challenge, particularly with respect to data collection, illustrated in the chapter. Once again the historical and regional context is an essential part of the analysis of the shuttle trading phenomenon. Cross-border cooperation in the western regions of Belarus with Poland, Latvia and Lithuania has deep roots in the history of the region.

The final part contains three chapters dealing with various policy perspectives. Chapter 9, by Peter Zashev, is concerned with cluster development and cluster policies in border regions. Having reviewed the main problems faced at the regional level in cluster development and policy making, the author offers a concrete set of recommended measures. There is much discussion these days about improving the relationship between research and policy as part of an attempt to make policy more evidence-based; as this chapter demonstrates clustering is one area where the gap between research evidence and public policy is the greatest.

In Chapter 10, Anna Rogut and Bogdan Piasecki shift the focus from policy intervention to the governance structures and practices, from the perspective of cross-border cooperation. Essentially the pressure for change stems, on the one hand, from regulatory arrangements shifting from the national scale upwards to supra-national or global scales downwards to the individual body, or local, urban or regional configurations; whilst on the other hand, economic activities and inter-firm networks are becoming simultaneously more localized/regionalized and transnational. Clearly such trends present a major challenge to traditional regional and industrial policies and more particularly to the governance of them.

In this context, the chapter outlines the diversity of governance structures and practices in Poland and presents their impact on the scale, intensity, nature, and effects of cross-border cooperation. The results presented indicate a degree of diversification in governance structures and practices in Poland in response to the diversity of political and socio-cultural contexts in which cross-border cooperation is conducted. The political context focuses on the implications of Poland's membership of the EU, which has changed the status of some borders, and the dissimilarity versus similarity of the political systems which form the principal framework conditions for cross-border cooperation in both Polish case study regions.

Finally, in Chapter 11, David Smallbone and Mirela Xheneti examine the role of public policy as an enabling or constraining influence on cross-border entrepreneurship. Creating a policy environment to facilitate productive forms of cross-border entrepreneurship may be viewed as a necessary part of the regional development strategies for these border regions. However, it is typically more difficult to achieve in situations where the border is a 'hard' external border of the EU where border controls represent a potential barrier to movement. A broad view is necessarily taken of what constitutes policy, in other words, the effects of government policies and actions on entrepreneurship and cross-border activity rather than a narrower focus on so-called entrepreneurship policies. This is operationalized by using a simple typology which divides policies into those that directly affect cross-border entrepreneurial activities (such as partner search facilities, cross-border databases, for example of regulations) and those that indirectly do so.

NOTES

1. Project One: Coordinator: Professor Dr Friederike Welter, at that time RWI Essen, Germany; Professor David Smallbone, Small Business Research Centre, Kingston University, UK; Dr Nina Isakova, Centre for Scientific and Technological Potential, Ukraine; Dr Anton Slonimski, Economic Research Institute, Belarus; Dr Elena Aculai, National Institute of Economy and Information, Moldova. Project Two: Coordinator: Professor David Smallbone, Small Business Research Centre, Kingston University, UK; Professor Dr Friederike Welter, at that time RWI Essen and University of Siegen, Germany; Professor Anna Rogut, Entrepreneurship and Economic Development Research Institute, Lodz, Poland; Professor Kari Liuhto, Pan-European Institute, Turku School of Economics and Business Administration, Finland; Professor Dr Kiril Todorov, Entrepreneurship Development Centre, University of National and World Economy, Bulgaria; Urve Venesaar, Department of Business Administration, School of Economics and Business Administration, Tallinn University of Technology, Estonia; Professor Lois Labrianidis, University of Macedonia (UoM).
2. INTAS is an independent international association whose members include the European Union (EU), the EU member states and further countries of the world. The primary objective of INTAS is the promotion of scientific cooperation between the INTAS member states and the members of the Commonwealth of Independent States.
3. http://epp.eurostat.ec.europa.eu/statistics_explained/index.php/National_accounts_%E2%80%93_GDP.

REFERENCES

Bellak, C. (2004), 'The impact of enlargement on the race for FDI', Vienna University of Economics and B.A. Working Paper no. 86, Vienna: University of Economics.

Brenton, P. (2002), 'The economic impact of enlargement on the European economy: problems and perspectives', CEPS Working Document no. 188, Brussels: Centre for European Policy Studies.

Brücker, H. (2001), 'The impact of Eastern enlargement on EU labour markets', German Institute for Economic Research (DIW Berlin), Berlin: Deutsch-Französisches Wirtschaftsforum.

Commission of the European Communities (2001), 'Communication from the Commission on the Impact of Enlargement on Regions Bordering Candidate Countries: community action for border regions', Brussels: Commission of the European Communities.

Dunford, M. and A. Smith (2000), 'Catching up or falling behind? Economic performance and regional trajectories in the "New Europe"', *Economic Geography*, **76**(2), 169–95.

Eczurra, R., P. Pascual and M. Rapun (2007), 'The dynamics of regional disparities in Central and Eastern Europe during transition', *European Planning Studies*, **15**(10), 1397–421.

European Commission (2007), 'EU enlargement and multi-level governance in European regional and environment policies: patterns of learning, adaptation and Europeanization among cohesion countries (Greece, Ireland, Portugal) and lessons for new members (Hungary, Poland): ADAPT', final report, Luxembourg: European Communities.

Fidrmuc, J., G. Moser, W. Pointner, D. Ritzberger-Grünwald, P. Schmidt, M. Schneider, A. Schober-Rhomberg and B. Weber (2002), 'EU enlargement to the East: effects on the EU-15 in general and on Austria in particular: an overview of the literature on selected aspects', *Focus on Transition*, **1**, 44–70.

Grabbe, H. and K. Hughes (1998), *Enlarging the EU Eastwards*, Chatham House Papers, London: RIIA/Printer.

Huber, P.B. (2003), 'On the determinants of cross-border cooperation of Austrian firms with Central and Eastern European partners', *Regional Studies*, **37**(9), 947–55.

Hughes J., G. Sasse and C. Gordon (2003), 'EU enlargement and power asymmetries: conditionality and the Commission's role in regionalisation in Central and Eastern Europe', ESRC 'One Europe or several?', Programme Working Paper no. 49/03, Sussex European Institute, University of Sussex.

Krätke, S. (2002), 'Cross-border cooperation and regional development in the German–Polish border area', in M. Perkmann and N.L. Sum (eds), *Globalization, Regionalization and Cross-border Regions*, Basingstoke: Palgrave, pp. 125–50.

Labrianidis, L. (1999), 'The investment activity of Greek companies in CEE countries: the situation beyond the myth', in E. Andrikopoulou and G. Kafkalas (eds), *Greece and the New European Space: The Enlargement and New Geography of European Development*, Athens: Themelio.

Lavigne, M. (1998), 'Conditions for accession to the EU', *Comparative Economic Systems*, **40**(3), 38–47.

Lejour, A.M., R.A. de Mooij and R. Nahuis (2001), 'EU Enlargement: economic implications for countries and industries', CPB Document no. 011, available at: http://www.cpb.nl/sites/default/files/publicaties/download/eu-enlargement-economic-implications-countries-and-industries.pdf, accessed 18 July 2011.

Monastiriotis, V. (2008), 'The emergence of regional policy in Bulgaria: regional problems, EU influences and domestic constraints', GreeSE Paper no. 15, Hellenic Observatory Papers on Greece and South East Europe, The European Institute, London School of Economics.

Niebuhr, A. (2005), 'The Impact of EU Enlargement on European Border Regions', HWWA Discussion Paper no. 330, Hamburg: Hamburg Institute of International Economics.

Perkmann, M. (2003), 'Cross-border regions in Europe: significance and drivers of regional cross border cooperation', *European Urban and Regional Planning Studies*, **10**(2), 153–71.

Perkmann, M. (2005), 'Cross-border co-operation as policy entrepreneurship: explaining the variable success of European cross-border regions', CSGR Working Paper no. 166/05, Warwick.

Petrakos, G. (2001), 'Patterns of regional inequality in transition economies', *European Planning Studies*, **9**(3), 359–83.

Rogut, A. (ed.) (2008), *Potencjał polskich MSP w zakresie absorbowania korzyści integracyjnych*, Lodz: Wydawnictwo Uniwersytetu Łodzkiego.

Rokicki, B. and A. Żołnowski (2008), 'Ogólne aspekty gospodarcze', in UKIE (ed.), *Cztery lata członkostwa Polcki w UE. Bilans kosztów i korzyści społecznogospodarczych*, Warsaw: Urząd Komitetu Integracji Europejskiej, pp. 15–33.

Smallbone, D., B. Piasecki, U. Venesaar, K. Todorov and L. Labrianidis (1999), 'Internationalisation and SME development in transition economies: an international comparison', *Journal of Small Business and Enterprise Development*, **5**(4), 363–75.

Trichet, J.C. (2004), 'EU enlargement: challenges and opportunities', keynote speech at the conference 'Europe's Frontiers: EU Enlargement – Its Implications and Consequences, 27 October, Lisbon: Calouste Gulbenkian Foundation.

Ze-Wen, G. et al. (1991), 'Technological characteristics and change in small industrial enterprises in Guangdong Province, China', in A. Bhalla (ed.), *Small and Medium Enterprises: Technology Policies and Options*, London: Intermediate Technology Publications.

PART I

Conceptual Issues

2. Consequences of EU enlargement for economic development in border regions

Urve Venesaar and Merle Pihlak

INTRODUCTION

Recent EU enlargements have changed the status of regions and borders in Europe by creating new internal and external border regions. The location of regions near the internal or external border of the EU determines the conditions for crossing the border for goods and people and consequently the challenges for cross-border cooperation. As many border regions are among the more disadvantaged regions in Europe, the development prospects of border regions are an important aspect of the enlargement process, emphasizing the potential importance of cross-border interaction and cooperation for economic development purposes.

In addition, the removal or emergence of border-related barriers that have accompanied EU enlargement has not been undertaken in isolation. There have also been other impacts and changes in the business environment, such as opening of the market, increased competition or decrease in the number of customers, that pose new opportunities but also threats for the development of entrepreneurship and cross-border cooperation (CBC) in economically less-developed border regions. EU enlargement has removed borders between member states, thereby opening markets whilst also increasing competition, but at the same time the EU has tightened external borders (that is, decreasing customers) to enhance its security (Williams, 2007). As external borders have become tighter, regional cooperation with neighbouring countries has become more difficult. In terms of the level of development and entrepreneurship activity, peripheral border regions tend to be lagging behind compared with other regions of the countries (Weise et al., 2001; Bachtler et al., 2000; Platon and Antonescu, 2001). At the same time the development of cross-border relations by the institutions of these regions and internationalization of enterprises through cross-border co-operation could provide additional possibilities for new developments in the future.

In a number of previous studies, authors have pointed out regional differences, which may be taken into account when analysing possible development prospects in border regions. Previous research has mainly concentrated on macroeconomic effects, labour market (for example migration issues), foreign trade and investment, or on particular regions (for example Baldwin and Venables, 1995; Bellak, 2004; Fidrmuc et al., 2002; Zuleeg, 2002). The evidence suggests that as far as Central and Eastern European economies are concerned, there is considerable variation among countries, reflecting differences in the types of industries, degrees of capital intensity, and ability to comply with the requirements of the *acquis communautaire* (Carlin et al., 1999; Kaitila, 2001). Both the needs and potential of border regions depend on a number of socio-economic characteristics (for example location, resources, economic, historical, social and cultural factors), which create an external environment for business development and may be a basis for an assessment of regional differences and EU enlargement effects. In this regard, one of the underlying hypotheses is that the potential for regional economic development, including the development of entrepreneurship and cross-border cooperation, is likely to be affected by characteristics of the regions themselves. This refers to a need for developing a relevant regional typology as a basis for further analysis and assessment of EU enlargement effects in different regions.

Based on the above-mentioned aspects, the objective of this chapter is to analyse the consequences of EU enlargement for economic development in border regions affected by border-related effects, such as the removal/emergence of visa requirements, customs duties, border queues, clearing formalities, quantitative and item restrictions on goods, and double tariffs. But border regions are also affected by wider socio-economic changes, such as changes in trade regimes, and in the institutional and business environment including competition, which in turn influence entrepreneurship and socio-economic development in these regions. Cross-border entrepreneurship may be viewed as a form of internationalization for enterprises, which can contribute to economic development in border regions, through the generation of external income with associated multiplier effects.

This chapter is based on a review of key literature relevant to the effects of EU enlargement on regional economic development in border regions. The initial review was undertaken in the EU's sixth framework programme project 'Challenges and Prospects of Cross-Border Cooperation in the Context of EU Enlargement' (CBCED, 2006–2008). Following the introduction, the next two sections are dedicated to the EU enlargement effects, associated with changes in border regulations and the socio-economic conditions of regions. After that, regional differences (that is, typology aspects) are considered as a key factor influencing the EU enlargement effect, and further regional development is analysed. Next, the idea for the development of a typology of cross-border regions is presented. The chapter ends with brief conclusions.

BORDER-RELATED EU ENLARGEMENT EFFECTS

EU enlargement effects related to border issues can be divided into: (1) measures of foreign trade policy related to the free movement of goods, services and capital between member states and common trade regulations for third countries; and (2) visa policy related to free movement of people between member states and restrictions for third country nationals. The process of economic integration has involved the removal of internal barriers, while strengthening external ones. The factors influencing the development of entrepreneurship at a regional level that were most influenced by changes in the status of borders, included the degree of complication of procedures, and the speed and cost of movement of goods, services and people across the border. The emergence of 'soft' borders inside the EU generally simplified matters, and 'hard' borders with third countries restricted cooperation and communication.

In a political sense, enlargement has changed the nature of relations between countries. For example, before enlargement, Central and Eastern European countries were dealt with by the EU as part of its external relations policy, but after EU entry, new member states have been dealt with as EU internal issues. Integration into the EU is viewed as crucial for the long-term stability and prosperity of individual countries, as well as for Europe as a whole. On the other hand, relations between new member states and third countries have been changed as a result of the implementation of EU common foreign trade and visa policy. These processes are influenced not just by political factors, but also by economic, cultural, historic and social conditions.

The main mechanisms by which enlargement impacts on regions are via trade flows, FDI and cross-border purchases, but also through commuter and migration flows and the acceleration of structural change processes (Fidrmuc et al., 2002, p. 59). The process of removing barriers to trade started at the beginning of the 1990s, when Central and Eastern European countries (CEECs) managed to redirect their exports away from the former COMECON members to the European Union. For example in Estonia, until 1991, exports to the former Soviet Union accounted for 90–95 per cent of total exports, but after four years it had dropped to 30 per cent (Venesaar and Hachey, 1995). The trade volume has increased significantly and the EU has become the most important trading partner of most CEECs, although with detailed variations between countries, regions and sectors. Geographical proximity has played a key role in influencing bilateral trade patterns (Weise et al., 2001). Changes have also occurred in the patterns of FDI and in capital and labour markets (including migration), alongside dramatic changes in the political and economic systems of new member countries. The process of transformation from socialist to market economies was associated with greater integration into the international division of labour, in general, and closer economic and political relations with the EU in particular (Weise et al., 2001; Bchir et al., 2003).

The removal of trade barriers has resulted in increased access to new markets, thus creating new opportunities for companies to expand their activities beyond their national borders, as well as providing consumers with a wider range and higher quality of products and services. On the other hand, the removal of trade barriers has also increased competition. The impact of joining the Single Market can be analysed by further detailing the effects of removing barriers to trade and movement of factors of production, on the one hand, and adoption of common EU standards, on the other. However, this distinction (which is sometimes referred to as negative and positive integration effects) is not always clear cut, since the removal of non-tariff barriers to trade is often linked to the adoption of product standards. At the same time, inside the EU enlargement has been accompanied by a continuing process of integration, which has affected regional production structures, the level of competition, as well as social conditions. Another group of integration measures includes the adoption of EU norms and policy principles (*acquis communautaire*). This means alignment with the external trade regime (including the adoption of the EU common external tariffs), the adoption of product and process standards (ranging from quality standards of products to safety at work and environmental standards), as well as other EU common policies, such as the common agricultural policy, transport policy, regional policy.

For enterprises in internal border regions EU enlargement simplified border crossing, clearing formalities, and facilitating the movement of persons and goods as customs fees and restrictions on quantities of goods and visa requirements were removed. By contrast, for external border regions a visa regime and restrictions on the movement of goods were introduced and/or tightened. However, in order to meet the requirements of the EU, double tariffs were abolished (for example for Estonian exports).

Another aspect of the trade regime that can have differentiated spatial effects is the implementation of customs tariffs and non-tariff barriers for

importing goods from third countries. However, the more open the economies of the acceding countries were before the enlargement (as in the case
of Estonia), the more trade barriers the joint foreign trade policy resulted in.
Widespread effects included the relocation of trade from more-efficient
non-EU countries to less-efficient EU member states. The alternative was a
decrease in the competitiveness of goods imported from third countries in
situations where the previous business relations persisted. Overall, it can be
concluded that border-related enlargement effects are heavily influenced by
the location and the level of development of cross-border regions.

EU ENLARGEMENT EFFECTS RELATED TO SOCIO-ECONOMIC FACTORS

In order to assess the effects of EU enlargement on entrepreneurship and
economic development in border regions and on cross-border cooperation,
in particular, it is necessary to consider the factors influencing the development of entrepreneurship at the regional level and how EU enlargement may
have affected these. These factors include the location of regions, the
conditions of the external business environment (for example business
regulations; economic environment; resources available, entrepreneurship
policy measures); historical, social and cultural factors, as well as the
awareness and competence of entrepreneurs to operate in a changing
business environment, in order to benefit from the challenges of cross-
border cooperation.

EU enlargement has brought together countries with different levels of
development, with the result that their integration into the EU has increased
regional disparities (Lackenbauer, 2004). Factor endowments (for example
technology, wages) and proximity to industrial centres (capital regions and
EU markets) both help to explain the economic geography of EU accession
countries. In most cases, metropolitan and urban areas (particularly, capital
city regions) have grown, while most rural and old industrial areas, as well
as those in Eastern peripheries, have performed less favourably (Bachtler et
al., 2000; Traistaru and Iara, 2002). It has been suggested that the processes
of internationalization and structural change are also expected to favour
Western regions, as well as regions with a strong industrial base and
countries near the East–West frontier (Petrakos, 2000).

Some assessments suggest that the overall impact of enlargement on the
'old' EU will be negligible, because the economies of the acceding countries are so small (Barysch, 2003; Bchir et al., 2003). At the same time, the
macroeconomic impact of enlargement is much more pronounced for
accession countries (Lejour et al., 2001; Niebuhr, 2008), because of the

limited level of initial efficiency, greater liberalization and small economic size. However, these countries have already reaped the short-term benefits from previous trade agreements with the EU. In this context the medium-term adjustment is likely to have adverse consequences for new member states, before efficiency gains increase overall welfare (Bchir et al., 2003). At the same time, new members in Central and Eastern Europe have already experienced wider benefits from being able to access the EU budget and the technology, know-how and capital markets of the EU (Fidrmuc and Nowotny, 2000).

The effect of EU enlargement on entrepreneurship development in border regions is also affected by the underlying regional variations in entre-preneurship in the country. There is considerable evidence from mature market economies to suggest that significant spatial variations exist in the extent to which SMEs contribute to employment growth and economic development. Mason (1991) has explained these spatial variations in new firm formation rates in terms of differences in economic and occupational structures, entrepreneurial culture, and economic factors with respect both to demand and the supply of factors of production. Differences in structural characteristics such as industrial sector, establishment size and occupa-tional structures also help to explain some of the spatial variations in new firm formation rates. Socio-cultural factors, such as the entrepreneurial orientation of the population and the entrepreneurial propensities of local institutions, are also recognized as potentially significant by Mason. Eco-nomic factors include both demand-related influences, such as the level of disposable income, the ownership structure and functional composition of industry, and supply-side factors, which affect the supply of the main factors of production and flows of information.

In addition, specific characteristics of individual border regions are likely to affect the opportunities for, and constraints on, the development of entrepreneurship within them. For example, the types of entrepreneurial activity that develop are likely to be affected by the economic development characteristics of adjacent regions and countries, as well as by the wider societal context. With respect to the internationalization of SMEs, both geographical and cultural distance is of importance, as firms tend to internationalize, initially into neighbouring regions. In this respect, regional economic cooperation can play an important role in increasing economic and investment activity within a particular cross-border region. This par-ticularly applies in the case of SMEs, which are usually even more oriented towards nearby countries than larger firms, because they may experience more internal constraints on international growth, such as limited capital, management, time and experience, than larger enterprises (Buckley, 1989). As a result, it is expected that the enlargement of the EU may be of particular relevance for the internationalization of European SMEs within Europe, with cross-border arrangements having an important role in this.

A study undertaken in South-Eastern Europe suggests that firms in border regions may have a higher level of interaction with other firms than the average for national firms in all countries. It also shows that trade relations and economic cooperation eventually depend on the level of specialization and the size of the markets (Dimitrov et al., 2003). At the same time, previous research also suggests that barriers to cooperation matter, and can negatively affect the performance of firms in border regions. Overall, firms in countries surveyed were less concerned about potential barriers, such as the quality of infrastructure (for example roads, proximity of checkpoints) and more concerned about the wider issues, such as a lack of assistance in developing cross-border relations, political instability, corruption and exchange rate variations, as well as the financial conditions prevailing in each country. Surveyed firms did not consider a lack of common language across the borders to be a major barrier for interaction. The previous empirical results suggest that the best policy to encourage cross-border cooperation is the development of the regional economies and the improvement in their economic environments (Dimitrov et al., 2003).

At the regional level, common problems and resources in constituent parts of a cross-border area can positively contribute to creating and sustaining cooperation across borders. For example, Nordic and Baltic cooperation is motivated by the need to tackle problems of nuclear waste management, long distances, harsh climate and environment (Saprykin, 2003). In the case of Italy and Slovenia, specific regional assets have played an important role in designing measures for achieving common development goals (Sfiligoj, 2000).

Cross-border cooperation can also be influenced by cultural, social, political and economic similarities or differences across borders. Dissimilarities between economic systems and in levels of economic development; dissimilar social systems; a lack of a common language and cultural tradition; poor knowledge of each other's attitudes and behavioural patterns (prejudices) can all contribute to a lack of trust between potential partners, inhibiting cooperation across borders (Krätke, 1998). Differences in values and mentalities influence entrepreneurship practices. People with a similar cultural background can more easily find a common language, which helps them to build trust-based relationships. Cultural background also influences institutional cooperation and the business and trade environment. People and institutions from different cultural backgrounds face difficulties at different levels: interpersonal, organizational and societal (Kirkman et al., 2006; Grilo and Thurik, 2006; Melnikas et al., 2006; Uhlaner and Thurik, 2003).

Ethnic and national identities are another enabling or constraining influence on cross-border cooperation, as well as on the propensity of individuals to engage in entrepreneurship itself. However, the direction of the causal relationship remains unclear. Häkli's research provides a clear case to support the claim that common identity is a predecessor of successful cooperation across national borders (Häkli, 2004). At the same time, the opposite, namely 'top-down' initiated and supported cooperation leading to a sense of belonging to the same community, might apply in some cases (Heddebaut, 2004). In fact, the promotion of a functional cross-border region does not presume a common identity among its inhabitants. At the same time, there can be particular challenges where cross-border cooperation involves individuals and/or organizations across the former East/West bloc divide, because the economic and social systems of the two blocs differed fundamentally. In terms of governance, for example, Soviet bloc countries were characterized by a domination of central authorities over local authorities. A disproportionately large share of tasks was accomplished by central authorities, at the expense of local authority activity. Another noteworthy feature was the weakness or virtual absence of civil society, so that a participative governance regime could not develop. Regarding entrepreneurship and the wider economic system, private enterprise activities were not tolerated in Soviet-style planned economies (Turnock, 2005; Bafoil, 1999).

Moreover, partly because of centralization and partly for ideological reasons, border areas were typically turned into zones of secrecy and separation. Many roads and railroads in border areas were closed in order to reduce cross-border communication to the minimum. The regions were closed to non-residents and the areas were frequently subjected to depopulation, which meant that infrastructure and industry in the border regions was often in a poor condition. This is the legacy many of the border regions of former socialist bloc countries inherited, which the newly independent states have to change as they seek to integrate themselves into the international system (Kennard, 2004).

A number of studies have focused on the implications of EU enlargement for SMEs (for example Smallbone et al., 1999; Smallbone and Rogut, 2005), including some that refer back to the experience of previous market integration (for example Smallbone et al., 1999). Their main conclusion is that whilst accession-related changes have important potential implications for firms of all sizes, the distinctive size-related characteristics of SMEs affect their ability to identify, cope with and respond to new sources of threat and opportunity.

REGIONAL DIFFERENCES AS A KEY FACTOR INFLUENCING EU ENLARGEMENT EFFECTS

Previous studies have made use of various bases for analysing regional differences in economic development in border regions. For example, according to Resmini (2002), border regions may be classified on the basis of their location, type or status of countries, for example, those bordering current EU members; those bordering other accession countries; those bordering external countries, as well as internal regions. This division was based on the analysis of the impact of the eastern enlargement of the EU border regions in Bulgaria, Estonia, Hungary, Romania and Slovenia (Resmini, 2002). Focusing on the specialization and growth patterns in border regions in accession countries, the Resmini research showed that enlargement processes have an uneven impact on border and non-border regions, with the greatest impact on regions bordering the EU, essentially because of their geographical proximity to large potential markets.

Border regions with other accession countries did not present serious concerns, because the competitiveness of manufacturing activity benefited from the higher wages in neighbouring countries, infrastructure, FDI, and the presence of service activities in the neighbouring region, although manufacturing mainly consisted of traditional, labour-intensive activities. However, regions with external borders did raise concerns because of their peripheral position, not only with regard to their respective countries but also with respect to the EU. However, low wages, FDI and infrastructure connections with the capital city enable economic activities to be attracted to these regions and also to overcome any negative effects generated by distance (Resmini, 2002). Internal border regions are relatively attractive economically because of a well-developed service sector and to a lesser extent by FDI and a skilled labour force, but there are differences between countries. Analysing the regional relocation of industries, previous research has shown that average regional specialization has decreased in Estonia, for example, during economic integration with the EU since 1990 (Traistaru et al., 2002). An important conclusion from this research was that for regions in accession countries, geographic proximity to European core regions matters, as far as locational attractiveness is concerned (ibid.).

Another relevant contribution is that of Krätke (1998), proceeding from the paradigm of new regionalism, whereby a region is partly understood as being both independent from a national economy and an integral part of the international system. In this view, the competitiveness of a region is to a large extent determined by the region's system of production and govern-ance. This refers, on the one hand, to the effectiveness of production within a region (which is influenced both by regionally based and externally owned enterprises), and on the other hand, to the particular system of regulation within the region. The latter is defined as the economic and social patterns of communication, industrial organization relationships and political coordination mechanisms. At the macro level, cross-border cooperation refers to connections between political and local authorities. At the level of entrepreneurs and firms (micro level), a cross-border region is characterized by a network of firms which cooperate across borders. A successful cross-border region is characterized by its inclusion in trade and business networks, which operate on a larger scale than simply across the border into a neighbouring region. Regions characterized by a poor structure of business networks, and which therefore remain relatively isolated from cooperation on a larger scale, are also likely to remain backward in terms of overall level of development (Krätke, 1998).

Krätke's scheme divided regions into two types: first, internationally competitive regions characterized by a high degree of integration into international networks; and secondly, regions characterized by a poor level of competitiveness because of their weak integration with international business. The level of the regions' GDP per capita was used for the purpose of international comparison, calculated according to 'purchasing power standards' (PPS) (Krätke, 1998). Other indicators used included the number of industrial jobs per inhabitant; the spatial distribution of FDI; the number of firms with foreign capital; the extent of privatization; private sector development; as well as the region's internal characteristics, such as institutional frameworks, trust between actors and attitudes of residents towards neighbours. Krätke (2002) proposed a typology of European regions based on a centre–periphery dimension, defined in terms of economic, technological and institutional resources. 'Centre' or structurally strong regions were characterized by a high level of economic, technological and institutional resources and social capital. Structurally strong regions were also characterized by the presence of some specific competence or specific stock of knowledge combined with a high capacity for innovation.

Krätke also suggested that in spite of the overall poor level of development of new EU member states, there are certain industrial locations that are characterized by high innovative capacity and a high level of concentration of capital. Across the enlarged EU, Krätke distinguished three types of regions: (1) structurally strong industrial centres in old European industrial states; (2) structurally weak regions of new member states; and (3) relatively strong industrial sites in the new member states.

Referring specifically to cross-border regions, Jessop (2002) offers a typology, based on the processes of how a cross-border region evolved, which involves examining the historical development of various regions. It was related to the idea that the complexity of cross-border regions cannot be captured easily. Jessop's emphasis was on the need to recognize the importance of preceding events and contextual factors. Cooperation and entrepreneurship near borders can be affected by various motivations, including historical relationships between companies, surplus generated from price differentials and the development of 'natural' economic spaces. This raises the question of what constitutes a cross-border region and also the nature of borders themselves. Although any bounded area contains various natural features, some of which might be well suited for demarcating a territorial border, it is human actions which are of primary significance when it comes to understanding borders (O'Dowd, 2003; van Houtum, 2003; Jauhiainen, 2000; Smouts, 1998), emphasizing their social construction.

A further contribution from previous research is that of Muller et al. (2006), who emphasized the heterogeneity of regions in new member states and candidate countries, which results not only from diversity at national level but also reflects some clear differences in the local situation. This particularly applies when considering innovation capacities; it is one of the reasons why it is important to consider the sub-national level in any analysis of innovation potential. Their main concept is that innovation capacity should not be reduced to R&D investment and related activities but rather should be understood as depending on, first, the capacity of a region to absorb, secondly, to diffuse, and thirdly, to demand new knowledge. The approach adopted in the analysis of Muller et al. (2006) aims at integrating the different components of innovation capacity at the regional level. In other words, an innovation system perspective is emphasized. In this view, the socio-economic development of a (national or regional) territory is seen as driven – at least partly – by its innovation capacity.

The analysis of Muller et al. (2006) relies on a theoretical basis developed at a European level by Radosevic (2004). Its further elaboration and application at the regional level for new member states and candidate countries allows the establishment of a multi-dimensional innovation capacity framework along five dimensions: knowledge creation; absorptive capacity; diffusion capacity; demand; and governance capacity (Muller and Nauwelaers, 2005). Five different types of regions result from their statistical analysis, with each group gaining a specific appellation (cf. Muller and Nauwelaers, 2005): capital regions; regions with tertiary growth potential; skilled manufacturing platform regions; industrially challenged regions; lagging-behind agricultural regions (Muller et al., 2006).

Analysis undertaken by Weise et al. (2001) has identified four inter-related types of regional disparity: a contrast between urban and rural areas; a core/periphery disparity, especially in countries with a monocentric urban structure; a West/East difference, which is particularly evident in border areas; and concentrations of restructuring problems in old-industrial areas (Bachtler and Downes, 1999). All of these patterns are important to consider as possible bases for differentiating enlargement effects and regional development. In terms of urban–rural contrasts, most of the available literature consistently identifies major CEE agglomerations and urban areas as leaders in the transformation process (for example Bachtler et al., 2000; Boeri and Brücker, 2000). Most prominent is the dominant role of core and capital city regions. Indeed in countries such as Hungary, the Czech Republic, Estonia and Latvia, there is no centre that rivals the capital city (Weise et al., 2001). The dominance of monocentric settlement structures is formidable: for example, the Tallinn area has 80–90 per cent of foreign investment and tourism and 40 per cent of all registered enterprises in Estonia. Boeri and Brücker (2000) found that, in comparison to the situation in established EU countries, CEE capitals were relatively small in terms of population share (except Hungary) but had significantly higher shares of overall GDP. The absence of major secondary centres in any of these CEECs means that, outside the capital cities, spatial disparities in growth are more limited and the economic geography is essentially a monocentric one (Bachtler et al., 2000).

EU enlargement effects are also influenced by factors of regional economic development in the domestic region as well as by conditions on the other side of the border. These include the human resource endowment, the level and types of economic activity, the policy environment for entrepreneurship and cross-border partnership, physical infrastructure, historical, cultural and other factors.

To summarize, our review of existing literature leads to the expectation that EU enlargement has different implications for different types of border regions. In this context, the development of an integrated typology of cross-border regions may help to better assess the consequences of EU enlargement for economic development in border regions.

A TYPOLOGY FOR ANALYSING THE CONSEQUENCES OF EU ENLARGEMENT FOR CROSS-BORDER REGIONS

The review of previous literature leads us to hypothesize that EU enlargement effects will be affected by various regional characteristics. Depending on the aims of the study, border regions may be classified on the basis of different criteria. These include the level of economic development, the system of governance and the policy environment, amongst others. Specific indicators can be selected to operationalize each dimension. An indicative list of regional characteristics that may influence EU enlargement effects includes:

1. *Economic Factors*
    a. levels of economic development, on the two sides of the border.
    b. hard or soft border.
    c. accessibility, for example to main markets; capital cities.
    d. education level of population.
    e. age structure.
    f. sector mix.
    g. size distribution of enterprises.
    h. degree of concentration/diversification of the economic structure.
2. *Policy Context*
    a. governance structure, for example Type I/II governance struc-tures; public–private partnerships.
    b. policy environment for entrepreneurship and cross-border part-nership, for example policies to promote entrepreneurship; time and cost of new business registration.
3. *Contextual Factors*
    a. historical factors, for example common history between two sides of the border.
    b. cultural factors, for example shared language(s), regional identity.
    c. level of institutional and personal trust.
4. *Infrastructure*
    a. physical infrastructure.
    b. knowledge-related infrastructure, for example innovation centres.
    c. evidence of an active regional innovation system.
    d. Internet access per capita.
    e. density of road and rail networks.
    f. distance from international airport.
    g. number of border crossing points per kilometre of border.

Previous literature has suggested that the effect of enlargement on cross-border entrepreneurial activities and regional development will depend on the changes with respect to the status of borders, the trade regimes, the structure of competition and the patterns of FDI and capital markets. Clearly, a key factor is the distinction between regions with hard (external) borders and regions with soft (internal) borders. A division of regions into external and internal border regions is connected, first, with border-related EU enlargement effects. This is because the border regime is a system of controls, regulating behaviour at the borders. It determines the conditions for crossing the border. The openness of a border refers to the degree of freedom of movement of goods and labour across the border. At the same time, different classes of goods and services cross borders under different conditions. While financial services meet virtually no barriers, material goods typically meet barriers in the form of taxes.

The location of regions in relation to the types (status) of countries is important. Defining regions at the NUTS III level, border regions were divided into three groups by Resmini (2002): (1) those bordering present EU members; (2) those bordering other candidate countries negotiating accession; (3) those bordering external countries, as well as internal regions. The location determines the adjacency of countries with different levels of economic development. Therefore, the level of economic development, regional capacity and development potential must be considered in the case of both internal and external regions (Krätke, 2002; Muller and Nauwelaers, 2005). Based on Krätke, border regions can be divided into developed/strong regions and undeveloped/weak regions. According to Muller and Nauwelaers, the potential of the regional innovation system is a characteristic of border regions that has an important influence on its development potential. Another important issue with respect to cross-border cooperation is the relative situation in the regions on the two sides of the border, for example with respect to levels of economic development. Considering the distinction of border regions on the basis of relative economic development, four regional types can be identified (illustrated in Table 2.1). Similar tables can be produced for the other dimensions listed above, which may be combined into multi-dimensional regional typologies.

The potential for cross-border cooperation contributing to the development of productive entrepreneurship is likely to be affected by a variety of other regional characteristics (of the regions on both sides of the border). Referring specifically to cross-border regions, Jessop (2002) offers a typology, based on the processes of how a cross-border region has evolved, emphasizing the importance of preceding events as well as contextual factors. Cooperation and entrepreneurship near borders can be based on various motivations, including historical relationships between companies. For example, the historical relationships between companies in Estonia and Russia were inherited from the Soviet time, acting as a motivational influence on their cooperation in the contemporary period.

Another example of the role of cultural affinity encouraging cross-border cooperation is in south-east Estonia, where a historical part of Setomaa comprising four municipalities makes up a region on the eastern border of Estonia. Part of the historical Seto land is situated in Pechory region (Russia) near the Estonian border. Today, a number of Estonians or

Table 2.1   Border region typology based on relative economic development levels

Region across the border		Domestic region	
		Regional characteristics	
		Developed/strong* regions	Undeveloped/weak regions
Regional character-istics	Developed/strong* regions	High potential for regional development assessed on the basis of various characteristics, which support cross-border cooperation (enterprises, institutions)	Differences in the level of development on the two sides of the border, where cross-border cooperation activities (e.g. households) may take advantage of these differences (e.g. prices, availability of jobs, goods etc.)
	Undeveloped/weak regions	Differences in the level of development of border regions where cross-border cooperation activities (e.g. enterprises) may take advantage of these differences (e.g. using cheap factor inputs, particularly labour) from the other side of the border	Weak regions, where the scope for household and/or enterprise-based cross-border cooperation is based mainly on survival reasons, here 'soft' (particularly historical and cultural) factors are important

Note: * Developed/strong regions are defined as those with a strong potential for entrepreneurship and cross-border cooperation.

Source: Smallbone et al. (2007).

descendants of Estonians live there. These historical and cultural factors are also influencing cross-border cooperation in the region. Setomaa has managed to retain its traditional face and identity. This supports the emergence of a totally unique handicraft cluster involving both Estonian and Russian border areas and the successful implementation of a handicraft training programme, based on the development of cross-border cooperative relations. The development of logistics to service transport flows going through Estonia has been stimulated as a result.

Some enlargement-related effects in border regions are direct, while others are more indirect. Direct effects result from a change in the status of a border that has affected the potential for interaction across it. The principal mechanisms by which the enlargement impacts on regions directly is via trade flows, FDI, cross-border purchasing, commuter and migration flows and through the acceleration of structural change processes. Indirect effects of enlargement include those resulting from the differential impacts of EU enlargement on firms of different sizes. Since there is evidence that large enterprises are better equipped than their small firm counterparts to deal with the sources of threat (such as compliance with a new regulatory regime) and also to take advantage of any new market opportunities, regions that are comprised mainly of small firms are likely to be disadvantaged. Another example of indirect effects of enlargement is where a (border) region is affected (either positively or negatively) through the effect of enlargement on the national territory, of which the region is part.

Previous research evidence suggests that since increased market integration tends to widen existing disparities, there is a sense in which, in the absence of policy intervention, enlargement may favour the economically strong firms and regions and challenge the weak. Characteristics of structurally strong regions include specific competences; specific stocks of knowledge and innovation capacity; and a high stock of economic and social capital. Cross-border cooperation should seek to enhance such characteristics in border regions.

CONCLUSIONS

The consequences of EU enlargement for entrepreneurship and economic development in border regions are related to the dynamic effects of changes in border status, such as the removal/emergence of visa requirements, customs duties, border queues, clearing formalities, quantitative and item restrictions on goods, and double tariffs, and wider socio-economic changes, such as changes in trade regimes and changes in the institutional and business environment, including the nature and sources of competition.

This review has shown that EU enlargement effects are expected to be different for internal regions with 'soft' borders and external regions with 'hard' borders, and for regions with different levels of economic development. Internal and external border regions are likely to be influenced differently by border-related effects. For enterprises in internal border regions, EU enlargement simplified border crossing, clearing formalities, and movement of persons and goods as customs fees as restrictions on quantities of goods and visa requirements are removed. The removal of trade barriers should result, on the one hand, in increased access to new markets, thus creating new opportunities for companies to expand their activities beyond their national borders, as well as providing consumers with a wider range and higher quality of products and services. On the positive side, firms acquire access to EU production and export subsidies according to the adoption of EU norms and policy principles (*acquis communautaire*). On the other hand, the removal of trade barriers will also increase competition in the domestic market.

The effects of EU enlargement for external border regions may be mostly negative because of the 'hard' border controls, the visa regime and restrictions on the movement of goods. The main problems are connected with quantitative restrictions on goods, complicated customs documentation, increased border queues and waiting time, increased customs duties for third countries and visas. Obtaining visas can be a significant obstacle for enterprises providing services for tourists, such as accommodation and recreational activities. In addition, according to EU rules, new member states have been required to implement customs tariffs and non-tariff barriers for imports from third countries, thereby limiting the possibilities for cross-border cooperation.

Regional characteristics are also a potentially important influence on likely enlargement-related effects. These characteristics include the location of border regions, type of country (that is, old or new EU members, candidate countries or 'third' countries), the level of economic development of the neighbouring cross-border region, as well as other regionally specific characteristics, such as historical and cultural factors. In addition, a variety of characteristics on both sides of the border, such as human resources, the policy environment for entrepreneurship and cross-border partnership and the physical infrastructure, are all part of the context for cross-border activity. Clearly, EU enlargement-related effects are highly differentiated at the regional level, reflecting the complexity of regional development processes.

REFERENCES

Bachtler, J. and R. Downes (1999), 'Regional policy in the transition countries: a comparative assessment', *European Planning Studies*, **7**(6), 793–808.

Bachtler, J., R. Downes and G. Corzelak (2000), *Transition, Cohesion and Regional Policy in Central and Eastern Europe*, Aldershot, UK: Ashgate Publishers.

Bafoil, F. (1999), 'Post-communist territories and borders: conflicts, learning and rule-building in Poland', *International Journal of Urban and Regional Research*, **23**(4), 567–82.

Baldwin, R.E. and A.J. Venables (1995), 'Regional economic integration', in G.M. Grossman and K. Rogoff (eds), *Handbook of International Economics*, Vol. 3, Amsterdam: Elsevier Science B.V.

Barysch, K. (2003), 'Does enlargement matter for the EU economy?', Centre for European Reform Policy Brief, available at: http://www.cer.org.uk, accessed 21 August 2006.

Bchir, H., L. Fontagne and P. Zanghieri (2003), 'The impact of EU enlargement on member states: a CGE approach', CEPII Working Paper no. 10, Paris: CEPII.

Bellak, C. (2004), 'The impact of enlargement on the race for FDI', Vienna University of Economics Working Paper no. 86, Vienna: Vienna University.

Boeri, T. and H. Brücker (2000), 'The impact of Eastern enlargement on employment and labour markets in the EU member states', Berlin, Germany and Milan, Italy: European Integration Consortium: DIW, CEPR, FIEF, IAS, IGIER.

Buckley, P.J. (1989), 'Foreign direct investment by small and medium sized enterprises: the theoretical background', *Small Business Economics*, **1**(2), 89–100.

Carlin, W., S. Estrin and M. Schaffer (1999), 'Measuring progress in transition and towards EU accession: a comparison of manufacturing firms in Poland, Romania and Spain', *Journal of Common Market Studies*, **38**(5), 699–728.

Dimitrov, M., G. Petrakos, S. Totev and M. Tsiapa (2003), 'Cross-border cooperation in South-eastern Europe: the enterprises' point of view', *Eastern European Economics*, **41**(6), 5–25.

Fidrmuc, J. and T. Nowotny (2000), 'The effects of the EU's Eastern European enlargement on Austria: Austria's specific position', *Focus on Transition*, **1**, 100–131.

Fidrmuc, J., G. Moser, W. Pointner, D. Ritzberger-Grünwald, P. Schmidt, M. Schneider, A. Schober-Rhomberg and B. Weber (2002), 'EU enlargement to the East: effects on the EU-15 in general and on Austria in particular: an overview of the literature on selected aspects', *Focus on Transition*, **1**, 44–70.

Grilo, I. and R. Thurik (2006), 'Entrepreneurship in the old and new Europe', SCALES-paper no. 200516, Zoetermeer: EIM Business & Policy Research.

Häkli, J. (2004), 'Governing the mountains: cross-border regionalisation in Catalonia', in O. Kramsch and B. Hooper (eds), *Cross-border Governance in the European Union*, London and New York: Routledge, pp. 56–69.

Heddebaut, O. (2004), 'The EUROREGION from 1991 to 2020: an ephemeral stamp?', in O. Kramsch and B. Hooper (eds), *Cross-border Governance in the European Union*, London and New York: Routledge, pp. 70–87.

Jauhiainen, J.S. (2000), *Regional Development and Regional Policy: European Union and the Baltic Sea Region*, Turku, Finland: Painosalama.

Jessop, B. (2002), 'The political economy of scale', in M. Perkmann and N.L. Sum (eds), *Globalisation, Regionalisation and Cross-Border Regions*, Houndmills, New York: Palgrave Macmillan, pp. 25–49.

Kaitila, V. (2001), 'Accession countries' comparative advantage in the internal market: a trade and factor analysis', Discussion Paper no. 3, Finland: Bank of Finland Institute in Transition (BOFIT).

Kennard, A. (2004), 'Cross-border governance at the future eastern edges of the EU: a regeneration project?', in O. Kramsch and B. Hooper (eds), *Cross-border Governance in the European Union*, London and New York: Routledge, pp. 107–20.

Kirkman, B.L., K.B. Lowe and C.B. Gibson (2006), 'A quarter century of *Culture's Consequences*: a review of empirical research incorporating Hofstede's cultural values framework', *Journal of International Business Studies*, **37**(3), 285–320.

Krätke, S. (1998), 'Problems of cross-border regional integration: the case of the German–Polish border area', *European Urban and Regional Studies*, **5**(3), 249–62.

Krätke, S. (2002), 'The regional impact of EU eastern enlargement: a view from Germany', *European Planning Studies*, **10**(5), 651–64.

Lackenbauer, J. (2004), 'Catching-up, regional disparities and EU cohesion policy: the case of Hungary', *Managing Global Transitions: International Research Journal*, **2**(2), 123–62.

Lejour, A.M., R.A. de Mooij and R. Nahuis (2001), 'EU enlargement: economic implications for countries and industries', CESifo Working Paper no. 585, Munich, Germany: Centre for Economic Studies and Ifo Institute for Economic Research.

Mason, C. (1991), 'Spatial variations in enterprise: the geography of new firm formation', in R. Burrows (ed.), *Deciphering the Enterprise Culture: Entrepreneurship, Petty Capitalism and the Restructuring of Britain*, London and New York: Routledge, pp. 74–106.

Melnikas, B., P. Baršauskas and V. Kvainauskaite (2006), 'Transition processes and integral cultural space development in Central and Eastern Europe: main problems and priorities', *Baltic Journal of Management*, **1**(2), 201–12.

Muller, E. and C. Nauwelaers (2005), 'Enlarging the ERA: identifying priorities for regional policy focusing on research and technological development in the new member states and candidate countries', Fraunhofer, Germany: ISI/MERIT.

Muller, E., A. Jappe, J.A. Heraud and A. Zenker (2006), 'A regional typology of innovation capacities in new member states and candidate countries', Working Papers Firms and Region no. R1/2006, Karlsruhe: Fraunhofer Institute Systems and Innovation Research.

Niebuhr, A. (2008), 'The impact of EU enlargement on European border regions', *International Journal of Public Policy*, **3**(3), 163–86.

O'Dowd, L. (2003), 'The changing significance of European borders', in J. Anderson, L. O'Dowd and T.M. Wilson (eds), *New Borders for a Changing Europe*, London and Portland, OR: Frank Cass, pp. 13–36.

Petrakos, G. (2000), 'The spatial impact of East–West integration in Europe', in G. Petrakos, G. Maier and G. Gorzelak (eds), *Integration and Transition in Europe: The Economic Geography of Interaction*, London: Routledge, pp. 38–68.

Platon, V. and D. Antonescu (2001), 'SMEs development in cross-border cooperation region Romania–Hungary', paper presented at the International Conference 'Restructuring, Stability and Development in South-Eastern Europe', University of Thessaly, Volos, Greece, 1–3 June, available at: http://www.seedcenter.gr/projects/MNE/1stconfer/1stconf_papers/Platon.pdf, accessed 1 June 2011.

Radosevic, S. (2004), 'A two-tier or multi-tier Europe? Assessing the innovation capacities of Central and East European countries in the enlarged EU', *Journal of Common Market Studies*, **42**(3), 641–66.

Resmini, L. (2002), 'Specialization and growth patterns in border regions of accession countries', ZEI Working Paper B17, available at: https://www.econstor.eu/dspace/bitstream/10419/39527/1/353916463.pdf, accessed 26 May 2011.

Saprykin, P. (2003), 'Cross-border cooperation after EU enlargement: possibilities for the experience of Nordic and Baltic countries and North-West Russia', final report of the conference 'Cross-border Cooperation after EU Enlargement', Tartu, Estonia, 16–18 June.

Sfiligoj, A. (2000), 'Systematic support for cooperation among SMEs located in the areas adjoining the border between Italy and Slovenia', PHARE CBC Slovenia–Italy 'SME Strategy' SL-9701.03.02.

Smallbone, D. and A. Rogut (2005), 'The challenge facing SMEs in the EU's new member states', *International Entrepreneurship and Management Journal*, **1**(2), 219–40.

Smallbone, D., L. Labrianidis, U. Venesaar, F. Welter and P. Zashev (2007), 'Challenges and prospects of cross border cooperation in the context of EU enlargement', Deliverable 7: State of the Art Review of Literature, Kingston, UK: Kingston University.

Smallbone, D., B. Piasecki, U. Venesaar, K. Todorov and L. Labrianidis (1999), 'Internationalisation and SME development in transition economies: an international comparison', *Journal of Small Business and Enterprise Development*, **5**(4), 363–75.

Smouts, M.C. (1998) 'The region as the new imagined community?', in P. le Gales and C. Lequesne (eds), *Regions in Europe*, London and New York: Routledge, pp. 22–8.

Traistaru, I. and A. Iara (2002), 'European integration, regional specialisation and location of industrial activity in accession countries: data and measurement', Bonn: ZEI-Centre for European Integration Studies, available at: http://www.zei.de/download/Phare/data.pdf, accessed 1 June 2011.

Traistaru, I., P. Nijkamp and S. Longhi (2002), 'Regional specialisation and concentration of industrial activity in accession countries', ZEI Working Paper B02-16, Bonn: Centre for European Integration Studies, University of Bonn.

Turnock, D. (2005), 'Regional development with particular reference to cohesion in cross-border regions', in D. Turnock (ed.), *Foreign Direct Investment and Regional Development in East–Central Europe and the Former Soviet Union*, Aldershot: Ashgate, pp. 181–244.

Uhlaner, L. and R. Thurik (2003), 'Post-materialism: a cultural factor influencing total entrepreneurial activity across nations', SCALES research report N200321, Zoetermeer, Netherlands: EIM Business and Policy Research.

van Houtum, H. (2003), 'Borders of comfort: spatial economic bordering processes in the European Union', in J. Anderson, L. O'Dowd and T.M. Wilson (eds), *New Borders for a Changing Europe*, London and Portland, OR: Frank Cass, pp. 37–58.

Venesaar, U. and G.A. Hachey (1995), *Economic and Social Changes in the Baltic States in 1992–1994*, Tallinn: Estonian Academy of Sciences, Institute of Economics.

Weise, C., J. Bachtler, R. Downes, I. McMaster and K. Toepel (2001), 'The impact of EU enlargement on cohesion', Berlin, Germany and Glasgow, Scotland:

German Institute for Economic Research (DIW) and European Policies Research Centre (EPRC).

Williams, M.B. (2007), 'On Europe's edge: changing borders in Central and Eastern Europe', in K. Fabian (ed.), *Globalization Perspectives from Central and Eastern Europe: Contemporary Studies in Economic and Financial Analysis*, Vol. 89, Oxford: Elsevier, pp. 137–71.

Zuleeg, F. (2002), 'Benefits and threats of EU enlargement for Scotland', Discussion Paper no. 1, Edinburgh, Scotland: Scottish Executive.

3. Trust, learning and cross-border entrepreneurship

Friederike Welter, Nadezhda Alex and Susanne Kolb

INTRODUCTION

In recent years, there has been a growth of interest in the role of trust in business behaviour, because of its potential influence on reducing transaction costs (for example, Fukuyama, 1995; Williamson, 1993; Höhmann and Welter, 2005; Welter and Smallbone, 2006). Related to business behaviour, trust is based on a perception of the probability that other agents will behave in a way that is expected (Gambetta, 1988). In a cross-border context, trust might be expected to play a particularly important role because of the risks inherent in cross border transactions. For example, implementation gaps in the legal framework leave scope for discretionary actions of officials. In such a context, trust assists individuals in controlling these risks and reducing the costs connected with each border crossing. Also, trust and learning are closely linked, with recursive relations. Although learning happens independently of trust, it also can be an outcome of trust and its context, and it influences trust-building.

Overall, the topic of trust and learning in relation to cross-border entrepreneurship has not been researched systematically, with most of the literature focusing on (inter)organizational and personal trust in the context of multinationals, but neglecting the regional component of international entrepreneurship.[1] As such, a conceptual and empirical investigation of the topic can contribute to greater understanding of the role of different forms of trust on cross-border entrepreneurial activities. This chapter reviews some empirical evidence from the project CBCED ('Challenges and Prospects of Cross-Border Cooperation in the Context of EU Enlargement', 2006–2008) in order to discuss factors influencing trust and learning in a cross-border context.

A CONCEPTUAL PERSPECTIVE ON TRUST AND LEARNING IN A CROSS-BORDER CONTEXT

Generally, trust can be differentiated into institutional and personal trust. *Personal trust* signals trust at the individual level, in the case of a cross-border partnership towards the partner enterprise or organization. Personal trust may result from the characteristics of a group such as an ethnic or kinship group, or personal networks of friendships. High levels of personal trust reflect repeated positive experiences made over time and long-standing relations, building on initial knowledge about the partner. But it also occurs in bilateral (business) relationships, often long-standing ones, where persons have come to know each other (Williamson, 1993). In both cases, they know or assume that the partner/friend will not behave in a way that is detrimental to the relationship, even when there are no written or explicit rules set out. This means that these relationships are governed by norms, values and codes of conduct inherent in a business environment and/or a wider society.

Institutional trust reflects trust in the functioning of the overall political, legal or economic framework and into its informal rules. Low levels of institutional trust are taken as indicators of a deficient institutional framework. Institutional trust is essential for the efficient operation of a market economy, because where high levels of institutional trust exist, individuals can enter into transactions with only limited information about their partner's specific attributes, which means that the scope of trust extends beyond the number of people that are known personally (Welter and Smallbone, 2006). In this regard, institutional trust is based on legal safeguards and sanctions in case the relationship fails.

Both forms of trust are of a dual nature, drawing attention to the complex nature of the trust phenomenon duality '(…) entails that trust and control each assume the existence of the other, refer to each other and create each other, but remain irreducible to each other' (Möllering, 2005, p. 283). With regard to institutional trust, we can further distinguish between trust in formal and informal institutions, where formal institutional trust represents systemic trust, complemented by legal safeguards. Informal institutional trust represents 'genuine' trust, itself complementing formal institutional trust. Similarly, personal trust consists of 'genuine' personal trust and a 'calculated' risk ensured by control mechanisms. Applying this duality of trust to a cross-border context allows a closer look at *factors influencing trust in cross-border activities*. Where partners are drawn from different national and cultural contexts, it is of particular interest to identify the factors which influence the ability of partners to cooperate effectively, and to analyse the processes through which trust is built. For example, research on cross-border trading in a post-Soviet environment has shown that risks can be minimized by drawing on relations of mutual trust. Apart from long-standing business and friendship relations, this includes family help (Hohnen, 2003; Humphrey, 2002; Wallace et al., 1997, 1999; Welter et al., 2006; Williams and Balaz, 2002) and ethnic and kinship ties (Thuen, 1999, Williams and Balaz, 2005).

Learning may happen independently of trust, but it may also influence trust-building, as well as being influenced by the existence of trust, which is of particular importance in a cross-border context. *Entrepreneurial learning* refers to changes of known and trusted patterns. Learning is generated if the entrepreneur's interpretation of what to do leads to an action that is no longer wanted by the external environment, for example, in cases where new regulations have made a particular action illegal. Internal or external events can act as triggers for a change in entrepreneurial behaviour, provided they exceed a threshold above which the entrepreneur recognizes a need for behavioural changes. This threshold depends on the entrepreneur's background and experiences and his/her business objectives, but entrepreneurial learning is also affected by the institutional environment.

In a cross-border context, there are some critical aspects of learning, which is influenced by commitment, trust and cross-cultural competencies. Learning experiences from past collaborations affect not only the willingness, but also the competency for cross-border learning. In this context, cultural and emotional misfits may counteract positive learning experiences, thus impeding trust-building. Moreover, tacit knowledge, which is one of the most crucial resources in achieving positive learning results, is difficult to transfer between individuals (Polanyi, 1966; Nonaka et al., 2001), and the cross-border context might act as a further impediment. A certain fit (in terms of resource, organizational and technological characteristics as well as in terms of trust and partner openness) between cooperating partners appears to be a necessary precondition for a mutual and beneficial knowledge transfer in these situations.

As previously mentioned, trust and learning are closely linked with recursive relations. First, the overall level of both personal and institutional trust within a region can impact on the ability, willingness and commitment of individuals and organizations to learn and also to de-learn. This also has consequences for learning processes in cross-border cooperation, particularly if regions in neighbouring countries demonstrate different levels of trust. In this regard, learning is an outcome of trust and its context: learning is facilitated by higher levels of trust and vice versa, which means that the requirements for trust to occur may indirectly have an impact on learning processes. Moreover, while personal and institutional trust can facilitate learning on different levels, personal trust can also be an outcome of learning through repeated interaction between individuals, in other words 'learning to trust' (Nooteboom, 2002). In this regard, institutional trust is also influenced by learning, as 'learning to trust' in institutions may develop over time, based on experiences with institutions.

TRUST AND LEARNING IN CROSS-BORDER PARTNERSHIPS: REVIEWING EMPIRICAL EVIDENCE

Data and Data Analysis

One must be aware that trust is not an 'objective' phenomenon, which can easily be measured and understood across cultures and countries (Welter and Smallbone, 2006). Trust, in particular its understanding and interpretation, is very much a socially constructed phenomenon, which renders its measurement and empirical analysis difficult. Key issues concern the operationalization of different concepts of trust and the choice of adequate empirical methods. Trust frequently results from habitual behaviour, where individuals implicitly draw on habits and norms without calculating or justifying their behaviour beforehand. Previous research in which some of the authors have been involved (Höhmann and Welter, 2005) has demonstrated the difficulties in using standardized surveys in order to study trust in entrepreneurial activities. Therefore, this project used a qualitative approach based on multiple case studies. Interviews were conducted on a semi-structured basis, using a topic guide, with respondents from households, enterprises and local support organizations and administrations. Household respondents were identified by researchers at random, through observation of petty trading activities at markets on both border sides and/or railway stations at border crossing points. Enterprises were mainly identified through assistance from institutions, in order to include firms where there was some expectation that they were, or had been, involved in cross-border activity. Enterprises were selected to represent different size, sector and age groups.

Two hundred and forty and 80 in-depth interviews were conducted with enterprises and households respectively (with the exception of the German and Finnish border regions) in twelve European border regions, two per country. Interviews were conducted face to face, and extensive interview protocols were kept; where possible, interviews were also recorded. Interview protocols have been translated into English and systematically analysed with the help of software for qualitative data analysis, which assists in detecting patterns. A detailed, cross case analysis concerning issues of trust and learning has been conducted by the authors of this chapter. The conceptual framework outlined in the previous section was the basis for developing coding nodes, which allowed a systematic search for patterns of trust, its origin, forms and role as well as for ways that trust is built and lost. Interviews have been coded by all members of the German research team and coding has been cross-checked for inconsistencies before progressing with the thematic analysis.

The Macro Context for Trust and Learning

At the regional level, the institutional framework, sectoral and economic factors, as well as cultural and spatial dimensions influence trust. They constitute the macro context for trust-building and consequently for learning.

The *institutional framework* includes legal and political frameworks, the respective culture and economies and historical experiences. All these factors can contribute to a high level of institutional trust, if and when individuals have had positive experiences, or where they are confident that the institutional environment is functioning well. Interviewees frequently compared their own business environment to those in Western Europe, which clearly draws attention to the benefits of a well-functioning institutional environment:

> Things would be completely different if we collaborated with a businessman from Western Europe, let's say an Italian one. When you export to Western-European countries you feel safe, you know there are guarantees. Things are planned well and properly organised from the early start. There are rules and formal procedures and there is no space for 'strange' agreements and informal activities. (Florina Enterprise 12)

Another respondent concluded that:

> I trust western institutions more than I trust the local ones. On the regional level there is less trust than on the national level. I trust eastern institutions very little. (Biała Podlaska Enterprise 5)

Such trust in the functioning of formal institutions is required for entrepreneurial activities to develop and thrive over time, because it allows entrepreneurs to go beyond a circle of trusted and well-known business partners (Welter and Smallbone, 2006), thus influencing the nature of cross-border activities and their development potential. This takes on particular importance in a cross-border context, where institutions across the border are unfamiliar. In situations where individuals feel that they cannot trust the formal framework, or where a rule of law does not exist, they will resort to personal trust. Personal trust allows partnerships to emerge regardless of the deficiencies of the institutional environment, but an over-reliance on personal trust also may restrict the development of cross-border partnerships in the longer run (Welter and Smallbone, 2009).

Political relations and political problems between neighbouring countries also influence institutional trust, as well as levels of personal trust, as is apparent in the case of the Estonian regions bordering Russia, or in the case of Greece and FYRoM (Republic of Macedonia) because of the so-called 'naming issue'.[2] This lowers the level of institutional trust: 'Political relations are rather negative at the moment, and this has decreased the trust of some partners' (Ida Viru Enterprise 11). A low level of institutional trust also influences personal trust because individuals may be reluctant to cooperate across the border: 'I feel that there is no way of creating trust between our company and the Russian partners – the Russian administration acts in an unpredictable way and we cannot help this at all' (South Karelia Enterprise 6), although interviewees clearly identify political distortions as the reason for this: 'It is a pity that poor relations between politicians influence communication between ordinary persons' (Ida Viru Enterprise 17).

Trust-building can be influenced, albeit indirectly, by *economic conditions*. For example, lower labour costs in the neighbouring country can trigger cross-border cooperation as evident in both of the German case study regions and in some of the Greek enterprise partnerships. The effect on trust and learning is an indirect one: if economic conditions are favourable, they facilitate cross-border cooperation with mutual benefits to both partners which in turn serves as a basis for trust-building. On the other hand, the economic situation in neighbouring regions can act as a deterrent for trust and learning. This applies especially in regions where low levels of economic development go hand in hand with still deficient legal and political frameworks, thus reinforcing institutional distrust.

In line with results from previous studies (for example, Bachmann, 2003; Chepurenko and Malieva, 2005; Lane, 1997; Lane and Bachmann, 1996; Radaev, 2004; Venesaar, 2005; Welter, 2005), our evidence illustrates how trust-building is facilitated in environments where legal frameworks exist and function well, leaving no room for discretionary decisions of officials, and where institutions fostering cross-border entrepreneurship exist. A negative influence is also visible in several of our case study regions. In cooperation between Poland and Belarus, respondents from households and enterprises alike complained about difficulties with customs officials and restrictive border regulations after Poland joined the EU: 'There is total lack of trust towards duty officials in Belarus, there is total freedom of legal interpretations among them' (Biała Podlaska Enterprise 1). But also between Greece and FYRoM or South Karelia and Russia, an uncertain environment impedes cross-border activities:

> Laws were different from month to month. I can remember that there was a law in the FYRoM which forced the foreign investor to have a local partner in order to establish a firm there. That was the reason why I did not follow an entrepreneurial idea I had, namely to open a building material retail shop in Skopje, even though I think it would be a totally new idea for the local consumers. (Florina Enterprise 18)

> The main problem in Russia, the uncertainty, has to do with the Russian officials. Their activities create most of the barriers we have faced in our CBC. [...] especially the way the local authorities interpret the law – they are not consistent in this way, the interpretations seem to change every day (if not every hour). (South Karelia Enterprise 6)

Thus, in hostile or turbulent environments, institutional deficiencies hinder the development potential of cross-border cooperation which indirectly restricts the potential for trust-building. Two examples, which not surprisingly are both examples of household cross-border cooperation (see also Welter and Smallbone, 2009), illustrate the influence of domestic and foreign institutions in this regard. For example, a household in Biała Podlaska (Biała Podlaska Household 14), trading with cigarettes and alcohol, complained about the risks involved in his illegal trading activities, while a Bulgarian household (Kyustendil Household 1) legalized his activities over the course of time. This reflects the context-specificity of trust-building, which, although ultimately an individual process, is highly influenced by the respective economic and institutional context.

Another macro-level factor influencing trust refers to *geographical (or spatial) proximity* which has a twofold role. On the one hand, it facilitates trust-building because it allows for (frequent) personal contacts. This is visible in examples from all regions. In enterprise cooperation entrepreneurs either emphasize the ease of crossing borders and meeting partners, or the advantage of producing in a border region which allows them to arrange 'just-in-time'-deliveries across the border. In households, geographical proximity is often the main trigger for their cross-border activities to develop:

> However, several Polish companies located near the border are customers of the considered enterprise in Görlitz as well. This results from the spatial proximity, shorter delivery times and the lead which the firm has regarding trust. (Görlitz Enterprise 2)

The geographical proximity matters, since they are able to visit me in 1–1½ hours; thus, they call me in the morning, asking me to "prepare" their orders till noon. (Florina Enterprise 17)

On the other hand, geographical proximity can also facilitate the supervision of business relations, which at first glance renders trust (building) superfluous. Empirical evidence indicates that trust often occurs as a calculated risk. The partners trust each other but they also have opportunities to check on the relationship because of geographical proximity. For example, a German interviewee explained how punctuality of delivery is facilitated by the spatial proximity of the Polish partner, which allowed for unannounced visits by the German director on the Polish site 'in order to secure the quality of the Polish products' (Görlitz Enterprise 1).

In this regard, two main patterns are visible in the data, indicating the duality of trust in the first case and the role of personal experiences and the background for trust and learning in the second case. First, 'calculated' trust occurs in the initial stages of a cross-border partnership, with genuine personal trust developing alongside 'calculated' trust in the later stages of the partnership. Secondly, in some cases, it is not geographical proximity as such that fosters 'calculated' trust, but negative experiences at the individual level, which forces entrepreneurs to reduce their level of initial trust and resort to safety and controls instead.

Finally, *cultural influences* can both facilitate and hinder trust-building. Where cultural proximity is supported by a functional institutional environment and political relationships, institutional trust in both its forms does not pose a problem, as for example in the Finnish–Swedish region of Tornio: 'Trust has never been an issue – in this way the Swedes are very much like the Finns – people consider oral contracts equally binding' (Tornio Enterprise 19), or similarly in the German–Polish region of Görlitz and Zgorzelec. This also holds true for many interviewees in the Finnish–Russian case study region of South Karelia, although personal trust dominates their cross-border relations, which confirms the important role of social capital and close ties in developing cooperation with partners from a post-Soviet context (see also Ledeneva, 1998, 2006; Schrader, 2004):

There is a saying about business in Russia, that before you know your partner thoroughly there is no point in starting to do business with him. (South Karelia Enterprise 14)

The only way to build trust is to have very close and personal relationships with the people involved – you have to be almost 'friends' before you can assume that things will work as promised. (South Karelia Enterprise 8).

Collective identities are an indicator for cultural proximity and are visible across most regions. In Southern European regions interviewees emphasized their 'Balkan identity' (Kyustendil Enterprise 19) as well as similarity in the languages used as a means of creating a common understanding in business relations across the border. In other regions, for example Sweden and Finland, cultural proximity is visible in common mentalities and behaviour. Interviewees mentioned traditions, religion, music, social habits, history and stories, heroes and national symbols, and common languages as the main facets of collective identities:

> A common background with Eastern countries helps to build trust. (...) They see the Slavic roots, similar language. Also, the perception of the world is similar (Polish–Belarusian border) (Biała Podlaska Enterprise 5).

> Common cultural habits helped in trust building. Balkan people are very close to us. I never felt fear or insecurity when in the FYRoM. They were never offensive towards us, unlike what many Greeks were expecting (Greek–Macedonian border) (Florina Enterprise 3).

> Don't forget that they are Balkans, just like us (Greek–Bulgarian border) (Serres Enterprise 6).

> Bulgarians and Macedonians have a common culture, common language and even common habits in eating and drinking, which facilitates the development of cross border activities (Bulgarian–Macedonian border) (Kyustendil Enterprise 3).

> A Finnish person and a Swedish person share exactly the same characteristics: they are equally honest, hardworking and also equally envious of other people (Finnish–Swedish border) (Tornio Enterprise 3).

The evidence also illustrates how cultural distance, as reflected in prejudices, retentions and stereotypes (for example, Adamczuk and Rymarczyk, 2003a; 2003b; Krätke, 1999), hinders trust-building. For example, most Polish respondents show a low level of informal institutional trust in their Belarusian partners, as apparent in interview statements such as: 'I always follow the rule of limited trust in contacts with Belarusians' (Biała Podlaska Enterprise 1) or another respondent claiming that 'they have it [cheating] in their blood' (Biała Podlaska Enterprise 3), even if over time partners might have come to know each other and have developed personal trust. Despite shared cultures, a lack of national identities might prevent trust to emerge in a cross-border cooperation:

Regarding trust, I can say that we did not trust them. Apart from the fact, they could not offer us a single safety valve and secure our payments, we have to bear in mind that they lack a clear, national identity. When you do business with them you cannot guess whether your partner is Slav, Muslim, Albanian, Roma or … whatever. You do not know who you have opposite to you and this makes you feel cautious. […] We could not understand each other and they could not guarantee for anything. (Florina Enterprise 12)

Typical Czech people with their cosiness, for instance, rather live in the heartland. After 1945, the formerly German settlements and cities located in the border region were filled with rather unwanted 'bad' people. Therefore, the Czechs living in this region seem a bit 'wilder' than those living in the heartland. People should pay attention with which they cooperate, for instance, and primarily inform on the previous history and the family of the possible cooperation partner. (Hochfranken Enterprise 3)

Interestingly, the evidence demonstrates an increase in cultural distance in regions with a mutual socialist history after EU accession, as illustrated in this quote where a Bulgarian entrepreneur describes the relationship with his Macedonian partners:

After Bulgaria's accession to the EU a role in building trust plays the respect that Macedonian people have to the Bulgarian ones. They already perceive the Bulgarians as people of a different class. (Kyustendil Enterprise 3)

Factors Influencing Trust at the Micro Level

Organizational and personal influences on trust form the micro context in which trust-building processes are embedded. In regions bordering countries with a turbulent and uncertain institutional environment, two behavioural patterns are visible, both signalling a lack of institutional trust, but with different implications for the role of personal trust and formal agreements. On the one hand, personal trust, signalled by informal agreements, can substitute for formal agreements. This is the case, for example, in both Estonian regions: 'A word given by a Russian businessman is worth more than an Estonian contract' (South-east Estonia Enterprise 19). On the other hand, personal trust is not necessary to complete business transactions because individuals resort to commercial regulations which allow them to forgo both personal and institutional trust. This refers to cooperation based on cash or advance payments. First of all, the nature of this cross-border cooperation (or the business field) explains such behaviour (see also Welter et al., 2004), but regional patterns are also to be found in the data. One such example refers to Biała Podlaska, bordering Belarus, where individuals and entrepreneurs display a high level of distrustful behaviour towards their

Belarusian partners, resulting in an overall dominance of regulations such as advance payments in cross-border partnerships. Nevertheless, our evidence on regulations of cross-border partnerships is not conclusive as to whether formal or informal (that is, handshake contracts) agreements foster trust-building. Geographical proximity facilitates the use of informal agreements, together with personal trust in the form of long-standing cooperation or previous knowledge of partners:

> As we have known each other now for years, the need for face-to-face meetings is not so great any more – we know the people we deal with personally and are also familiar with their ways of action. (South Karelia Enterprise 4)

Formal contracts are seen as a guarantee for long-term cooperation, setting out the general terms of the partnership such as delivery terms, prices and quality level. Respondents recognize that the validity of formal, written contracts depends on the overall institutional environment, which means that in many cases such agreements have to go hand in hand with personal trust, as illustrated by entrepreneurs in South Karelia and Görlitz:

> Making contracts with Russians can be rather problematic at times – you need to have good personal relations with your partners and once this level of trust has been achieved formal/written agreements are not really necessary, but even written contracts do not guarantee that things will go accordingly. The Russians can very abruptly claim that the contracts have become invalid. (South Karelia Enterprise 8)

> If you present a contract to Polish businessmen as the basis of a potential deal at the beginning of the negotiation, the deal will probably not be closed. That is why contracts in Poland should be handled with care. There, a promise is worth more than a signed contract. (Görlitz Enterprise 11)

Trust also emerges when both partners benefit from the cross-border cooperation. This is facilitated when there are friendships or previous knowledge of (potential) partners, suggesting that personal trust existed before the cross-border partnership started. This is apparent when interviewees discuss how they selected partners: 'The most important criterion to select my partners is the fact that I know them well, since they used to be my customers' (Florina Enterprise 17). Friendships also evolve over time, and well-functioning personal relations are considered an important success factor:

Concrete aims and opinions on side of the partners as well as implicit honesty are prerequisites for well-working collaboration. Only when interpersonal relationships work well, businesses can be successful and both partners are able to reach their aims. (Görlitz Enterprise 1)

Social relationships developed along with our entrepreneurial cooperation. You had to visit them, drink and eat once every time, etc. Our relations are better with our constant partners. (Florina Enterprise 3)

In some cases, interviewees perceived the objectives of partners to be detrimental to both their own goals and/or to the cross-border cooperation. This is vividly illustrated by a Greek entrepreneur discussing the nature of his cooperation with Macedonians and the implications this has for trust:

Most of the entrepreneurs engaged in retailing businesses are opportunists, focused on short-term relationships and profits, without caring about the future. They are not interested in getting improved and become professionals. This is the result of their past experiences, since the status quo there made them adopt a narrow minded perception on how to do business. In my opinion, you can't trust them. (Florina Enterprise 15)

Not surprisingly, trust-building is fostered by *regular communication*: 'Neither contracts, lawyers nor seminars can be as helpful as personal communication between partners' (Görlitz Enterprise 1), which itself is facilitated by geographical and cultural proximity. Geographical proximity allows for frequent face-to-face meetings, which have been shown above as important factors for building trust (Welter et al., 2004), while cultural proximity at the level of communication is reflected in common language skills. It also means being familiar with the other's mentality, either because of a common culture, or due to shared experiences during Soviet times. This is apparent in the Estonian border regions, where many entrepreneurs and household traders had worked in Russia during the Soviet period, or they were Russian by origin. This draws attention to the close links between the macro and micro contexts of trust-building and learning, as illustrated by a Greek entrepreneur in describing his cooperation with an enterprise in the FYRoM:

One of the most important trust building factors is the common cultural background. If you ever go there and attend a marriage or a funeral, you will see that they are alike to us. In addition […], language is another fostering factor for cross-border cooperation and trust building in general, allowing us to come closer, even though we always have to be careful when selecting a partner, just like in every other cooperation. (Florina Enterprise 17)

Personal factors are the final component of the micro context for trust-building. The background and behaviour of both partners, the nature of their relationship and experiences with current and previous cross-border cooperation, influence trust and learning. Such factors are seen as sources of reliability and reliance, reflecting individual (or organizational) trustworthiness (Nooteboom, 2002, pp. 63–6). The background of partners, reflected in, for example, their professional experiences, schooling and language skills as well as in experience living abroad, in some cases signals openness towards other cultures, but it also draws attention to the skills and knowledge required for building cross-border partnerships. The behaviour of partners refers to personal characteristics and feelings emphasized in many interviews, which included honesty or loyalty, often mentioned alongside sympathy and empathy (Nooteboom, 2007), but also to partners acting in a business-like manner. In this respect, Western 'entrepreneurial identities', in the sense of 'trusted' and familiar behaviour, which is visible in, for example, payment on time, quality of products and timely deliveries, facilitate the emergence of trust; these Western entrepreneurial identities are requirements for trust to emerge. Partners have to earn trust through adhering to 'trusted' entrepreneurial behaviour:

> Trust is very important and it's impossible to work without that on the Russian market. The best way to create trust is to provide good products. Then it's also easier to sell. (South East Estonia Enterprise 7)

> Matters of trust are always present in every partnership. Concretely, certain factors exist that positively contribute. Our own reliability and good payment terms make them feel secure. Thus, they trust us. From our own point of view, the fact that they are always on time, within the given quality standards, holds an important role as well. (Florina Enterprise 11)

Where there is a clash between a 'Western' and 'Eastern' (unknown) entrepreneurial identity, trust-building is hindered, as seen in this example from the Finnish–Karelian border:

> Cooperation with Russian entrepreneurs has not been easy. The problems arise mostly from the fact that the Russians do not understand what Western companies expect from them – these misunderstandings about the 'rules' of doing business are what cause the most common problems. The Russians' commitment for doing business is not always admirable – I think this is something that the local culture does not emphasize, and this will surely be a problem also in the future. (South Karelia Enterprise 18)

Some respondents, mainly enterprises with vested interests in their cross-border cooperation, assist their partners to develop the skills and knowledge required for the partnership to flourish: 'when I see that they are not able to respond to my needs and requirements I try to instruct them on how to become better. Thus, cross-border cooperation becomes a great learning process for them' (Florina Enterprise 8). Another example from Hoch-franken illustrates this further: the firm cooperates with Czech companies, depending on their quality and reliable deliveries. The entrepreneur (Hoch-franken Enterprise 9) therefore organized training for his Czech partner and raised their quality processes to a level that he was satisfied with. This brings us to the next topic, namely learning in a cross-border context.

Learning in a Cross-Border Context

Two patterns of learning are visible in cross-border partnerships (Welter and Smallbone, 2008). One refers to enterprises and households 'learning (international) entrepreneurship', the second refers to 'learning to trust'. In case study regions with a socialist history (that is, Bulgaria, Estonia, Poland), the first pattern mainly consists of 'learning entrepreneurship' and this particularly applies at the level of household cooperation. To some extent, Poland is an exception because of early reforms in socialist times, which meant that the process of 'learning entrepreneurship' may have started as early as the 1970s. In regions belonging to mature market economies (Finland, Germany, Greece) and in Poland, this process is also related to 'learning international entrepreneurship'.

'Learning to trade' (Hohnen, 2003, p. 33) allows for the routinization and institutionalization of entrepreneurial practices, even where these result from simple cross-border trading activities (Welter and Smallbone, 2009). Entrepreneurial learning starts with recognizing opportunities in cross-border activity, realizing such ideas through cross-border petty trading activities, which are frequently illegal or semi-legal, and building up to a more substantial business over time. For example, one household in Bul-garia (Petrich Household 6) was importing processed olives from Greece. His intentions were to import unprocessed olives directly from Greek producers, process them in Bulgaria and distribute them on the local market in Petrich through a firm specifically registered for this activity. The other side of 'learning entrepreneurship' concerns 'learning international entre-preneurship' in different country contexts. This is especially to be seen in enterprise partnerships, regardless of the border region:

> The experience we have gained by entering foreign markets has taught us many things. Starting from the Balkans, we are planning to establish a network throughout Europe. It is very important to know your way around foreign markets. As I've already mentioned, this cooperation with Bulgaria has attracted

our interest to further expand our presence in the country, perhaps by establishing a branch there. (Serres Enterprise 8)

The second learning pattern refers to 'learning to trust'. In this regard, the empirical evidence illustrates that learning is often needed for trust to evolve, but it also shows that in some cases learning may need trust.

> In the course of time, trust is starting to build up. After each trip, both parties learn and profit from this experience. The other day, they asked me to give them a deposit of €1500 for a group of Greek people that would travel to Ohrid and then take the money from the Greeks. OK, I wasn't happy to do so, but I would have never done it if there weren't a certain degree of trust between us. (Florina Enterprise 8)

Not surprisingly, the background and behaviour of partners, the nature of their relationship and experiences with current and previous cross-border cooperation influence this type of learning, as emphasized by a Polish entrepreneur cooperating with a partner in Görlitz, Germany: 'Trust has been already built and is still being built on the basis of payment terms, reliability, our stability and long period of being in the market' (Zgorzelec Enterprise 4). In this context, it is the above-mentioned 'Western entrepreneurial identities' which may facilitate or impede 'learning to trust'. This is best illustrated by Greek entrepreneurs describing relations with partners in Bulgaria: 'Bulgarians are not familiar with the Western type of doing business. They are not used to make agreements. In many cases they drive a hard bargain after we have signed the related contracts' (Serres Enterprise 14); and only over time does a 'common business language with our Bulgarian partners' (Serres Enterprise 2) develop, resulting in entrepreneurs feeling 'more secure' (Serres Enterprise 2). Thus, 'learning entrepreneurship' and 'learning to trust' are closely linked; especially where one of the partners comes from a post-Soviet context, which is often reinforced by historical experiences and animosities, as in the Balkan context. Learning entrepreneurship contributes to post-Soviet partners 'earning trust' over time with their partners from an advanced market context 'learning trust' at the same time, thereby indicating the importance of understanding learning and trust as a process.

'Learning to trust' often appears to be restricted to single-loop learning because the trust needed for higher-level learning to occur is missing or cannot evolve. In all case study regions, individuals with negative experiences are often among those bringing forward stereotypes and cultural prejudices as the major explanation why their cross-border cooperation did not work. This is visible in the example described below, although the reasons might also have been their lack of experience, their risk-behaviour, a badly planned market entry, or a lack of cross-cultural competencies.

> Once we cooperated with a transport company from Belarus. We helped him to buy two Scania trucks in Sweden. The company was developing until somebody stole their trucks and the whole load [...]. Some half year later their drivers came to us and said that they wanted to cooperate, that he is the boss right now. It was obvious for us that this load was stolen by the drivers. This told us that this nation is not worth trusting. It is a black hole on the map. (Biała Podlaska Enterprise 11)

In some cases, individuals who have had negative experiences continue their partnership or develop new partnerships, therefore displaying a capacity for double-loop learning by adapting their underlying actions and strategies, even if the negative experience has resulted in them losing trust. In other words, although fraud and cheating breed distrust, it can also trigger positive entrepreneurial learning. This is illustrated in examples across all surveyed regions where entrepreneurs, when asked for learning experiences from their partnerships, emphasized the need to survey markets properly before concluding cross-border partnerships, to formalize business partnerships or simply to be 'more cautious' in dealing with unknown partners:

> On the other hand, our company has learned a lot from this process. We are more experienced now and we know we can't trust anyone. We have now learned that we have to conduct a proper market survey before we enter a foreign market. Of course, this experience makes us a little cautious for the future ones, particularly with foreign collaborators. We are circumspect and I believe this is reasonable. (Florina Enterprise 10)

Learning can occur on both sides, as illustrated by this entrepreneur from Greece, who displayed a proactive approach when summarizing his learning experiences:

> Every single step we take in our cross-border cooperation is a big lesson for us. The learning experience is extremely helpful, since we get familiarized with their mentality, the legal framework and we adapt to this environment. We also learn to distinguish between our partners and choose the one that fits best in our strategic plan. Taken for granted that our intention is the expansion to the Balkan market, every single partnership is a great lesson for us and surely affects our behaviour in the future. We create what we call 'experience network'. The previous experience gives us the green light to continue, or an orange-alert-light to warn us for possible risks. [...] We view this cooperation as know-how exchange. There are things that we offer and things that we learn by our Bulgarian partners, which are extremely useful for us. Just think of how they realize and exploit the opportunities in the mountain areas. Just look at how they

have developed the ski centre in Bansko. They are also familiar with the procedures involving joint ventures between private entities and State agencies and we cannot be compared to them. They have also specialized knowledge and if you approach your cooperation in a positive manner, there are a lot of things to gain. (Serres Enterprise 2)

CONCLUSIONS AND IMPLICATIONS

It has been shown that the factors influencing trust and learning in cross-border entrepreneurial activities operate at both macro and micro levels. At the macro level, the institutional framework, economic factors, as well as cultural and spatial dimensions influence trust and learning. At the micro level organizational and personal factors are important for trust to emerge and learning to occur.

In this regard, our evidence illustrates a twofold role for personal trust in cross-border cooperation: cross-border cooperation is mainly triggered at the personal level, which means that, in many cases, personal trust is a necessary 'ingredient' for cross-border cooperation to emerge, especially in institutional environments, which does not encourage the development of institutional trust in the wider sense. Personal trust emerges as a result of repeated actions in cross-border cooperation, leaving us with an apparent dilemma: how can cross-border cooperation come about if personal trust does not exist at the beginning? Möllering (2006, p. 191) argues that at the 'heart of the concept of trust is the suspension of vulnerability and uncertainty (the leap of faith), which enables actors to have positive expectations of others'. This perspective allows us to solve the dilemma of the recursive nature of personal trust, and is an important facet drawing attention to a much required process perspective on trust in a cross-border context. Interestingly, our empirical evidence also demonstrates that 'genuine' personal trust, based on friendship, empathy and habituation, rarely dominates in business relations. Personal trust is typically complemented by 'calculated' trust, thus apparently confirming Williamson's conclusion that it is not personal trust, but rather 'calculated' trust which dominates in business relationships (Williamson, 1993). The evidence presented in this chapter shows personal trust in a cross-border context as having both calculative and non-calculative, routinized and habitual, elements, thus confirming its dual nature. Genuine trust and control can co-exist and co-evolve (see also Möllering, 2005).

Moreover, the empirical results show that both personal and institutional trust may be required for learning to occur. 'Learning to trust' in institutions at all levels (individuals, organizations, regions) is triggered by experience with institutions at the individual level. This draws attention to the links between macro factors influencing trust and learning and their impact on learning and trust-building at the micro level. All this takes on particular importance in a cross-border context, where learning and trust are needed for the cooperation to develop successfully over time. It draws attention to the factors which would need to be addressed in order to ensure that participants are able to realize the full potential of their cross-border entrepreneurial activities over time. One of the main points emerging from the empirical data concerns the complexity and reciprocal nature of the interrelations between personal and institutional trust and levels of learning.

In terms of implications for theory and future research, the results illustrate that the duality of trust, as stipulated by Möllering for trust and control (that is, personal trust), also exists for institutional trust. In this regard, future research could seek to analyse further the extent to which such differences in the nature of trust in cross-border entrepreneurship foster or impede the development potential of cross-border activities. Additionally, further research needs to pay more attention to the duality of genuine personal trust and control. Conceptually, the multi-dimensionality of the trust phenomenon poses challenges for understanding and researching trust. In this regard, another research implication concerns methods and methodologies of researching trust and learning. Taking into account the context- and process-nature of the phenomena in question, future research needs to study trust and learning, both qualitatively and longitudinally, in order to gain deeper insights into its nature.

NOTES

1. See Smallbone et al. (2007) for a detailed literature review. Exceptions in this regard include a recently finished project on cross-border cooperation in Belarus, Moldova and Ukraine (cf. Welter et al., 2007a; 2007b; Welter and Smallbone, 2008, 2009), and a project researching German–Ukrainian business relationships with particular emphasis on their links to the overall institutional framework (cf. Möllering and Stache, 2007).
2. In 1944, Marshal Tito created Yugoslavia's southern republic and called it 'Socialist Republic of Macedonia'. However, 'Macedonia' was already the name of one of Greece's Northern provinces. After 1991 the country was temporarily named 'The Former Yugoslav Republic of Macedonia (The FYRoM)', but its people continue to call it Macedonia. Neither the Greek government nor the Greek people agree with this.

REFERENCES

Adamczuk, F. and J. Rymarczyk (2003a), 'Local aspects of European integration on the example of Zgorzelec/Görlitz cross-border co-operation', in G. Dieckheuer (ed.), *Eastward Enlargement of the European Union. Economic Aspects*, Frankfurt am Main: Peter Lang, pp. 137–46.

Adamczuk, F. and J. Rymarczyk (2003b), 'Transborder cooperation in Europe based on the example of Poland and Germany', in G. Dieckheuer (ed.), *Eastward Enlargement of the European Union. Economic Aspects*, Frankfurt am Main: Peter Lang, pp. 147–57.

Bachmann, R. (2003), 'The role of trust and power in the institutional regulation of territorial business systems', in D. Fornahl and T. Brenner (eds), *Cooperation, Networks and Institutions in Regional Innovation Systems*, Cheltenham, UK and Northampton, MA, USA: Edward Elgar, pp. 58–81.

Chepurenko, A. and E. Malieva (2005), 'Trust milieus of Russian SMEs: cross-regional comparisons', in H.-H. Höhmann and F. Welter (eds), *Trust and Entrepreneurship: A West–East Perspective*, Cheltenham, UK and Northampton, MA, USA: Edward Elgar, pp. 136–55.

Fukuyama, F. (1995), *Trust: the Social Virtues and the Creation of Prosperity*, New York: Free Press.

Gambetta, D. (1988), 'Can we trust trust?', in D. Gambetta (ed.), *Trust: Making and Breaking, Co-operative Relations*, Oxford: Blackwell Publishers, pp. 213–37.

Höhmann, H-H. and F. Welter (eds) (2005), *Trust and Entrepreneurship: A West–East Perspective*, Cheltenham, UK and Northampton, MA, USA: Edward Elgar.

Hohnen, P. (2003), *A Market out of Place? Remaking Economic, Social and Symbolic Boundaries in Post-Communist Lithuania*, Oxford: Oxford University Press.

Humphrey, C. (2002), *The Unmaking of Soviet Life: Everyday Economies after Socialism*, Ithaca, NY and London: Cornell University Press.

Krätke, S. (1999), 'Regional integration or fragmentation? The German–Polish border region in a new Europe', *Regional Studies*, **33**(7), 631–41.

Lane, C. (1997), 'The social regulation of inter-firm relations in Britain and Germany: market rules, legal norms and technical standards', *Cambridge Journal of Economics*, **21**(2), 197–215.

Lane, C. and R. Bachmann (1996), 'The social constitution of trust: supplier relations in Britain and Germany', *Organization Studies*, **17**, 365–95.

Ledeneva, A.V. (1998), *Russia's Economy of Favours: Blat, Networking and Informal Exchange*, Cambridge: Cambridge University Press.

Ledeneva, A.V. (2006), *How Russia Really Works: The Informal Practices that shaped Post-Soviet Politics and Business*, Ithaca, NY: Cornell University Press.

Möllering, G. (2005), 'The trust/control duality: an integrative perspective on positive expectations of others', *International Sociology*, **20**(3), 283–305.

Möllering, G. (2006), *Trust: Reason, Routine, Reflexivity,* Amsterdam: Elsevier.

Möllering, G. and F. Stache (2007), 'German–Ukrainian business relationships: trust development in the face of institutional uncertainty and cultural differences', MPIfG Discussion Paper 07/11, Cologne: MPIfG.

Nonaka, I., R. Toyama and P. Byosière (2001), 'A theory of organizational knowledge creation: understanding the dynamic process of creating knowledge', in M. Dierkes, A. Berthoin Antal, J. Child and I. Nonaka (eds), *Handbook of Organizational Learning and Knowledge*, Oxford: Oxford University Press, pp. 491–517.

Nooteboom, B. (2002), *Trust: Forms, Foundations, Functions, Failures and Figures*, Cheltenham, UK and Northampton, MA, USA: Edward Elgar.

Nooteboom, B. (2007), 'Social capital, institutions and trust', *Review of Social Economy*, **65**(1), 29–53.

Polanyi, M. (1966), *The Tacit Dimension*, Garden City, NY: Doubleday.

Radaev, V. (2004), 'How trust is established in economic relationships when institutions and individuals are not trustworthy: the case of Russia', in J. Kornai, B. Rothstein and S. Rose-Ackerman (eds), *Creating Social Trust in Post-Socialist Transition*, New York: Palgrave Macmillan, pp. 91–110.

Schrader, H. (2004), 'Spheres of trust, social capital and transformation in Russia', in H. Schrader (ed.), *Trust and Social Transformation*, Münster: Lit, pp. 79–101.

Smallbone, D., L. Labrianidis, U. Venesaar, F. Welter and P. Zashev (2007), 'Challenges and prospects of cross border cooperation in the context of EU enlargement', Deliverable 7: State of the Art Review of Literature, Kingston, UK: Kingston University.

Thuen, T. (1999), 'The significance of borders in the East European transition', *International Journal of Urban and Regional Research*, **23**(4), 738–50.

Venesaar, U. (2005), 'Emergence of and changes in trust in Estonian SMEs', in H.-H. Höhmann and F. Welter (eds), *Trust and Entrepreneurship: A West-East Perspective*, Cheltenham, UK and Northampton, MA, USA: Edward Elgar, pp. 176–96.

Wallace, C., V. Bedzir and O. Chmouliar (1997), 'Spending, saving or investing social capital: the case of shuttle traders in post-communist Central Europe', East European Series No. 43/June 1997, Vienna: Institute for Advanced Studies.

Wallace, C., in association with O. Shmulyar and V. Bedzir (1999), 'Investing in social capital: the case of small-scale, cross-border traders in post-communist Central Europe', *International Journal of Urban and Regional Research*, **23**(4), 751–70.

Welter, F. (2005), 'Culture versus branch? Looking at trust and entrepreneurial behaviour from a cultural and sectoral perspective', in H.-H. Höhmann and F. Welter (eds), *Trust and Entrepreneurship: A West-East Perspective*, Cheltenham, UK and Northampton, MA, USA: Edward Elgar, pp. 24–38.

Welter, F. and D. Smallbone (2006), 'Exploring the role of trust in entrepreneurial activity', *Entrepreneurship Theory and Practice*, **30**(4), 465–75.

Welter, F. and D. Smallbone (2008), 'Entrepreneurship in a cross border context: the example of transition countries', paper presented to the ICSB World Conference, Halifax, June.

Welter, F. and D. Smallbone (2009), 'The emergence of entrepreneurial potential in transition environments: a challenge for entrepreneurship theory or a developmental perspective?', in D. Smallbone, H. Landström and D. Jones-Evans (eds), *Entrepreneurship and Growth in Local, Regional and National Economies*, Frontiers in European Entrepreneurship Research, Cheltenham, UK and Northampton, MA, USA: Edward Elgar, pp. 339–53.

Welter, F., T. Kautonen, A. Chepurenko, E. Malieva and U. Venesaar (2004), 'Trust environments and entrepreneurial behaviour: exploratory evidence from Estonia, Germany and Russia', *Journal of Enterprising Culture*, **12**(4), 327–49.

Welter, F., D. Smallbone, A. Slonimski, O. Linchevskaya, A. Pobol and M. Slonimska (2006), 'Enterprising households in a cross-border context', paper presented at RENT, Brussels, 22–24 November.

Welter, F., D. Smallbone, E. Aculai, N. Isakova and A. Slonimski (2007a), 'Cross-border partnerships in Belarus, Moldova and Ukraine and the consequences of EU enlargement: state of the art literature review', Beiträge zur KMU-Forschung 3, Siegen: PRO KMU.

Welter, F., D. Smallbone, E. Aculai, N. Isakova and A. Slonimski (2007b), 'Cross-border cooperations in Belarus, Moldova and the Ukraine and EU enlargement', Summary Report for INTAS 04-79-6991, Siegen: PRO KMU.

Williams, A. and V. Balaz (2002), 'International petty trading: changing practices in trans-Carpathian Ukraine', *International Journal of Urban and Regional Research*, **26**(2), 323–42.

Williams, A. and V. Balaz (2005), 'Winning, then losing, the battle with globalization: Vietnamese petty traders in Slovakia', *International Journal of Urban and Regional Research*, **29**(3), 533–49.

Williamson, O.E. (1993), 'Calculativeness, trust and economic organization', *Journal of Law and Economics*, **XXXVI**, 453–86.

PART II

Regional Case Studies from the EU

4. Cross-border cooperation within an enlarged Europe: Görlitz–Zgorzelec

Anna Rogut and Friederike Welter

INTRODUCTION

Although it is the barrier effects that are more often emphasized, state borders represent a potential asset which provides cross-border regions with an opportunity to become centres of growth (ESPON and Interact, 2007). At the German–Polish border, Görlitz and Zgorzelec have taken advantage of this opportunity, and for two decades they have been participating in various forms of cross-border cooperation defined as 'any concerted action designed to reinforce and foster neighbourly relations between territorial communities or authorities [...] and the conclusion of any agreement and arrangement necessary for this purpose' (Council of Europe, 1980, article 2).

Institutional cooperation of both regions has been supported by a number of EU initiatives. One of the first was the PHARE CBC[1] programme, which financed a wide range of activities, including transport, telecommunications, small infrastructural projects, and the development of local authorities' competence (WWPE, 2007). However, all the projects were 'linked to measures supported by INTERREG or by other Community external assistance programmes and/or [...] projects agreed by the countries concerned, that have a cross-border impact, contribute to the development of structures in border regions and facilitate cooperation between the countries as a whole' (European Commission, 2004, pp. 6/7). In the years 2004–06, similar support was provided under the INTERREG IIIA programme, which was designed to stimulate the development of cross-border economic and social centres; to finance the development of industries of entrepreneurship and small companies; to improve the cross-border system of environmental protection, the modernization and development of transport links, fostering small local initiatives; to develop human capital and institutional forms of cross-border cooperation, as well as to expand cooperation in research, technological development, education and culture (Gorzelak et al., 2004; Taylor et al., 2005). In the years 2007–13, such assistance is provided under European Territorial Cooperation,[2] financing, amongst others, the bilateral Cross-Border Cooperation Programme Poland–Saxony 2007–2013. This programme aims at administrative cooperation and the integration of local communities. This is achieved through the delivery of joint actions on the labour market: support for entrepreneurship and development of small and medium-sized enterprises (SMEs), tourism, culture and cross-border trade, information and communication networks and development and common use of infrastructure, especially in such areas as health protection, culture and education (Saxon State Ministry for Economy and Labour, 2008).

Institutional cooperation has been accompanied by the development of spontaneous cooperation between companies and households, undertaken with or without the support of programmes and public resources (Guz-Vetter, 2002; Małachowski, 1997; Szromnik, 1993). This type of cooperation has become an element of a wider range of structural transformations resulting from global trends (Kofman and Youngs, 2003; Swyngedouw, 2004; Waters, 2001). For a long time, such cross-border activity was stimulated by the differences in prices, labour costs as well as in institutional regulations (particularly with reference to the labour markets). However, in the post-accession period (since 2004), such differences have been gradually declining (European Commission, 2008; Rogut, 2008; Rokicki and Żołnowski, 2008), which in turn has led to seeking new sources of mutual benefits.

This chapter aims to provide an empirical overview of future prospects of development of, first, institutional and, second, enterprise cross-border cooperation between Görlitz and Zgorzelec, with a particular focus on challenges and barriers. The data are drawn from the CBCED project (Challenges and Prospects of Cross-Border Cooperation in the Context of EU Enlargement, 2006–2008). The chapter begins with a short description of the cross-border regions studied, highlighting the experience with cross-border cooperation, followed by an assessment of the challenges to institutional and enterprise-based cross-border activity. It concludes with brief policy recommendations.

GÖRLITZ–ZGORZELEC: TOWARDS A CROSS-BORDER REGION

Görlitz and Zgorzelec are twin cities (and counties) separated by the Neisse/Nysa River, which since 1945 has formed the border between Germany and Poland. Prior to that, Görlitz was the economic, political and cultural centre of the Prussian Upper Lusatia and home to large industrial firms, as well as SMEs, although the two world wars halted this favourable development. The treaty of Potsdam in 1945 confirmed the Oder–Neisse Line as the new border between Poland and Germany, dividing Görlitz into a German zone on the western side of the river, and a Polish zone, named Zgorzelec. Since then, both towns have diverged in terms of their economies: Görlitz remained home to the main industries while Zgorzelec 'inherited' some municipal utility works and a few manufacturing workshops (Adamczuk and Rymarczyk, 2003a).

Until 1990 Görlitz was part of the GDR (German Democratic Republic). Although the GDR and Poland were both socialist countries, neither the political nor the social ramifications of the border were reduced after the division. Consequently, the cities developed independently of one another (Friedrich et al., 2005). The national boundary remained an external, EU hard border until 1989. The demarcation along the Neisse in 1945 was a strong symbol of separation. As a result, for a long time, cooperation between Görlitz and Zgorzelec was 'virtually non-existent' and the first steps in that direction were not taken until 1970 (Adamczuk and Rymarczyk, 2003a). Since that time, cross-border cooperation has been gaining in momentum and significance, albeit with some periods of stagnation. For instance, in the mid-1980s, approximately 1600 to 2000 inhabitants of Zgorzelec and the surrounding areas were employed on the German side of the border. In the autumn of 1980, cooperation came to an almost complete standstill because of the Solidarity movement in Poland, but in 1984, when the political situation calmed down, it resumed anew. In the late 1980s, ties between the cities were further strengthened by the formation of a Polish–German municipal bus line and taxi service across the border (Adamczuk and Rymarczyk, 2003a; Friedrich et al., 2005).

The political breakthrough of 1990 gave hope and offered prospects for Görlitz to rise as an intermediary between East and West Europe. Since 1989, the border has been open with no visa requirements (Galasinska et al., 2002). Additionally, in 1991 the German and Polish governments signed a 'treaty on good neighbourhood relations and friendly cooperation' and an agreement concerning regional and cross-border cooperation (Adamczuk and Rymarczyk, 2003b). On the regional level, the installation of a cross-border commission for the coordination of the city councils of Görlitz and Zgorzelec institutionalized the formerly loose and project-oriented cooperation that had been going on since the mid-1990s. In 1998, the cooperation of the cities culminated in the proclamation of the 'European City of Görlitz–Zgorzelec', which had an important symbolic dimension (Friedrich et al., 2005). The cities aimed to jointly solve problems concerning education, culture, sports, economy and municipal services while, at the same time, respecting their mutual national interests. This political rapprochement was accompanied by the development of the transport infrastructure between the regions, which led to a high density of border crossing points.

The breakthrough of 1990 and the subsequent steps towards EU membership have paved the way for intensive institutional and enterprise cross-border cooperation. This has been additionally enhanced by a challenge common to both regions, that is, the disadvantage of being geographically located in between the much bigger cities of Dresden (Germany) and Wrocław (Poland), which attract investors and skilled professionals and are seen as 'boom towns'. This has been compounded by changes in the age structure towards an ageing population and a decreasing population of employable age groups (Kathke et al., 2005; Niebuhr and Stiller, 2004). Additionally, both regions have experienced a high emigration rate of young people.

These threats are fully reflected in the development scenario for the Polish–German border areas, which forecasts increased spatial concentration around large cities, including Dresden and Wrocław, which will attract new inhabitants and new types of businesses to become regional metropolitan areas (Lammers et al., 2006). The scenario also predicts the possibility of a high growth rate of medium-sized cities, and in particular of the Polish–German twin cities of Görlitz and Zgorzelec. However, it will be much easier to take advantage of this opportunity if the regions are able to create a common cross-border region defined not only in terms of geographical proximity (ESPON and Interact, 2007), but also in terms of a 'more or less explicit strategic objective pursued by social forces within and beyond border regions' (Perkmann, 2007, p. 254; see also Kramach and Hooper, 2004; Leibenath et al., 2008; Perkmann and Sum, 2002).

The first steps in this direction have already been taken, and the twenty-year long institutional cross-border cooperation has given rise to the first cross-border structures.[3] However, according to an international study (ESPON, 2006), in both regions there still remains some untapped potential. This is reflected in the relatively low level of membership in transnational activities, even though 'the membership alone does not say anything about the quality and quantity of activities' (ESPON, 2006, p. 113). The next step would be to merge both regions into a single functional cross-border region with a high 'ability to create and achieve appropriate internal interactions while pursuing common interests for the future' (ESPON and Interact, 2007, p. 8). However, in order to achieve this it would be necessary to tackle the challenges hindering the existing scale and scope of institutional and enterprise cross-border cooperation.

CHALLENGES TO INSTITUTIONAL CROSS-BORDER COOPERATION

The challenges to institutional cross-border cooperation include both policy-driven and market-driven mechanisms. The former refer to the ability to build 'co-operative relationships between public and other bodies that share certain interests, such as coping with environmental interdependencies or creating cross-border economic spaces' (Perkmann, 2005, p. 5). The basis for building such relationships has been a long process, although the ongoing process of European integration impacts on 'domestic institutions and their political cultures' (Cowles et al., 2001, p. 1; see also Bukowski et al., 2003; Featherstone and Radaelli, 2003; Gualini, 2004).

As in the majority of Central and Eastern European EU member countries, in Poland the process of Europeanization began with transformation in the early 1990s. Initially, it was based on the Europe Agreements[4] and the decision of the European Council taken at the summit in Copenhagen (June 1993), which opened the door to the European Union for those countries.[5] Another step was the development (1994) of additional (the Europe Agreements notwithstanding) forms and rules of cooperation under the so-called structural dialogue, which aimed to support the processes of adjustment to EU standards and in particular to the requirements of the Single Market. The subsequent stage included the adoption of the so-called reinforced pre-accession strategy aimed at the combination of different forms of EU support into a uniform framework of the Accession Partnership Programme. It also aimed to familiarize candidate countries with European Union policies and procedures (European Commission, 1997), which was significant from the perspective of Europeanization. It was achieved through the broad involvement of candidates in all Community programmes, the implementation of two new forms of pre-accession aid,[6] as of 2000, and the focusing of PHARE aid on projects directly contributing to the acceleration of integration with the European Union. As regards Poland, this meant focusing on, among others, the operation of public administration, particularly the degree of fit of the existing administrative arrangements with European requirements (Hille and Knill, 2006). Consequently, when Poland became an EU member, it had relatively well-prepared administration structures (Leiber, 2007; MWH Consortium, 2007), including such areas as regional policy and the coordination of structural instruments; the development of an efficient administration system and adjustment to the EU standards, together with the rules and procedures of programming, financing, monitoring and evaluation (MRRiB, 2000).

However, CBCED findings, in particular the key informant interviews with representatives of municipalities, support organizations and similar bodies in both Görlitz and Zgorzelec, indicate that some of the challenges that persist with respect to institutional cross-border cooperation are differences in administrative systems. This may be figuratively illustrated with reference to the following interview fragment:

> The Mayor of Zawidów cooperates with a Czech County Head. But the Saxon self-government is different. [...] It is not clear whether they are peers or not. It would seem that the question of titles is not that important, but it still constitutes a certain barrier and occasionally delays some actions.

In addition, there is a degree of dualism of the Polish governmental and self-governmental authorities,[7] which leads to competence conflicts and political disputes, shorter experience in preparing projects, behavioural differences due to different business models, and a subordination of economic interests to political interests (Box 4.1). As a result, it is not surprising that German interviewees reported the following: the main problem concerns the centralized organization of Poland. Many decisions are only confirmed after consulting Warsaw. Institutional cooperation is hampered in those cases where contracts and feedback from the Polish government are required. The Polish administrative procedures often result in long time lags. Many Polish institutions used every opportunity to gain profit themselves, either legally or illegally. Despite goodwill and interest, conflicts arise where both sides put their own interests first.

BOX 4.1   DIFFERENCES IN ADMINISTRATIVE SYSTEMS

Different business models: 'Polish people are hot-blooded by nature. Once they have an idea, a concept, they would like to pull it through quickly, arrive at concrete decisions as to action or division of responsibilities. On the other hand, Germans take a lot of time, they need a timetable, several meetings, everything needs to be planned well in advance and discussed. Recently, the Regional Contact Point revealed that it had some savings from other projects, and it needed to file an application very soon – within a week. The Commune quickly came up with an idea – the only remaining thing was to discuss it with the city of Görlitz. So we called the City Office, and they say all right, we could meet in three weeks. However, finally we managed to get around it, and the project was eventually granted financing.' (Key informant, Zgorzelec Communal Office).

Subordination of economic interests to political interests: 'Cooperation with other local authorities in nearby areas is uneven. It would be much better without politics, and once someone's political beliefs have come into play, cooperation does not go smoothly any more. If you strictly adhere to your party lines, nothing good comes out of it; your actions do not tend to be factual.' (Key informant, Zawidów Communal Office).

This situation is compounded by the differences in the levels of socioeconomic development (ESPON, 2006) which lead to diverging goals and interests of the regional authorities. These differences surfaced in the protracted negotiations concerning the Cross-Border Cooperation Operational Programme Poland–Saxony 2007–2013, and differences in the prioritization of objectives for the next few years. In Poland, the most important projects are infrastructural, whereas in Germany they are focused on soft programmes: social, cultural and educational.

On the Polish side, institutional cross-border cooperation is also hampered by the scarcity of national financial resources, which is felt particularly strongly by entrepreneurs' organizations, and a lack of support from public funds (Box 4.2).

BOX 4.2   FINANCIAL BARRIERS TO CROSS-BORDER COOPERATION

Local authorities: 'The problem is that German partners are given some resources for their business activities from the state authorities, but the Association does not have such aid from the government. This vast difference in potential is particularly visible if the resources assigned to particular types of outlays are compared, e.g. on human resources. While in Poland, the outlays amount to approximately 2000 euros, in Germany they amount to 10 000 euros, which causes a feeling of injustice.' (Key informant, South-Western Local Government Forum).

Business organizations: 'Another factor impairing the development of cooperation between chambers of commerce and entrepreneurs across the border is the much higher financial potential of German chambers as compared to their Polish counterparts. In Germany, the membership of entrepreneurs in chambers of commerce is guaranteed by law (obligatory), and that is why German chambers are wealthy (membership fees) and have a very strong influence on the development of their regions. For example, it is virtually impossible to carry out a major investment without obtaining the opinion of a chamber of commerce first. The issuance of such an opinion is legally guaranteed. Thus, the law is helpful to entrepreneurs in Germany. On the other hand, in Poland there are many small chambers of commerce; there are chambers of commerce in every major city, including three in Wrocław alone. Moreover, in cities there are also numerous regional development agencies, which make it difficult for foreign (German) companies to decide who to approach and talk to about investment. The existence of numerous small business support institutions in the region should be treated as an important detriment to the development of cross-border cooperation and entrepreneurship.' (Key informant, West Chamber of Commerce).

An important factor in cooperation between local authorities is the fact that the main source of financing for that cooperation is individual projects. It is often the case that a lack of continuity between particular projects leads to frequent rotation of contact persons, especially on the Polish side, which makes it difficult to establish long-standing relationships. On the other hand, cooperation between business organizations, (mainly chambers of commerce), is affected by the differences in the ways they operate. For example, while craft enterprises are obliged to become members of the Chamber of Crafts in Germany, Poland has a voluntary membership, and the chamber system varies from region to region. Therefore, German institutions have difficulties in identifying potential Polish partners for German enterprises that are interested in cross-border cooperation. Additionally, because of the large number of chambers in Poland, institutional partnerships are mainly driven by the initiative of single persons and groups.

Further challenges are posed by market-driven mechanisms based on 'the proliferation and/or reactivation of social or economic relationships' (Perkmann, 2005, p. 5), the most important ones being prejudices of people living on both sides of the border, involving negative stereotypes and mentality (Box 4.3).

BOX 4.3   CHALLENGES RELATED TO
             MARKET-DRIVEN MECHANISMS

Prejudices: On the German side, those Germans who had
been banished from their former homeland still hold prejudices
against the neighbouring Polish regions. Therefore, Poland's
entry into the EU was viewed with great suspicion in the region
and many people voiced their concern. They assumed crime
rates would rise and the labour market would be overwhelmed
by cheaper competitors from Poland, leading to the destruction
of the German price level. It was particularly craftsmen who
feared EU enlargement. On the Polish side some people say
that: 'The decision makers or sports people do not have historically motivated prejudices. There are only some isolated cases
of bad behaviour – mostly on the German side' (Key informant,
Zgorzelec County Office). However, most respondents pointed
out that 'there are prejudices between partners which are
historically motivated. Lower Silesia once belonged to Germany, so there was the problem of displaced people who hoped
to go back to their home towns. As a result they treated this
region as a temporary place of residence and thus did not try
hard to work creatively. In this respect, prejudices have resulted
from the War; overcoming them takes time. The Germans will
remember that they had their car stolen in Poland, but don't
care if at the same time ten of their cars were stolen in
Germany' (Key informant, Consulting company Eurotransfer-
und Beratungsring Neisse e.V.). Furthermore, there are contemporary controversies. 'Situations such as the opening of the
Silesian Museum in Görlitz (which met with disapproval or even
disdain on the part of Polish people) surely have a negative
effect on cooperation and mutual trust. An important role is also
played by national politics with regard to Germany and German
claims on areas now inhabited by Polish people. Due to bad
legislation some Poles inhabiting the border areas have lost
court cases and there is little help from the government in this
respect. These problems are still surfacing and do not help to
build trust or good relations with the neighbours.' (Key informant, Zgorzelec Municipal Office)

Negative stereotypes: 'The perception of one's neighbour is
often created on the basis of stereotypes. [...] Until now, there

is still a difference between Eastern and Western states in the perception of Polish people. In the West, everything's fine, but in Eastern Germany there are still strange behaviours like atavisms. You can feel that they don't like us [Poles].' (Key informant, Polish employers' federation of Western Poland)

Mental barriers (mostly characteristic of older generations): 'The mentality of young people functions in a completely different way. For example, there was a meeting of architecture students who were supposed to create a vision of the future of Zgorzelec and Görlitz. In the meeting, there were also many invited guests: the authorities of the cities of Zgorzelec and Görlitz, representatives of local institutions, associations, and chambers. The students presented a wonderful vision of one city, of course preserving the existing administrative division' (Key informant, Zgorzelec Trade Guiding). 'For young people who were born in Lower Silesia, this region is their motherland, and that is why prejudices are not so widespread in the young generation.' (Key informant, Consulting company Eurotransfer- und Beratungsring Neisse e.V.)

A universal barrier to cross-border cooperation, for local authorities, business organizations, as well as for individual entrepreneurs, is the linguistic barrier, particularly for the older generation. German and Polish belong to very different language groups and there are disparities in language competence on both sides of the border. Most Polish cooperation partners have at least a rudimentary command of the German language or have translators, but the Polish language is too difficult to learn for German partners, so most of the analysed cooperation talks are held in German. Consequently, one of the main problems of German people concerns the language difference. Difficulties in communication which are due to the language barrier hinder the building of confidence between the partners. In addition, negotiations often depend on very small nuances, which are hard to understand, even for interpreters. The Polish language also constitutes a special problem regarding the law and tax issues. But language is also important when German and Polish partners meet in private contexts outside business. Of course, the language problem also exists on the Polish side.

Young people tend to study foreign languages, and if they do not know Polish or German they usually switch to English:

The language barrier is a real problem. A lot of people in Poland speak English, and many Germans also, so it [English] might be a viable communication channel. However, in rural areas the knowledge of languages is still low. It is important that young people study foreign languages at school, and that is already bearing fruit. (Key informant, Zgorzelec Communal Office)

Clearly, it will be necessary to take a range of measures to tackle the above-mentioned challenges, but now it will be much easier than twenty years ago, as the first elements of a (cross-border) regional identity have begun to emerge (van Houtum and Lagendijk, 2001) due to many joint initiatives (Box 4.4). While this process seems to be blocked by some 'revival' of national prejudices, this meets with a less and less favourable response from the younger generations. Consequently, such initiatives make Görlitz and Zgorzelec a contemporary 'laboratory' in terms of re-scaling space (Brenner, 1999; Gualini, 2006; Swyngedouw, 2004) and identity.

BOX 4.4   EXAMPLES OF JOINT INITIATIVES IN VARIOUS FIELDS CONTRIBUTING TO BUILDING A CROSS-BORDER REGIONAL IDENTITY

Common area and common identity: This initiative dates back to 1998, when a cross-border municipal association Europe-City Zgorzelec/Görlitz was established. It was meant to be a supra- and multinational, bilingual city, an educational rather than an industrial centre, a kind of municipal bridge spanning Germany and Poland. Recently, Europe-City decided to vie for the title of the European Capital of Culture in the year 2010. That way it wanted to present a vision of European cultural integration and aspiration for a new, common identity, as well as development of teamwork skills across the existing borders. In order to get the title, several joint projects were prepared, the most important being called the 'Park of Bridges'. This was supposed to be both a symbolic and a real place; a new common centre of Europe-City; a green belt along the border river with shared educational, cultural, and sports facilities; a German gate to Polish culture and a Polish gate to German culture. Further on, the idea was meant to be developed through many modern installations and artistic events. Another scheduled project was 'the Polish–German Salon' organized by

---

the Görlitz Theatre, where the inhabitants of both cities were supposed to tell each other the stories of their lives. People were supposed to free themselves of past limitations and feel the desire for a common future. This was also designed to be an element in the difficult process of Polish–German reconciliation (see: http://www.bip.zgorzelec.iap.pl/2219,5783/5783/art2058. html)

Trust built from scratch: 'Before Poland's accession to the European Union, they had been cooperating with a partner guild from Görlitz, when the Master of the Guild was Mr X. [...] Meetings at that time were frequent. Ultimately, it depends on the people who cooperate with each other. What is important is trust, which you build over the years, and also mentality. Meetings were both formal and informal. They were not only professional; there were balls, parties, meetings in the guild houses, joint celebrations of public holidays. Informal meetings prevailed, although there were also agreements signed by the City Authorities, for instance the Partner Cities Agreement. After the fall of the Berlin Wall, the situation changed. [...] The partner Guild of Görlitz was very big, they had problems with financing, and the Guild suspended its activities for some time. Thus, the cooperation was terminated, and we lost touch with the Guild. Nevertheless, just before Poland's accession to the European Union in 2004, the Guild seemed to revive, under new leadership. I was invited to the opening, and that was the only invitation from the Görlitz Guild so far. The current Guild Master has a different mentality. Mr X was brave and was not afraid of criticism from his craftsmen. The current Guild Master is cautious, he is afraid of Polish competition. I also had my worries before Poland joined the EU. I was worried that we did not have as much money as the Germans. On the other hand, we are not afraid of competition, while the German craftsmen were and continue to be afraid of Polish competition. That is why our contacts with the Guild are not as good as they used to be.' (Key informant, Zgorzelec Trade Guiding)

Development of cooperation abilities: 'The South-Western Forum of Territorial Self-Government prepared itself for cross-border cooperation through participation in projects. An example is the actions carried out within the project "Lower Silesians Closer to Europe" co-financed with the Small Project Fund Phare CBC. This was designed to create a cooperation platform for border rural areas and develop bilateral initiatives and projects of both associations, as well as to establish contacts between the rural areas in the Lower Silesian–Saxon–Czech border region through organizing new organizational and technological solutions for agriculture, building a new network system of rural cross-border cooperation, and building a production and information cooperation platform for agriculture and the food industry.' (Key informant, South-Western Local Government Forum)

CHALLENGES TO CROSS-BORDER ENTERPRISE COOPERATION

Even though cooperation between companies dates back to the 1990s, 2004 brought a new reality. It also brought one of the most serious challenges for entrepreneurs from both regions, that is the increasing costs and prices in Poland and the question of reorientation of motivation for cross-border cooperation. Poland's accession to the EU and joining the Internal Market accelerated the process of rising prices, forcing companies to reconsider their cooperation strategies. For example, in previous years differences in labour costs constituted the main motivation inducing German companies towards cooperation, as cheaper labour on the Polish side encouraged them to move production (subcontracting), with geographical proximity being a favourable factor. In particular that helped small companies to manage their dispersed value chain. In this way, enterprises were able to offer cheaper products compared to their competitors, securing their German location, and increasing their market share, sales and profits. In the region there are good examples of how this works. In one case, different components for a German enterprise's products (in the automotive industry) are manufactured in Poland and subsequently delivered to Görlitz. Another example refers to a German manufacturer of ropes that sends intermediate products to his Polish partner who processes them into end products, which is cheaper for the German firm than manufacturing the ropes in Germany. For one of these German entrepreneurs, ordering in Poland means 30 to 50 per cent cost savings in comparison to Germany. However, differences in labour costs are slowly disappearing, which means that if enterprise cooperation is to continue, it will be necessary to find new sources of mutual benefit. These opportunities have been observed by some entrepreneurs, particularly in Germany, who believe that cooperation is necessary to maintain business contacts in Poland, for example with the intention of using the Polish market to facilitate the penetration of markets further to the east. In this regard, geographic proximity emerges as a benefit to cooperation between German and Polish enterprises; this fosters partnership, because it allows frequent face-to-face visits, thus helping trust to emerge over time (also see Welter et al., Chapter 3 in this volume).

Additional challenges are posed by the aforementioned market-driven mechanisms (including prejudices and the linguistic barrier), which could be collectively defined as a lack of knowledge about German and Polish mentalities and a lack of intercultural skills. This in turn leads to the rise of potentially contentious issues, such as the different understanding of contracts. According to most of the interviewed Germans, Polish people have a different understanding of the value of contracts than Germans. Therefore, 'Germans are regarded with suspicion if they come to an initial partner meeting with a contract, because Polish partners often wonder whether the Germans want to hedge themselves against the Poles or do business with them', as emphasized by one of the interviewees, who stressed that a promise in Poland is worth more than a written contract.

Similar differences occur in respect of mentality. All German interviewees pointed to differences in Polish mentality which they believe to lead to 'non-business-like' behaviour hindering cross-border cooperation. Mostly, Polish people are seen as friendly, helpful, hospitable and correct partners. However, some of the German entrepreneurs voiced concerns about their reliability, as they deviate from the strict and schedule-oriented business behaviour of the Germans: 'Polish firms rely on the attitude that if we cannot do it today, we will do it tomorrow'. In the case of subcontracting, such delays may result in additional costs for the German partner, so they need to learn to be patient with the Polish partners. In some cases, quality issues arise, as stated by this German entrepreneur: 'Delivery reliability and the quality of products from Poland are further problems. It just works there if a German engineer is watching everything. Just-in-time businesses are very important but it takes too long with Polish deliveries.' In contrast, Polish entrepreneurs say: 'We work fast and stick to deadlines. The Germans are a bit slower in this respect.'

Another important area is trust. A German entrepreneur explicitly stated that he did not trust contracts with Polish businessmen, though he had made friends with his cooperation partners over time. Money is the only thing he trusts in doing business with Polish enterprises. His 'mistrusting' behaviour is explained by his previous negative experiences, both in a private and business context. At the closing of a contract, for instance, his former employer had remitted 10 000 euros from Germany to his Polish partner on a notary trust account, but never received any kind of service in return. What is more, the Polish company could not be found ever again. However, some Polish entrepreneurs have also experienced similar situations, as this interviewee explained: 'You have got to be careful as certain customers from Germany did not pay us for our work, and we sued them [...] It has turned out that you have to carefully check contracts with German clients.' Thus, most entrepreneurs treat trust as an indispensable basis for successful cooperation, even though they are aware of the fact that it takes time to build trust and that it depends on a number of factors, including the foreign partner's solvency, well-drafted contracts and previous contacts (Box 4.5, also see Chapter 3). Trust on a personal level depends on the willingness and openness of individuals to learn about their partners and their respective cultures. This is reflected in cross-border relationships arising from personal relations and/or extending beyond mere 'business' cooperation, as in the case of an entrepreneur from Görlitz who was invited to a public EU enlargement celebration that took place in Poland. Another entrepreneur quoted his first conversation with his Polish partner as an example of the role trust plays in cooperation between the partners from the beginning. The Polish director took a notepad and wrote down the Polish translation of the word 'trust', and the German partner added the German word. According to him, by this the parties manifested their belief that cooperation should mainly be based on trust, which has been the case until today.

BOX 4.5   OPINIONS OF POLISH ENTREPRENEURS CONCERNING TRUST-BUILDING FACTORS

Payment: 'Trust has always been built on the basis of payment deadlines, reliability and the duration of the company's presence on the Polish market. In addition, trust is built on the basis of abiding by certain rules, that is, we receive a confirmation of delivery dates from Germany, and German companies keep to these dates, and this creates trust. The Germans are very conscientious and care about Polish clients.'

Contracts: 'Trust between our companies is built on the basis of well-prepared documents and contracts, exact measurements concerning where windows/doors should be placed, as well as on the contract. Previously, I had worked with a Czech employee of the company, and our cooperation was successful,

> which is why we trust each other. My past experience in the field of cooperation with the Czech Republic enhances future growth of trust.'
>
> *Previous experiences:* 'Trust is built with our German partner through a representative in Görlitz on the basis of long-lasting cooperation, as I already knew this person and had worked with him. In addition, he is an active member of the cooperative and this has also helped mutual trust. Trust grows as cooperation becomes closer, through receiving more orders/contracts from the representative. Trust is built through economic and cultural factors; there is nothing that could hamper the development of trust.'

Yet another important area is with respect to German understanding of Polish culture. Cooperation with Polish partners has to take place on the business, personal and emotional levels. Arrogant and presumptuous behaviour on the German side would be counterproductive, as one of our German interviewees explains: 'Reliability, honesty, loyalty and readiness for action are the most important factors which influence trust building in cooperation. Collaboration works better if people do not behave as if they believe they are more important than the Polish partners but are honest and correct.' Also if German entrepreneurs transport their values and business behaviour to the Polish business world, then problems are imminent. According to one interviewee, his main mistake was to believe that his enterprise could offer the same payment terms for Polish customers as for the German ones. Because the Polish customers did not act accordingly, his enterprise lost a lot of money.

One of the factors that hinder cross-border cooperation is the different legal and fiscal systems on either side of the border However, according to results from the CBCED project, these challenges are the easiest to overcome for entrepreneurs, and some may even see business opportunities in some of them. This may be illustrated by the mechanism spurred by labour market regulations. Officially, the German labour market is closed to Polish employees. However, it is not closed to Polish companies. This leads to a solution which is satisfactory for both sides. Polish employees seeking jobs in Germany set up one-man companies there (typical self-employment) and offer services to German employers, thus becoming subcontractors. As a result, the post-EU integration period on the German side is characterized by a boom of start-up (Polish) micro-enterprises. The regulations on the German labour market also create good opportunities for larger Polish companies which, upon starting their operations there, are entitled to using cheaper (relative to Poland) business loans during their first five years of operation, as well as loans granted by German employment agencies to companies which employ jobless German residents.

Both Polish and German entrepreneurs are familiar with most of the challenges above and understand the necessity to take action. However, both sides highlight the fact that prior cooperation and Poland's accession to the European Union have made these challenges less acute. This cooperation has initiated processes of learning and trust-building, while EU enlargement has ensured a level playing field in terms of legal and administrative conditions for starting and running businesses on both sides of the border. The next steps should therefore be aimed at improving the processes of learning and trust-building and at increasing the efficiency of the support infrastructure for cross-border cooperation.

CONCLUSIONS

A number of developmental problems common to Görlitz and Zgorzelec have long inspired a variety of cross-border cooperation initiatives. An additional impulse was provided by EU enlargement, which paved the way for the authorities in both regions, and for the local communities, to tap into new short- and long-term benefits following a joint vision, which could assist in building a cross-border regional identity and thus facilitate the concerted development of this border area. The timing for creating a joint regional identity is encouraging since historical prejudices and reservations are fading away in the younger generations on both sides, who perceive the region as their genuine homeland. The local administrations are cooperating successfully across the border, offering manifold possibilities to develop cross-regional processes of learning and building trust. Further tightening of cooperation is welcomed, as both sides understand that 'the goal of cooperation [...] is not to create a new administrative level, but instead to develop cooperative structures, procedures and instruments that facilitate the removal of obstacles and foster the elimination of divisive factors' (AGEG, AEBR and ARFE, 2004, p. 7). However, this requires continued effort to eliminate the barriers which now restrict the efficiency of joint actions. Many of these barriers and many measures to be taken have been identified in the European Charter for border and cross-border regions (AGEG et al., 2004). Nevertheless, empirical evidence from the CBCED project makes it possible to go a step further and formulate some place-based (Barca, 2009) policy recommendations designed to do the following.

At a local/regional level the region's manifold advantages as 'a gate to the East and West' should be actively promoted and the quality of life raised in order to attract enterprises interested in investing in the region. This includes a joint understanding of regional strengths and weaknesses for a cross-border development strategy in the economic area as well, and the development of a local/regional integrated learning strategy (Committee of Regions, 2007) in order to facilitate cross-border cooperation and governance. This would include: (i) supporting common institutions to facilitate the development of a cross-border strategy for the region; (ii) creating cross-border working groups where policy makers and administration officers could meet and discuss policy-related problems hindering CBC at enterprise level; and (iii) developing an overall cooperation strategy (instead of project-based cooperation).

At national and EU levels: (i) use EU funding as leverage for regional and private money; (ii) actively promote the European Grouping of Territorial Cooperation (EU, 2006) to foster cross-border administrative regions.

EU enlargement in 2004 opened up new perspectives for cross-border cooperation in Görlitz. The region moved from the periphery back to being a region in the middle of Europe, although perceptions about this may differ. The integration of Poland into the European Union offers Görlitz and Zgorzelec an opportunity to step out of their perceived peripheral situation, instead acting as a gateway to the East and West.

NOTES

1. Separate financing line for the PHARE programme (Poland and Hungary: Assistance for Reconstructing of their Economies), a pre-accession fund aimed at the preparation of new countries for European Union membership and elimination of economic disparities.
2. New objective (Objective 3) of the cohesion policy of the European Union, promoting transborder, international and interregional cooperation.
3. Institutional cross-border cooperation is presented at length in Chapter 10 (Rogut and Piasecki) in this volume.
4. Association Agreements aimed at the establishment of a framework suitable for political dialogue and gradual integration with the European Union; they were concluded by the European Union initially with Poland, Hungary and Czechoslovakia (1991), and subsequently with other countries of Central and Eastern Europe: Bulgaria, the Czech Republic, Slovakia and Romania in 1993; Estonia, Lithuania and Latvia in 1995, and with Slovenia in 1996.
5. First accession applications were submitted by Hungary (March 1994) and Poland (April 1994). Bulgaria, Estonia, Lithuania, Latvia, Romania and Slovakia applied in 1995, and the Czech Republic and Slovakia in 1996.
6. Aid for agricultural development and structural aid directed mainly towards aligning these applicant countries with Community infrastructure standards, particularly in the transport and environmental spheres.

7. See information on Polish administrative reform in Chapter 10 (Rogut and Piasecki in this volume).

REFERENCES

Adamczuk, F. and J. Rymarczyk (2003a), 'Local aspects of European integration on the example of Zgorzelec–Görlitz cross-border co-operation', in G. Dieckheuer (ed.), *Eastward Enlargement of the European Union*, Frankfurt am Main: Lang, pp. 137–46.

Adamczuk, F. and J. Rymarczyk (2003b), 'Transborder cooperation in Europe based on the example of Poland and Germany', in G. Dieckheuer (ed.), *Eastward Enlargement of the European Union*, Frankfurt am Main: Lang, pp. 147–57.

AGEG, AEBR, ARFE (2004), 'European charter for border and cross-border regions. New version', available at: http://www.aebr.net/publikationen/pdfs/Charta_Final_071004.gb.pdf, accessed 2 April 2007.

Barca, F. (2009), 'An agenda for a reformed cohesion policy: a place-based approach to meeting European Union challenges and expectations', available at: http://www.rgre.de/pdf/barca_report_v2104.pdf, accessed 14 October 2009.

Brenner, N. (1999), 'Globalization as reterritorialisation: the re-scaling of urban governance in the European Union', *Urban Studies*, **36**(3), 431–51.

Bukowski, J., S. Piattoni and M. Smyrl (eds) (2003), *Between Europeanization and Local Societies. The Space for Territorial Governance*, Lanham, MD: Rowman & Littlefield Publishers.

Committee of Regions (2007), 'Study on structural capacity and motivation of regions and local and regional authorities in R&D', available at: http://www.eulib.com/documents/Study+research_en.pdf, accessed 2 October 2008.

Council of Europe (1980), 'European outline convention on trans-frontier co-operation between territorial communities or authorities', available at: http://conventions.coe.int/Treaty/en/Treaties/Html/106.htm, accessed 19 August 2009.

Cowles, M.G., J. Caporaso and T. Risse (eds) (2001), *Transforming Europe: Europeanization and Domestic Change*, New York: Cornell University.

ESPON (2006), 'Enlargement of the European Union and the wider European perspective as regards its polycentric spatial structure', available at: http://www.espon.eu/export/sites/default/Documents/Projects/ESPON2006Projects/ThematicProjects/EnlargementPolycentrism/full_revised_version_113.pdf, accessed 8 February 2008.

ESPON and Interact (2007), 'Cross-border cooperation. Cross-thematic study of INTERREG and ESPON activities', available at: http://www.espon.eu/mmp/online/website/content/interact/1316/80/file_2792/CrossBorder_Cooperation_web.pdf, accessed 9 November 2008.

European Commission (1997), 'Agenda 2000 for a stronger and wider Union', COM (97) 2000 final, vol. I, Brussels: Commission of the European Communities.

European Commission (2004), 'PHARE cross-border co-operation. Interim evaluation of PHARE support allocated in 1999–2002 and implemented until November 2003', available at: http://ec.europa.eu/enlargement/pdf/financial_assistance/phare/fv_zz_cbc_0381_en.pdf, accessed 6 June 2011.

European Commission (2008), 'Labour market and wage developments in 2007', European Economy Series 5, available at: http://ec.europa.eu/economy_finance/publications/publication13227_en.pdf, accessed 22 July 2009.

EU (2006) Regulation (EC) No. 1082/2006 of the European Parliament and of the Council of 5 July 2006 on a European Grouping of Territorial Cooperation (EGTC), *Official Journal of the European Union*, 31 July 2006.

Featherstone, K. and C.M. Radaelli (eds) (2003), *The Politics of Europeanization*, Oxford and New York: Oxford University Press.

Friedrich, K., R. Knippschild, M. Kunert, M. Meyer-Künzel and I. Neumann (2005), 'Auf dem Weg zu einem gemeinsamen Leitbild für die Europastadt Görlitz/Zgorzelec', in K. Friedrich, R. Knippschild and M. Kunert (eds), *Zwei Grenzstädte wachsen zusammen*, Munich: ökom-Verlag, pp. 13–27.

Galasinska, A., C. Rollo and U.H. Meinhof (2002), 'Urban space and the construction of identity on the German–Polish border', in U.H. Meinhof (ed.), *Living (with) Borders*, Aldershot, UK: Ashgate, pp. 119–39.

Gorzelak, G., J. Bachtler and M. Kasprzyk (2004), *Współpraca Transgraniczna Unii Europejskiej: Doświadczenia Polsko-Niemieckie*, Warsaw: Scholar.

Gualini, E. (2004), *Multi-level Governance and Institutional Change. The Europeanization of Regional Policy in Italy*, Aldershot, UK and Burlington, VT: Ashgate.

Gualini, E. (2006), 'The rescaling of governance in Europe: new spatial and institutional rationales', *European Planning Studies*, **14**(7), 881–904.

Guz-Vetter, M. (2002), *Polsko-niemieckie pogranicze. Szanse i zagrożenia w perspektywie przystąpienia Polski do Unii Europejskiej*, Warsaw: Instytut Spraw Publicznych.

Hille, P. and C. Knill (2006), '"It's the bureaucracy, stupid". The implementation of the Acquis Communautaire in EU candidate countries, 1999–2003', *European Union Politics*, **7**(4), 531–52.

Kathke, S., K. Heinz and D. Andree (2005), 'Rozwój transgranicznych, zintegrowanych systemów komunikacji (TZSK) na przykładzie miast Görlitz/Zgorzelec oraz Frankfurt n. Odrą/Słubice. Streszczenie raportu', available at: http://www.forum-miast-granicznych.net/pl/files/Kurzbericht_05-05-25_endfassung_pl.pdf, accessed 11 April 2010.

Kofman, E. and G. Youngs (2003), *Globalization: Theory and Practice*, London and New York: Continuum.

Kramach, O. and B. Hooper (eds) (2004), *Cross-border Governance in the European Union*, Abingdon, UK: Routledge.

Lammers, K., A. Niebuhr, A. Polkowski, S. Stiller, A. Hildebrandt, M. Nowicki, P. Susmarski and M. Tarkowski (2006), *Polsko-niemiecki obszar przygraniczny w roku 2020 – Scenariusz rozwoju i zalecenia odnośnie jego realizacji*, Hamburg: Hamburg Institute of International Economics.

Leibenath, M., E. Korcelli-Olejniczak and R. Knippschild (2008), *Cross-border Governance and Sustainable Spatial Development. Mind the Gaps!*, Berlin: Springer.

Leiber, S. (2007), 'Transposition of EU social policy in Poland: are there different "worlds of compliance" in East and West?', *Journal of European Social Policy*, **17**(4), 349–60.

Małachowski, W. (ed.) (1997), *Polska – Niemcy a transformacja systemowa*, Warsaw: Szkoła Główna Handlowa.

MRRiB (2000), 'Narodowa Strategia Rozwoju Regionalnego', Ministerstwo Rozwoju Regionalnego i Budownictwa, available at: http://www.nsrr.gov.pl/NR/rdonlyres/385E4AAA-08EC-4D93-A639-5942772B261F/0/6536_nsrr01.pdf, accessed 5 February 2003.

MWH Consortium (2007), 'PHARE Cross-Border Cooperation Programmes 1999–2003. Thematic Evaluation', available at: http://ec.europa.eu/enlargement/pdf/financial_assistance/phare/evaluation/cbc_thematic_final_may_2007_en.pdf, accessed 22 April 2010.

Niebuhr, A. and S. Stiller (2004), 'The impact of Poland's EU accession on labour supply in the German–Polish border region: what can we expect?', European Regional Science Association Conference Papers, available at: http://www-sre.wu-wien.ac.at/ersa/ersaconfs/ersa04/PDF/234.pdf, accessed 6 June 2011.

Perkmann, M. (2005), 'Cross-border co-operation as policy entrepreneurship: explaining the variable success of European cross-border regions', CSGR Working Paper No. 166/05, available at: http://www2.warwick.ac.uk/fac/soc/csgr/research/workingpapers/2005/wp16605.pdf, accessed 13 May 2010.

Perkmann, M. (2007), 'Construction of new territorial scales: a framework and case study of the Euregio cross-border region', *Regional Studies*, **41**(2), 253–66.

Perkmann, M. and N.-L. Sum (2002), 'Globalization, regionalization and cross-border regions: scales, discourses and governance', in M. Perkmann and N.-L. Sum (eds), *Globalization, Regionalization and Cross-border Regions*, Houndmills, UK: Palgrave, pp. 3–21.

Rogut, A. (ed.) (2008), *Potencjał polskich MSP w zakresie absorbowania korzyści integracyjnych*, Lodz: Wydawnictwo Uniwersytetu Łódzkiego.

Rokicki, B. and A. Żołnowski (2008), 'Ogólne aspekty gospodarcze', in UKIE (ed.), *Cztery lata członkostwa Polski w UE. Bilans kosztów i korzyści społeczno-gospodarczych*, Warsaw: Urząd Komitetu Integracji Europejskiej, pp. 15–33.

Saxon State Ministry for Economy and Labour (2008), 'Program Operacyjny Współpracy Transgranicznej Polska–Saksonia 2007–2013', available at: http://www.ewt.gov.pl/Dokumenty/Lists/Dokumentyprogramowe/Attachments/90/Program_PL_SN_5sierp08.pdf, accessed 5 January 2009.

Swyngedouw, E. (2004), 'Globalisation or "glocalisation"? Networks, territories and rescaling', *Cambridge Review of International Affairs*, **17**(1), 25–48.

Szromnik, A. (1993), *Rynki Europy Wschodniej w oczach niemieckich przedsiębiorców*, Warsaw: Friedrich Ebert Stiftung Przedstawicielstwo w Polsce.

Taylor, S., K. Olejniczak and J. Bachtler (2005), 'A study of the mid-term evaluations of INTERREG programmes for the programming period 2000–2006', Austria: INTERACT Programme.

van Houtum, H. and A. Lagendijk (2001), 'Contextualising regional identity and imagination in the construction of polycentric urban regions: the cases of the Ruhr Area and the Basque', *Urban Studies*, **38**(4), 747–67.

Waters, M. (2001), *Globalization: Key Ideas*, 2nd edn, New York: Routledge.

WWPE (2007), 'Raport zamykający wdrażanie Programów Współpracy Przygran-icznej, Sprawiedliwosci i Spraw Wewnętrznych oraz Spójności Społeczno-Gospodarczej Phare realizowanych przez Władzę Wdrażającą Program Współpracy Przygranicznej Phare/Władzę Wdrażającą Programy Europejskie', Warsaw: Władza Wdrążająca Programy Europejskie.

5. Cross-border cooperation in the Bulgaria–Greece–FYR of Macedonia triangle

Lois Labrianidis, Kiril Todorov, Georgios Agelopoulos, Efi Voutira, Kostadin Kolarov and Nikos Vogiatzis

INTRODUCTION

In the last ten years, the Balkan region has undergone a series of radical changes owing to the various interacting forces of political, economic and social post-socialist transformation, as well as the European Union's (EU) enlargement process. This chapter focuses on an analysis of empirical research conducted in the context of cross-border cooperation (CBC) between Greece, Bulgaria and the Former Yugoslavian Republic of Macedonia (FYR of Macedonia). It outlines the unique features that characterize this south-eastern European border region when compared with other similar examples within Europe. The relevance of the case study is that it examines one of the most fragmented areas in Europe based on small regional economies with competing historical memories about the past and conflicting notions of ownership and belonging perpetuated through the presence of ethnic minorities that inhabit shared borders. Paradoxically, on the level of entrepreneurial interaction, social agents exhibit an unanticipated level of 'aggressive expansionism' which suggests new patterns of capital flow between the more and less developed areas in the Balkan region as a whole. Accordingly, it is argued that a long-term development strategy for the Balkans should be based on a closer reading of cross-border activities occurring in such 'subaltern' areas.[1] In general terms, during the post-1989 period, the existing barriers concerning the human and capital flows across the borders have been gradually removed, together with the previously dominant political divide in the area.[2] These events have led to the simplification of formalities and the establishment of new crossing points in the Balkan countries, aiming to foster CBC and, thus, reduce the isolation of neighbouring societies and economies.

Under these circumstances, the countries under investigation have implemented restructuring plans, which include the adjustments of their economic systems in order to adapt to the new conditions of the market economy. Consequently, a new economic geography has emerged in the area, where interaction between developed and less-developed regions has intensified and proved to be of crucial importance for both sides. This phenomenon marks a new era for border areas, which are traditionally viewed as disadvantaged and low-opportunity regions,[3] enabling cooperation to develop across borders and creating chances for local firms to participate in the new, EU and globalized economy.

The south-eastern part of Europe presents a telling example of the trend described above, in which a strong West–East interaction has been observable in recent years between Greece, Bulgaria and the FYR of Macedonia. CBC between these countries is not a new phenomenon, given the rigorous Greek investment activity that has been directed towards Bulgaria and the FYR of Macedonia during these years, as well as the established trade relationships between the three countries. What remains a novel phenomenon, however, is the proactive investment activity on the part of the former state socialist economies.

The available statistical data reveal, for example, that although Greece's share of global volumes of outward FDI is very small, namely 0.267 per cent in 2007 (UNCTAD, 2008), the country holds a leading position among Balkan countries and especially in Bulgaria and the FYR of Macedonia. Concretely, Greece is the third largest foreign investor in Bulgaria (following Austria and the Netherlands), having invested US$1598.2 million in total during the period 1992–2005 (Embassy of the Republic of Bulgaria in London, 2005), while it is in second position in terms of FDI in the FYR of Macedonia (following Austria), with €159.9 million during the period 2003–07 (National Bank of the Republic of Macedonia, 2008). Bulgaria has also contributed to a large extent to the FYR of Macedonia's restructuring processes, through investments in different sectors (including banks and the sugar industry). Trade volumes between the three countries have also increased significantly during these years.

On the regional level, the spatial concentration of cross-border activities, which also includes Albania, led to the formation of a regional market with international specialization, in which Albania's agricultural resources are combined with Bulgaria's and the FYR of Macedonia's manufacturing, as well as Greece's tertiary sector, creating the conditions for the port of Thessaloniki to become a major transportation hub in the area (Petrakos, 1996, p. 18). The specific market involves cooperation between local firms seeking to exploit the advantages derived from neighbouring regions of different levels of economic development. This phenomenon was particularly evident in sectors such as manufacturing, and more specifically the garment industry, in which Greek firms hold the position of second-layer subcontracting assigner to Bulgaria and FYR of Macedonia, thus creating a form of 'triangular manufacturing' (Labrianidis, 1996; 2001), although its importance has decreased over time.

Although the initiatives mentioned above were originally undertaken solely at firm level, European,[4] national and regional policies have been designed and implemented in order to encourage CBC between Greece, Bulgaria and the FYR of Macedonia. EU support under the three INTER-REG programmes, as well as PHARE/CARDS initiative,[5] has contributed to a large extent to stimulating interregional cooperation and fostering balanced development within the area. A significant share of funds has been directed to infrastructure improvement projects, thus enabling the transportation of goods across the borders. Moreover, cooperation at an institutional level (including local authorities and business support organizations) is likely to provide a foundation for enterprise-based CBC in the future. However, cross-border policies do not always reflect the specialized needs of local stakeholders (organizations, institutions and enterprises), since their opinions are rarely taken into consideration (Dimitrov et al., 2003, p. 20).

This chapter aims to provide an empirical assessment of CBC that has developed between Greece, Bulgaria and the FYR of Macedonia.[6] Special attention is given to the bordering areas of the countries, since, on the one hand, they comprise all the negative aspects of peripheral regions, and, on the other hand, they possess the advantages of geographical proximity and familiarity with the other side of the borders, advantages which can constitute enabling factors for CBC.

The structure of this chapter is as follows: the first section contains a short presentation of the case study regions (CSRs) and some methodological notes on the fieldwork conducted there, while the next section constitutes an empirical assessment of CBC in the area, accompanied by a discussion of the main findings. In the third section the major concluding points are presented and key implications for policy drawn. Our analysis reveals the advantages and opportunities created for local enterprises, institutions and neighbouring societies in a context, which during recent decades, has not encouraged CBC.

THE CASE STUDY REGIONS (CSRS)

Geography, Social Characteristics and Economic Development

The area under investigation involves the bordering regions of Greece, Bulgaria and the FYR of Macedonia (Figure 5.1). More specifically, the first CSR includes the bordering regions between northern Greece and southern Bulgaria: the Prefectures of Serres, Drama and Thessaloniki in Greece and the District of Blagoevgrad in Bulgaria. There are two crossing points in this area (Kulata-Promachonas and Ilinden-Exohi), with the latter starting operation in 2006.

The second CSR includes the border regions between north-western Greece and southern FYR of Macedonia: the Prefectures of Florina and Pella, together with Thessaloniki in Greece and the region of Pelagonia, which mainly includes the neighbouring Municipalities of Bitola and Prilep in the FYR of Macedonia. This area includes one crossing point: the border station of Metjitlija-Niki.

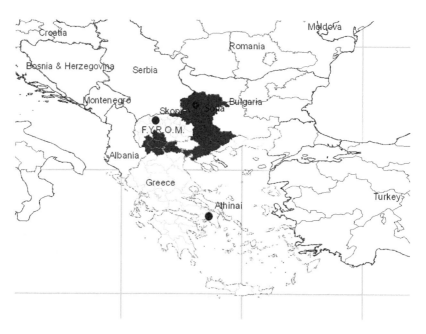

Figure 5.1   The case study regions (CSRs)

The third area under study involves the border regions between Bulgaria and the FYR of Macedonia, specifically the District of Kyustendil in the south-western part of Bulgaria and the north-eastern region of the FYR of Macedonia.

It is in these areas that the majority of cross-border cooperation between the three countries takes place. The area covered by the CSRs constitutes quite a fragmented space in both social and economic terms, since all the regions examined – perhaps with the exception of Thessaloniki – present similar characteristics of small size, restricted shares in total population and national Gross Domestic Product (GDP), as well as low population density and percentages of urban population.

An examination of the available data confirms the widely held view that border regions are traditionally disadvantaged, facing significant developmental problems and constraints. The CSRs are economies of small size and low contribution to total added value on the national level, while all three countries have a lower than EU-27 average of GDP/capita for the period 2000–08. Moreover, even though Greece holds a notably enhanced position when compared to Bulgaria and the FYR of Macedonia, it still lags behind the EU-27 average figure. It is worth mentioning that the grey economy in all three countries has a significant share, reaching 37 and 36.7 per cent of GDP in the case of Bulgaria's GDP[7] and Greece (Tatsos 2001), respectively.

With the exception of Thessaloniki and the Region of Pelagonia the other regions also present a significantly lower percentage of the regional GDP than the national average, ranging from 50.3 per cent for the case of the north-east region in the FYR of Macedonia to 76.4 per cent for Blagoevgrad on average during 2000–05 (Figure 5.2). Hence, it is clear that we are talking about relatively small sizes of the local economies on both sides of the borders.

Unemployment constitutes another crucial developmental barrier in the CSRs, especially for the Greek regions, where the relevant rate reached 17.5 per cent for Drama in 2007, compared to 9.8 per cent in 2000 (Eurostat, 2009). A similar situation is also apparent in Serres and Florina, where in both regions unemployment exceeds 15 per cent; and in Pella, in which unemployment rates among the labour force reached a two-digit number during recent years. These figures primarily represent the 'dark side' of the Greek firms' opening to the Balkans and particularly the delocalization of garment manufacturing firms during the 1990s to Southern Bulgaria (and more recently to the FYR of Macedonia).

At the same time, unemployment rates among the active population constitute one of the most unsettling barriers to growth in the FYR of Macedonia, boosting social disparities between the regions and increasing the gap with neighbouring European areas. According to official data

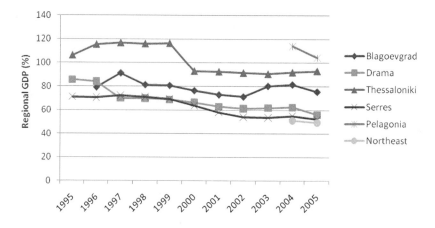

Source: Eurostat, General and Regional Statistics (2009).

Figure 5.2 *Regional GDP in percentage of the countries' average (1995–2005)*

provided by the State Statistical Office (2007), national unemployment reached 34.9 per cent in 2007, compared with 36 per cent in 2006. According to the same source, unemployment was 39.7 and 48.6 per cent for the regions of Pelagonia and the north-east region respectively during 2002.

Unemployment in the Bulgarian CSRs is relatively low, amounting to 6.7 per cent for Blagoevgrad Province (Petrich CSR) and 8.2 per cent for Kyustendil Province (Employment Agency, 2008). On one hand this could be partially attributed to the level of foreign direct investment in these areas, which has created new working positions there. On the other hand, low unemployment can encourage local cross-border activities, since low unemployment corresponds with increased purchasing power as well as with increasing interest in economic activities on the other side of the border. By contrast, high unemployment leads to reduced CBC as in the case of the Bulgarian–Serbian border.

These bordering regions are characterized by the existence of various bilingual ethnic minorities,[8] due to immigration and population exchanges in the area (particularly after the Balkan wars from 1912–13), populations that are sometimes considered to be the main source of national tensions. It is useful to note that this area was part of the Ottoman Empire from the early fifteenth to the early twentieth century, which brought together previously separated peoples and cultures and produced an amalgamation of populations out of which new social groups emerged, thereby creating an impact on CBC development in the wider Balkan region. The most dramatic effects on the social and economic structures in the regions studied were associated with the nationalistic policies implemented by the governments after the end of Ottoman rule and the twentieth-century wars, which caused mass migration processes, mutual animosity and disorientation, together with isolating cross-border populations and regimes. Although the socio-political context has changed with the events of the late nineteenth to mid-twentieth centuries, the longer-term historical legacy needs to be taken into account as a significant factor on CBC, even today. It is important to clarify that the 'leftovers' of the past may positively contribute to CBC. For example, the fact that some populations of this area are bilingual allows the development of closer communication and trust networks to occur.

SAMPLE AND METHODOLOGY

The findings presented and discussed below are primarily the outcome of fieldwork conducted in the CSRs from March–October 2007, which involved semi-structured interviews with both entrepreneurs and key informants currently or previously engaged in CBC. Specifically for the Greece–Bulgaria CSRs, the sample comprised 79 enterprises, of which 40 are located on the Greek side of the borders and 39 in Bulgaria. The first phase of the research also involved 42 key informant, semi-structured interviews conducted on both sides of the borders: 24 in Greece and 18 in Bulgaria, including representatives from the local authorities (municipalities and prefectures), chambers of commerce and industry, exporters' associations, commercial unions and NGOs that have experience of CBC with their counterparts on the other side.

The data collection instrument employed involved a semi-structured questionnaire in order to encourage the interlocutors to express freely their views on issues related with CBC and to recount their experiences during face-to-face interviews. Interviews were mainly conducted in the informants' native languages but English was also occasionally used. Our sample of enterprises was constructed on the basis of information provided through key-informant interviews as well as from available information in business directories on the Internet; the 'snowball' technique was also used in order to complete our database from the CSRs. It is worth mentioning that most cases (51 per cent) involved firms operating in manufacturing and more specifically within the garment industry, in which subcontracting is the basic form of cooperation (see Figure 5.3).

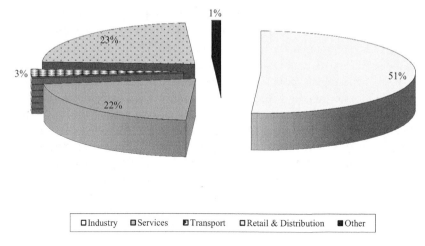

Source: Authors.

Figure 5.3   Share of firms per sector

A common type of CBC identified at the enterprise level in Petrich (Bulgarian–Greek border) is based on long-term relations between partners. The most widespread type of these relations is between supplier (Greek enterprise) and buyer (Bulgarian enterprise). By contrast, enterprises registered in Kyustendil and involved in CBC (Bulgarian–FYR of Macedonia border) operate mainly in light industries and the service sector (including wholesale and retail).

Concerning the age of the participants, most were between 36 and 50 years, although 21 per cent were younger entrepreneurs and employees (18–35 years old) working in firms engaged in CBC. The vast majority of our interviewees were male (88 per cent). A noteworthy feature referred to the linguistic skills of the people engaged in CBC (Figure 5.4), since common language constitutes an extremely important factor for developing partnerships. More specifically, knowledge of the dominant language of the cross-border region was common among all our interlocutors. However, the relevant percentage was distinctly higher in the case of entrepreneurs aged 51–65 (84.2 per cent), compared to 56 per cent for people aged 18–35 and 36–50, and only 33.3 per cent for interviewees aged over 65.

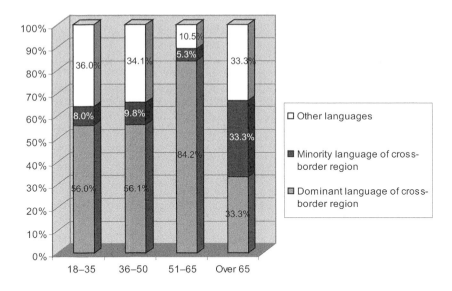

Source: Authors.

Figure 5.4   Distribution of interviewees according to linguistic skills

EMPIRICAL FINDINGS AND DISCUSSION

The Effects of EU Enlargement on Cross-Border Activity

One of the most important elements regarding CBC involves trust and security in transactions between enterprises located at the borders, as pointed out by several entrepreneurs who participated in the fieldwork. Given the fact that the physical distance between them is relatively small in all cases, interpersonal relations and familiarization are easily facilitated. However, CBC is easier to achieve if the regions on either side of the border are both part of the EU. At the same time, this argument is not as strong in the case of entrepreneurs as in the case of institutions, since the former are able to overcome barriers in a more effective way, compared to institutions where the problems experienced are sometimes national issues.

Bulgaria's accession to the EU proved to be a stimulating factor for CBC since it encouraged Greek firms either to develop or retain CBC, compared to the case of firms located in the FYR of Macedonia. Entrepreneurs identified several positive effects of EU enlargement among the wider socio-economic environment of Bulgaria:

> On a commercial level, EU enlargement to include Bulgaria and Romania is very positive, due to the fact that there are many new consumers with improved purchasing power. This is not the case in the FYR of Macedonia, where there still is unemployment and economic problems. Consequently, our commercial activities are not very good there. The residents of FYR of Macedonia mostly consume 60–70 per cent cheaper products from Turkey and China. (Florina Enterprise 3)

It could be argued that Bulgaria's accession to the EU created an important 'pull' factor for Greek enterprises to establish CBC in Bulgaria, since a new potential market emerged in the neighbouring region. Apart from the fact that this could lead to an extension of the customer base, it was also suggested that Bulgarian consumers gradually turn to more expensive, higher-quality products. Consequently, this phenomenon could also encourage Greek entrepreneurs to abandon the low-cost strategies implemented during the early years of expansion in the Balkan market and focus on higher value-added activities.

> As regards CBC in general and more specifically in northern Greece, the highest interest is presented in knowledge transfer and product exporting. We should focus on knowledge transfer and high-quality product exporting, if we are able to produce them. The service sector is also of great importance, as Bulgarian citizens will begin to search for higher quality, just like all the other European citizens. (Thessaloniki Key informant 24)

Increased access to the Balkan markets could be seen as an opportunity that will help companies in Greece to confront the deeper problems facing the Greek economy. It has previously been argued that the low-cost strategies implemented in the neighbouring markets cannot provide Greek firms with a sustainable competitive advantage. Instead, they tend to produce rather negative results, such as lost jobs reported in Greece in the short term, as well as longer-term negative effects. The latter include postponing the restructuring of firms necessary to upgrade them in order to produce more value-added products and to become internationally competitive (Labrianidis, 2001a, p. 4), ultimately leading to the absence of new and innovative investments in Bulgaria and FYR of Macedonia. In other words, CBC could be considered as an excellent chance for Greek companies to move up the value chain and produce for the upper segment of the market. The short-term effects, which include increased bankruptcies and unemployment in

Greece as a result of the companies' delocalization to the other side of the borders, could be cushioned (Labrianidis, 1996).

For Bulgarian companies the CBC opportunities created by EU accession are mostly related to the diversification of their supply sources and access to new markets. Bulgarian accession to the EU meant that Greek–Bulgarian CBC now involves simplified procedures at the borders, which facilitates product transport. Therefore, entrepreneurs sense their exports are better secured and trust levels are enhanced. There are also shorter delivery times now for exported products across the Greek–Bulgarian borders.

> The most serious problem you come across when cooperating with the other side of the border has to do with the transportation of the products, because of the problems that occur at the customs houses. After EU enlargement and the accession of Bulgaria, things have improved; the whole procedure is much simpler now and also it costs us less to transport goods from Bulgaria. (Florina Enterprise 5)

> Bulgaria's accession to the EU, overall, has had a positive influence on firms' activities in relation to a number of dimensions: facilitated regime of VAT taxation, delivery in a shorter-term, facilitated crossing of the border and fewer border checks. (Petrich Enterprise 19)

In contrast, in the case of the FYR of Macedonia–Greece, there are still crucial barriers regarding human and capital flows. The above statements are highly representative of the changes that occurred after the EU enlargement and the consequent improvement in CBC between Greece and Bulgaria. With Bulgaria's membership of the EU, the regulatory regimes concerning CBC between Bulgaria and Greece became equipotent, thereby creating a better position for Bulgarian entrepreneurs. This argument is further enforced by the examination of the case of the CBC with the FYR of Macedonia, since entrepreneurs recognize that since the country is not part of the EU, there is little evidence of radical changes in their cooperation.

Bulgarian entrepreneurs reported that their accession to the EU not only lacks any positive effects in terms of increasing CBC between them and entrepreneurs in the FYR of Macedonia, but that it has also increased fragmentation in the Balkan region. EU membership created additional barriers for CBC between member and non-member countries, which include new visa regimes, border controls and adjustments to the legal systems. This trend was particularly clear in the responses of Bulgarian entrepreneurs:

> EU enlargement creates new barriers for CBC with Serbia and Macedonia. For example, firms lose their clients because visas are necessary for both countries.

> Bulgarian visas should be free of charge but in fact they require payment. So, the main problem is the visa regime. In this regard, a subscription to a '50 km non-visa zone' is being discussed. But this is absurd because 'another border in the country could not be made'. Furthermore, Macedonian people changed their interaction with Bulgarians after EU enlargement. (Kyustendil Enterprise 15)

As a result, it could be argued that EU membership has a twofold effect, either negative or positive depending on whether the CBC dyad includes parts of an EU member or non-member country (Bulgaria–the FYR of Macedonia) or two members (Greece–Bulgaria) respectively. At the same time, this argument highlights the need for an integrated strategy for the development of the post-1989 Balkan region. Countries such as the FYR of Macedonia are obliged to pay serious attention to intra-Balkan economic relations (Petrakos and Totev, 2001, pp. 24–25). Given the country's distance from the EU core, together with the fact that it shares common borders with two member states (Greece and Bulgaria), cutting off the trade linkages with them poses severe threats to local economic development.

In addition, harmonization with the EU's legislative framework resulted in Bulgaria developing an image of a more secure business environment than previously. Common business codes and symbols emerged as a result of adjustment in the legal systems, while, additionally, signs of corruption are no longer considered by Greek entrepreneurs to be a significant barrier in Bulgaria.

> The elimination of corruption that has been actively pursued in the past years [in Bulgaria], particularly following the EU enlargement, creates a sense of security. (Serres Enterprise 9)

> The accession of Bulgaria has had a negative impact on the firm's CBC with its Macedonian partners. The number of the orders fell drastically and as a consequence so did the profit. The main reason was the introduction of trade restrictions for the Macedonian merchants. (Kyustendil Enterprise 7)

However, a completely different attitude was reported towards the FYR of Macedonia by both Bulgarian and Greek entrepreneurs, who judge that the country still lags behind other European countries in terms of economic development and governance structures. In the case of CBC between Greece and the FYR of Macedonia, national and political barriers have had a negative impact on trust levels and consequently on CBC development, due to the ongoing dispute over the name 'Macedonia' (see Europa 2000, pp. 2335–7). This issue creates enormous difficulties for CBC between the two sides, as clearly stated during the interviews:

> When importing products from the other side of the borders [FYRoM], we usually come across two major problems. Our partner is forced by the domestic legislation to mention on the invoices the constitutional name of the country, in other words 'Macedonia'. But Greece doesn't recognize this name, so it's as if this country doesn't exist. Hence, you can't really establish any cooperation with a non-existent country. (Pella Enterprise 11)

However, despite the important barriers it creates, it was also apparent during the fieldwork that most entrepreneurs recognize that they are not able to influence the situation, and furthermore do not consider it an obstacle to conducting business. They try hard to retain their partnerships due to the fact that they see significant economic advantages for themselves.

The Flexibility of Entrepreneurs in the Face of External Barriers

The entrepreneurs interviewed seem to be able to overcome such barriers by being more flexible than the institutions and by taking advantage of the business opportunities arising in the border regions. Most of the time these opportunities are based on what may be termed 'implicit agreements' between the two sides, namely a mutual consent not to touch the 'hot subjects' and to overlook the issues that separate the two regions at the national level:

> the issue concerning the name of 'Macedonia' creates some problems only in the customs and nowhere else. There is a mutual profit for both sides, and when you really want to cooperate there are no barriers; you can always find alternative solutions. (Florina Enterprise 11)

Business people want this name issue to be resolved, because they believe that this resolution would help both sides in several ways. It would both assist the efforts to promote development in the neighbouring regions, and stimulate their cross-border activities by increasing the flows of both products and people across the borders. In addition, they express their concern about competition pressures and ask for financial support, through tax relief and financing for investment projects by the government. One of their key priorities is infrastructural improvement for business expansion, while an acknowledged weakness is the lack of a specialized workforce. Finally, their relative inexperience and lack of know-how with respect to CBC leads them to apply for assistance on partner-search facilities and business-support organizations to act as intermediaries in their transactions with the other side of the border.

Institutional Cross-Border Cooperation

In the case of Bulgaria, following the country's accession in the EU, another field for CBC to develop emerged, namely the implementation of European-funded cross-border programmes and the possible transfer of knowledge between Greece and Bulgaria, since the former has been a member of the EU since 1981. On the other hand, in the case of Greece and the FYR of Macedonia, institutions appeared less flexible than local entrepreneurs, since the former appeared trapped by the political barriers associated with the name issue.

Specifically, common implementation of projects between Greece and Bulgaria was decisively facilitated by Bulgaria's accession to the EU. This has led to the formation of tighter bonds between institutions on the two sides of the border, reflected in training schemes for entrepreneurs, the provision of advisory services and knowledge-transfer projects.

> This lack of know-how is their [Bulgaria's] major incentive to cooperate with us. Being a member of the EU for so long is our [Greece's] main advantage, since we have the experience and the know-how to assist them and offer our services. (Thessaloniki Key informant 2)

Needless to say, there is a link between initiatives undertaken at the institutional level and enterprise-based CBC. Although institutional projects initially focused on establishing cooperation between chambers of commerce, the final beneficiaries include local enterprises. The dominant view expressed by representatives of local authorities, business support organizations and NGOs was that cooperation between institutions primarily involves 'soft' issues, such as culture, sports, twin-cities projects, but it can ultimately be a route to 'hard' issues, such as economic cooperation.

In short, it could be argued that Bulgaria's accession to the EU created greater opportunities and prospects for CBC with another EU member (Greece), both at the enterprise and institutional levels. At the same time, EU membership emphasized the gap between Bulgarian regions and neighbouring areas of the FYR of Macedonia, introducing new barriers and obstacles. As regards CBC between Greece and the FYR of Macedonia, not surprisingly, local institutions proved less flexible than entrepreneurs in their response to constraints associated with the name issue.

CBC as a Form of Local Delocalization

During the last six decades, an ongoing rapid change in the global map of production has been taking place. Specifically, the share of Less Developed

Countries (LDCs) in global manufacturing volume has risen significantly, accounting for 23.7 per cent in 2001, up from 13.7 per cent in 1980 (UNCTAD Globstat, 2002). However, a closer look at the available data reveals that this trend is primarily the result of the growing significance of nations such as China and India, while the share of Central and Eastern European Countries (CEECs) in world manufacturing value-added is down to 2.7 per cent from 19.3 per cent in 1980 (UNCTAD Globstat, 2002). Globalization of production has emerged and the participation of LDCs, especially within the CEECs, remains a key challenge.

This trend constitutes an enormously significant issue for areas and firms within the Balkans, given the developing character of the local economies and the relatively small size of the business entities located there. Moreover, labour-intensive industries, which are dominant in several Balkan countries, are mainly affected by the changing new geography of production (Kalogeresis and Labrianidis, 2008). Thus, it is of crucial importance for countries and regions among the CEECs to ensure their participation in what Gerrefi and Kornzeniewicz (1994, p. 2) have defined as Global Commodity Chains (GCC), meaning a 'set of inter-organizational networks clustered around one commodity or product, linking households, enterprises and states to one another within the world economy'. This chain involves Global Production Networks (GPN), a 'nexus of interconnected functions and operations through which goods and services are produced, distributed and consumed' (Henderson et al., 2002, p. 445).

CBC could be the means to achieve the above-mentioned goal, since it seems to enhance the role of Balkan countries among the GPN, thus creating the opportunities for local firms to cooperate with partners from more developed countries across the border (for example the case of the FYR of Macedonia–Greece and Bulgaria–Greece). Conversely, Greek and Bulgarian firms can take advantage of the fact that their neighbouring regions (in the FYR of Macedonia) are less developed and consequently costs are relatively lower there. In a sense, the border could become the competitive advantage of the regions, supplementing the role of local firms within the globalized economy. What is even more significant is that local firms located near the border manage to go international, despite their small size, due to their specific geographic location.

CBC could, therefore, be seen as a wider form of what Labrianidis has defined as 'local delocalization', involving the spatial restructuring of an industry at a regional or national level, across the border (2008, pp. 4, 41, 50–52). 'Local delocalization' includes small firms with very limited human and financial resources that manage to go international by taking advantage of the short physical distance between the mother company and the subsidiary (Labrianidis and Kalogeresis, 2009).

As a rule, SMEs internationalize their business starting from less capital-engaging operations (such as import and export) and gradually develop more complex establishments – such as joint ventures and foreign subsidiaries (Todorov, 2001). Although the relevant literature on globalization and delocalization is often focused on large enterprises, chains and networks, the important aspect of CBC in our case is that it involves, on the one hand, small firms that manage to go international and, on the other, firms that can also play an important role in local development. It is therefore interesting to examine the nature of 'local delocalization' across borders, in order to offer some useful empirical insights for future policy directions.

The examination of entrepreneurship development in the CSRs could also assist the efforts to complete the picture of the local economies. Business entities recorded there are for the most part micro- and small-sized firms,[9] which can face a variety of constraints on growth, such as restricted access to financing (Smallbone and Wyer, 1995), as well as an inability to control prices because of a lack of market power, a dependency on a relatively smaller customer base and finally limited access to policy makers (Labrianidis, 2001, p. 6). In addition, the extent to which financial and legal underdevelopment as well as corruption constrains small firm growth depends on a firm's size, since it is the smallest firms that are consistently the most adversely affected by all obstacles (Beck et al., 2005). It is therefore useful to investigate the type of firms that are engaged in CBC in the CSRs.

The available data show that almost all of the firms investigated in the CSRs were small- and medium-sized entities, employing up to 250 workers (95 per cent). Assessing the firms' size in terms of annual turnover, the results are quite similar, since 71 per cent of them reported an annual turnover of less than €2 million in 2007. These findings, combined with the data presented regarding the macroeconomic environment of the regions, illustrate the disadvantages faced by these local economies. One cannot expect these firms to manage to internationalize easily, compared to large enterprises with a well established brand name, greater availability of resources and more extensive know-how. For example, data for SMEs' development in Bulgaria support the correlation between firm size and the export capabilities, given the fact that the average increase in number of export-oriented SMEs between 2003 and 2007 is 6 per cent compared to 18.8 per cent for medium-size enterprises.[10]

However, an intensified trend towards expansion in the neighbouring markets by firms located near the borders was evident during the fieldwork. In spite of the handicaps of the local business environment, which pose barriers for small local firms, some were able to internationalize their activities through CBC. This form of 'local delocalization' includes several different types.

More specifically, a large share of the firms (41 per cent) engaged in the CSRs manage to enter into trade agreements, including sales on the other side of the border through intermediaries or importers (Figure 5.5). Another prevailing form of CBC involves subcontracting assignments (23 per cent), reflecting intensified cooperation between Greece–Bulgaria and the FYR of Macedonia in the garment manufacturing sector. Agreements on project-based cooperation and service provision, for example consultancy services, logistics or tourism services, also proved to be important in the CSRs. The latter type of CBC was particularly evident among tourist agencies located in the regions of Serres, Drama and Blagoevgrad, which has led to the formation of an informal cluster there, mainly due to the growing tourism demand from both sides of the borders. It is worth mentioning that tourist operators not only capitalize on existing infrastructures (such as hotels, sites, resorts and shopping malls), but also on the cultural heritage of the bordering regions. One example is the case of the ancient mythological figure, Orpheus, a subject of dispute according to national rhetoric, as to whether he was Thracian or Greek. Instead of going deeply into this unproductive dispute, Bulgarian and Greek tour operators have decided to jointly exploit his name. Such CBC was unthinkable before the EU-membership of Bulgaria.

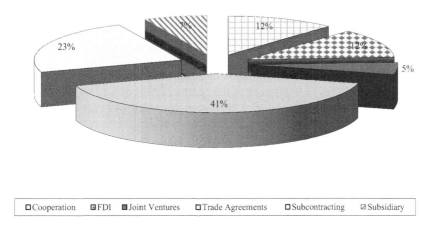

Source: Authors.

Figure 5.5   Forms of CBC evident in the CSRs

As far as the motivations for local firms to engage in CBC are concerned, low costs in the neighbouring markets were stated as the main (32.1 per cent) attraction. Given the fact that most firms face extensive price competition and cost pressures, the solution of delocalizing the labour-intensive parts of their production into neighbouring regions can provide them with a short-term competitive advantage. This policy mainly applies to the Greek firms, but also some Bulgarian ones that cooperate with the FYR of Macedonia:

> Naturally, the first incentive for us is the much lower cost, which equals 1/3 of the labour cost in Greece. (Florina Enterprise 2)

> One of the main reasons for starting CBC was the price of materials, which are cheaper in Macedonia and Serbia. (Kyustendil Enterprise 8)

At the same time, Bulgarian entrepreneurs view cooperation with Greek enterprises as an excellent chance to expand their client base and take advantage of their partner's connections with buyers throughout Europe. To put it in another way:

> CBC offers free access to a big market in Greece and a chance to sell the products directly to our customers without any intermediaries. (Petrich Enterprise 8)

Therefore, although differences can be observed in initial motivation between developed and less developed regions, the final result is common for all firms, namely a better position in the globalized market. Apart from lower costs, another significant motivating force for 'local delocalization' and CBC development has been geographic proximity. This was clearly pointed out by several entrepreneurs engaged in cooperation with the other side of the border (23.9 per cent of the cases examined).

Spatial proximity creates several advantages, such as better control and monitoring of the partner, short delivery times and higher levels of trust as a derived effect (also see Welter et al., Chapter 3 in this volume). Furthermore, spatial proximity allows entrepreneurs, as well as a few highly skilled employees from the 'parent' company to commute back and forth (between Greece, where they live and have the parent company, and Bulgaria and FYR Macedonia, where they have their subsidiary) on a daily basis, so as to run their company. This advantage is extremely important, particularly for smaller family-owned firms that go international and to a great extent for the less-developed economies as well (Labrianidis, 2001).

The firm avoided bankruptcy because of its location near the borders with Serbia and Macedonia. Other firms in central Bulgaria like that in Sevlievo were not so lucky. (Kyustendil Enterprise 12)

Lower transport costs needed – the distance between Petrich and Serres is 100 km (both ways), while the distance between Petrich and Sofia is more than three times longer – 360 km. This is a basic factor for choosing a Greek supplier but not a domestic one, situated in the Sofia capital, for example. (Petrich Enterprise 7)

In conclusion, it is precisely the border that creates the major incentive for an entrepreneur to engage in CBC. Neighbouring with a region of lower or higher economic development offers advantages in terms of differences in costs and opportunity for expansion into a new market as well as spatial proximity. In spite of the barriers that the size of the local economy poses, as well as those associated with the size of the firm itself, entrepreneurs in the CSRs manage to implement a strategy of local delocalization. This offers a major opportunity to these small companies to internationalize part of their activities and follow a procedure that fits their needs exactly, for example exploit lower labour costs and remain competitive. At the same time, one should bear in mind that due to their small size, these firms are not able to follow different internationalization strategies (for example subcontracting to Chinese firms). Given the fact that organizational difficulties during this process are enormous, the familiarization that geographic proximity enables is of considerable importance for the local entrepreneurs, who manage to better adapt to the socio-economic and institutional framework of the other side, on top of the much lower organizational costs involved in managing the subsidiary. Thus, they are able to overcome size-related constraints and become part of the globalized economy.

Lastly, it is also worth mentioning that signs of a possible reversal of flows between Bulgaria, Greece and the FYR of Macedonia were evident during the fieldwork. In the case of Greek–Bulgarian CBC, while this mostly referred to sales of final products from the more developed areas (the Greek side) to the less developed ones (Bulgaria), the opposite trend has also started to happen, due to the rising power of Bulgarian firms. These signs were particularly visible in the construction sector, in which Greek firms initially entered the Bulgarian market, providing local firms with building materials. However, during the last two to three years, Bulgarian firms have also been able to sell materials of high quality at competitive prices in the Greek market. Therefore, a reverse flow which reflects the dynamic character of CBC in the CSR is also observed:

> We are supplying a Bulgarian company with aluminium and iron material. However, this has tended to change over the course of time; nowadays, they are also supplying us with some other material. Let me just tell you that this is a very powerful and large enterprise that, if it chooses to make an opening towards the Greek market, will run most of the Greek commercial companies of the sector out of business. (Serres Enterprise 7)

An example of an opposite movement is the increasing activity of Bulgarian companies and individuals that are buying property in northern Greece – mostly along the seaside. A trend of transfer of commercial registration and activities of some of them in northern Greece, depending on their increasing resources, might be expected.

At the same time, even though the market of the FYR of Macedonia primarily includes the localities where Greek entrepreneurs are able to find lower labour costs, an opposite flow involves a large number of consumers from Greece who travel to the other side of the border seeking to buy cheap products. This movement is particularly evident in areas such as Bitola, which have become popular destinations for shopping and leisure activities for Greek travellers. However, this phenomenon was particularly evident during the decade 1995–2005, gradually fading out after 2000. An opposite flow is also apparent in the case of Greece–Bulgaria, involving the case of Sandanski, which is located in the immediate proximity of the Bansko ski resort, attracting a large share of Greek excursionists at weekends.

It is, therefore, useful to note that CBC in these cases cannot be restricted to the exploitation of the less developed areas, due to lower costs. Gradual improvement of conditions in the less developed areas can create new potential and opposite capital flows between more and less developed areas. This fact highlights, once more, the need for a long-term strategy for the development of the Balkan region as a whole, which could create positive effects for all sides. In addition, it contributes to questioning some of the established views regarding the factors which contribute to CBC and models of cross-border development.

CONCLUSIONS

As argued in this chapter, CBC between Greece, Bulgaria and the FYR of Macedonia presents some peculiarities and unique characteristics when compared to similar examples within Europe. This situation is primarily the outcome of the various interacting forces on several levels, including economic, social, cultural, political and historical perspectives. The whole area under investigation comprises one of the most fragmented spaces within Europe, involving small regional economies, while a strong presence of ethnic minorities in the shared borders and memories of the past has sometimes created tensions and rivalries on national and regional levels.

Despite the obvious disadvantages, a strong tendency by local entrepreneurs to exploit the available resources was evident during the fieldwork conducted in the CSRs. CBC in this case constitutes a form of what could be called 'local delocalization', which seems to fit the needs and capabilities of the small firms located in the CSRs. EU membership emerges as a vital (twofold) shaping factor for CBC in the CSR. It is clear that the derived benefits are more positive when both sides involve EU members (for example the case of Greece and Bulgaria), but on the other hand, a different outcome can emerge in a member–non-member situation, such as where Bulgaria's accession contributed to the deterioration of the country's cross-border relations with a non-EU country, that is, the FYR of Macedonia. This finding is of crucial importance for future policy development, bearing in mind the fundamental target of the EU enlargement process, namely balanced development and cohesion among European regions.

Some interesting findings also emerged from an examination of the nature of existing CBC in the area. Perhaps the most important attribute of CBC is related to the fact that it constitutes a form of 'local delocalization'. Firms located near the border manage to go international through CBC despite the fact that they are extremely small, simply by taking advantage of their location. What is even more important is that they would almost certainly not have managed to go international any other way, due to the constraints of the macroeconomic environment of the area and their small size. In other words, local entrepreneurs have managed to implement a strategy that fits their requirements, taking advantage of their proximity in regions of different economic development according to their needs.

In the case of Greek firms located in areas neighbouring Bulgaria and the FYR of Macedonia, this presented a major opportunity to exploit lower labour costs. This enabled CBC in labour-intensive industries, on a 'triangular manufacturing' basis, which to be sustainable has to be beneficial to all parties involved. Firms from less developed regions manage to acquire a better position among the GPN through collaboration with firms located in more developed regions and, thus, participate in the globalized economy. At the same time, proximity to a region of different economic development entailed another advantage for Greek firms: the gradual rise of Bulgarian citizens' purchasing power and, hence, the emergence of a newly formed market. This trend was particularly evident in the tourism sector, where strong cooperation between travel agencies on both sides of the border exists as a result of the increased tourism demands by the Bulgarian side. Spatial proximity also enables easier and more cost-effective transportation of goods across the borders, thus reducing both time and costs. It can also facilitate partner-search procedures by making monitoring and partner control easier, as well as enhancing trust levels due to familiarization with the other side, while reframing the common socio-cultural idioms as a bridge of communication rather than fuelling inter-ethnic tensions. Overall, entrepreneurs are able to commute back and forth, even on a daily basis, to visit their partners and their subsidiary company in the neighbouring country. Given the fact that organizational difficulties are enormous in the case of delocalization, geographic proximity enables enhanced adaptation to the new socio-economic environment of the cross-border market.

It should be noted, however, that even if local firms manage to establish cross-border cooperation, it does not mean that local, national and European policies are satisfactory for them. These findings are valuable for future policy development and highlight the need for an integrated development strategy for the Balkan region as a whole. Thus far, CBC is mainly promoted on an individual level, driven primarily by the entrepreneurs' ability to exploit the competitive advantage that the border offers. However, as argued in this chapter, there is a clear need to support these initiatives on a regional level, creating the basis for all regions to benefit equally from CBC. This presupposes an integrated approach based on closer cooperation between European, national and local (CBC) levels, while keeping in mind the rapid changes already on the way and the dynamic character of cooperation evidenced in the border regions.

Evidently, time and reflection are necessary prerequisites for the creation of viable structures and sustainable economic relations in the Balkans. The particular regions analysed in this chapter should be relevant for a European regional policy aiming at reducing disparities on the level of regional development.

NOTES

1. As is well known, the Western cultural imagination of the Balkans as an underdeveloped region fraught with conflict and corruption has created a series of stereotypes that remain dominant in the public perception of the area. In this respect, the research presented in this chapter aims at deconstructing this dominant Western notion (Todorova, 1997). The concept of 'subaltern', inspired by Gramsci, was introduced in the Western social sciences in the mid-1990s, mainly by Indian academics who redress the colonial imbalance in a post-colonial perspective (Gupta and Ferguson, 1997). Conceiving of the Balkans as a 'subaltern' region implies a reconceptualization from the standpoint of regional engagement, which involves mutual initiatives on the part of cross-border actors.
2. Cross-border migration in the region for EU citizens remains an open option. Schengen visa restrictions apply to non-EU citizens. This puts the entrepreneurs from the FYR of Macedonia in an underprivileged position; in the present study, mobility among the three states is guaranteed by bilateral agreements.

3. Conceptualizing borders as disadvantaged and low-opportunity regions involves, in the case of the Balkans, additional negative stereotypes. The dominant approaches of the Balkans in the 1990s presented Balkan border regions as low-opportunity, socially backward areas of national and political tension (see for example Kennan, 1993; Kaplan, 1994).
4. In this context the terms 'Europe' and 'European' stand for the EU and the EU policies.
5. The PHARE Programme is financed by the European Union to assist the applicant countries of Central and Eastern Europe in their preparations for joining the European Union. The CARDS programme is the EU's main instrument of financial assistance to the Western Balkans, covering specifically Croatia, Bosnia and Herzegovina, Serbia, Montenegro, Macedonia, Kosovo and Albania.
6. Almost all of the fieldwork interviews were conducted with Bulgarian and Greek respondents and thus the empirical assessment mainly reflects the Bulgarian and Greek views about CBC activities.
7. According to a study by AT Kearney and Visa Europe, stated by Peter Ayliffe, president and chief executive of Visa Europe in an interview with *Dnevnik* newspaper, 24 June 2009.
8. Recently recognized as such after decades of suppression of their identity by the national doctrines emerging after the end of the Ottoman Empire.
9. For example, according to official data, enterprises employing up to 50 persons constitute approximately 99.6 per cent of the total number of enterprises in Greece (Hellenic Organization of Small and Medium Sized Enterprises and Handicraft, n.d.).
10. Annual Report for the Condition and Development of SMEs in Bulgaria, 2008 (Ministry of Economy, Energy and Tourism, 2010).

REFERENCES

Beck, T., A. Demirguc-Kunt and V. Maksimovic (2005), 'Financial and legal constraints to growth: does firm size matter?', *The Journal of Finance*, **60**(1), 137–77.

Dimitrov, M., G. Petrakos, S. Totev and M. Tsiapa (2003), 'Cross-border cooperation in Southeastern Europe: the enterprises' point of view', *South and East European Development Centre* (SEED), **9**(2), 17–38.

Embassy of the Republic of Bulgaria in London (2005), 'Foreign direct investment inflow in Bulgaria by country and by year in USD m', available at: http://www.bulgarianembassy-london.org/pdf/FDI_inflow.pdf, accessed 23 February 2009.

Employment Agency (2008), 'Year-book 2007', Sofia: Ministry of Labour and Social Policy (in Bulgarian), available at: http://www.az.government.bg/Analyses/Anapro/2007/year/zaetost_2007.pdf, accessed 7 June 2012.

Europa (2000), *The Europa World Year Book 2000*, London: Europa.

Eurostat (2009), 'General and regional statistics', available at: http://epp.eurostat.ec.europa.eu/portal/page?_pageid=0,1136162,0_45572076&_dad=portal&_schema=PORTAL, accessed 11 January 2009.

Gerrefi, G. and M. Kornzeniewicz (1994), 'Introduction: global commodity chains', in G. Gerrefi and M. Kornzeniewicz (eds), *Commodity Chains and Global Capitalism*, Westport, CT: Greenwood Press, pp. 95–122.

Gupta, A. and J. Ferguson (eds) (1997), *Culture, Power, Place: Explorations in Critical Anthropology*, Durham, NC: Duke University Press.

Hellenic Organization of Small and Medium Sized Enterprises and Handicraft (n.d.), 'The SMEs sector in Greece', available at: http://www.eommex.gr/english/new/index.htm, accessed 12 March 2007.

Henderson, J., P. Dicken, M. Hess, N. Coe and H.W. Yeung (2002), 'Global production networks and the analysis of economic development', *Review of International Political Economy*, **9**(3), 436–63.

Kalogeresis, A. and L. Labrianidis (2008), 'Delocalization and development in Europe: conceptual issues and empirical findings', in L. Labrianidis (ed.), *The Moving Frontier: The Changing Geography of Production in Labour-Intensive Industries*, Aldershot, UK: Ashgate, pp. 23–58.

Kaplan, R. (1994), *Balkan Ghosts: A Journey Through History*, New York: Vintage Books.

Kennan, G. (1993), *The Other Balkan Wars: A 1913 Carnegie Endowment Inquiry in Retrospect with a New Introduction and Reflections on the Present Conflict by George F. Kennan*, Washington, DC: Carnegie Endowment for International Peace.

Labrianidis, L. (1996), 'Subcontracting in Greek manufacturing and the opening of the Balkan markets', *Cyprus Journal of Economics*, **9**(1), 29–45.

Labrianidis, L. (2001), 'Delocalisation of labour intensive industries. An argument in favour of 'triangular manufacturing' between developed countries–Greece–Balkans', in *Proceedings of the International Conference on Restructuring, Stability and Development in Southeastern Europe*, Volos: University of Thessaly.

Labrianidis, L. (2008), 'Introduction', in L. Labrianidis (ed.), *The Moving Frontier: The Changing Geography of Production in Labour-Intensive Industries*, Aldershot, UK: Ashgate, pp. 3–11.

Labrianidis, L. and T. Kalogeresis (2009), 'De-localisation', in R. Kitchin and N. Thrift (eds), *International Encyclopaedia of Human Geography*, Oxford: Elsevier.

National Bank of the Republic of Macedonia (2008) 'Data for foreign direct investment', available at: http://www.nbrm.gov.mk/default-en.asp?ItemID=8140DD0DAC749D4C8266412BE8822F50, accessed 22 February 2009.

Petrakos, G. (1996), *The New Geography of the Balkans: Cross-border Cooperation between Albania, Bulgaria and Greece*, Volos: University of Thessaly, Department of Planning and Regional Development.

Petrakos, G. and S. Totev (2001), 'Economic performance and structure in the Balkan region', in G. Petrakos and S. Totev (eds), *The Development of the Balkan Region*, Aldershot, UK: Ashgate, pp. 3–29.

Smallbone, D. and P. Wyer (1995), 'Export activity in SMEs', *CEEDR*, Working Paper Series, no. 9.

State Statistical Office of the Republic of Macedonia (2007) 'Active Population in the Republic of Macedonia', available at: http://www.stat.gov.mk/english/statistiki_eng.asp?ss=07.01&rbs=1, accessed 12 February 2009.

Tatsos, N. (2001), *Informal Economy and Tax Evasion in Greece*, Athens: Papazisis.

Todorov, K. (2001), *Strategic Management in Small and Medium Sized Companies – Theory and Practice*, 2 vols, Sofia: Ciela Soft and Publishing Co.

Todorova, M. (1997), *Imagining the Balkans*, New York: Oxford University Press.

UNCTAD (2008) 'Major FDI Indicators', available at: http://stats.unctad.org/FDI/TableViewer/tableView.aspx, accessed 20 February 2009.
UNCTAD Globstat (2002) 'Production of manufactures', available at: http://globstat.unctad.org/html/index.html, accessed 21 February 2009.

PART III

Regional Case Studies from the NIS

6. EU enlargement and SME development in Moldovan border regions

Elena Aculai and Adela Bulgac

INTRODUCTION

Important changes such as the EU enlargement can have an enormous impact on the situation of small firms in non-member states. In particular, these changes affect countries neighbouring the EU. When Romania joined the European Union (EU) in January 2007, the border between the Republic of Moldova and Romania, its neighbour, became the new border of the EU. This geographical proximity to the EU has influenced different aspects of socio-economic activity in the Republic of Moldova, in particular the development of entrepreneurship in its border regions. In this chapter we will discuss the effects of EU enlargement on the activity of Moldovan small and medium enterprises (SMEs). In particular, we will show that the entrance of Romania into the EU has created additional barriers and risks for the economic cooperation between Moldovan and Romanian SMEs. Our specific focus will be on businesses operating mainly in the border districts of Moldova that are either already involved in international business cooperation or planning to do so. We will juxtapose the expectations Moldovan entrepreneurs expressed before Romania joined the EU and the actual changes which took place after January 2007 and affected the cross-border cooperation of Moldovan SMEs. Empirically, the chapter will draw on the results of a series of interviews with entrepreneurs conducted between 2006 and mid-2009. Cross-border cooperation of small and medium businesses is defined as any form of contact or cooperation between entrepreneurs, including those involved only in export and/or import. We assume that prevailing export and import relationships between Moldovan and Romanian SMEs can serve as a basis for more complex forms of cross-border cooperation in the future. Finally, we will offer recommendations which may be employed by the government in order to promote and support the growth of cross-border cooperation.

DYNAMICS OF THE RELATIONSHIP BETWEEN MOLDOVA AND THE EU

After the EU enlargement in 2007 the western border between Moldova and Romania became the border between Moldova and the EU. With regard to the specifics of the relations between Moldova and Romania within the larger context of the relations between Moldova and the EU, we will consider first the relations between Moldova and the EU in general, and secondly, the relations of the two neighbouring countries, Moldova and Romania. This approach is important because of the specifics of interstate politics between Moldova and Romania. For example, in summer 2009 Moldova introduced a visa regime exclusively for Romanian citizens, despite the fact that since 2007 no EU citizens had to obtain a visa in order to enter Moldova. At the same time the President of Romania publicly announced that Romanian citizenship would be granted to one million Moldovan citizens, without having consulted with other EU members.

Moldovan–EU Relations

After Moldova, a former republic of the Soviet Union, gained its independence in 1991, it first concentrated on developing close economic cooperation with other Newly Independent States (NIS) countries. The choice of the West (namely, EU countries) as a strategic political partner over the East (namely, NIS countries) was not made in the early 1990s. In the late 1990s, Moldova, along with other transition countries in Central and Eastern Europe, defined its relations with the EU by signing a Partnership and Cooperation Agreement. The Agreement was ratified in 1998 for a period of ten years. After 2001, the Moldovan government announced the new political orientation of the country towards Europe. From that time, the relationship between Moldova and the EU started to develop. For example, Moldova was included in the European Neighbourhood Policy adopted by the EU in order to promote stability and security at the external borders of the European Union. As part of the European Neighbourhood Policy, in 2004 the EU–Moldova Action Plan was signed and approved by the European Commission (EC, 2004). The plan aims to strengthen the cooperation in social, economic, political, legislative and cultural areas. After the Action Plan was signed, the relationship between Moldova and the EU significantly improved compared to the previous period, which was regulated by the Partnership and Cooperation Agreement conditions. According to the Report on the Implementation of the EU–Moldova Action Plan, Moldovan legislation is adjusting to EU norms, and reforms have been introduced, all of which supported the decision of the EU to offer Moldova a preferential trade regime (GRM, 2008). In 2006 the Generalized System of Preferences+ (GSP+) was introduced, which replaced the old Generalized System of Preferences (GSP). A comparative analysis of the Ministry of Economy and Trade demonstrates that, after its introduction, the GSP+ covered 88 per cent of the value of Moldovan exports to the EU market, as compared to the GSP, which only covered 55 per cent (ADEPT and EXPERT-GROUP, 2008). In January 2008 Moldova was offered an asymmetrical trade regime with the EU countries. Other practical results of the cooperation with the EU include the construction of a bridge across the Prut River and of a customs office in the northern part of the country as part of an EU project. Currently because both Action Plan and Partnership and Cooperation Agreement have expired, the EU and Moldova are seeking a new framework to define their future cooperation. The EU expects more proactive measures and actions to be taken by the Moldovan side.

In 2006, the EU launched the Border Assistance Mission and a new customs regime at the Moldovan–Ukrainian border, which established greater control over and order along the border and correspondingly reduced contraband activity. The new customs regime indirectly forced Trans-Dniester companies to register in Chisinau. At the same time and as a consequence of the facilitated trade within the GPS+ and the asymmetrical trade regime, enterprises from the Trans-Dniester region oriented their exports towards the EU. In 2006–08, the region registered a growth of exports to the EU of 59 per cent, which was higher than the growth of exports to Russia, which has always been the main sales market for the aforementioned enterprises (Popescu, 2008). In general, the actions taken by the EU have contributed to the increase of exports and imports into the EU, but mainly larger enterprises benefited from them.

During the 1990s, Moldovan companies were more active exporting and importing into NIS countries, mainly as a result of trading relationships originating from the former Soviet Union. Over time this changed: for example, in 1997 imports from the NIS countries exceeded EU imports, but in 1998 EU imports dominated and have exceeded imports from the NIS countries ever since. In 2008 EU imports constituted 43 per cent of all imports, in comparison with 35.5 per cent of imports from the NIS (NBS, 2009a).

Exports were also reoriented from the NIS to EU markets, although it is only since 2006 that Moldovan enterprises have started to export more intensively to EU markets. In 2008, the share of Moldovan exports to the

NIS was 39.2 per cent, and to the EU 51.5 per cent of total Moldovan exports. This may partly result from the integration of Bulgaria and Romania into the EU, especially because Romania remained one of the main commercial partners of Moldova. Consequently, the changed export orientation of Moldovan enterprises towards EU markets is determined to a large extent by the preferences the EU offers to Moldovan businesses.

Moldovan–Romanian Relations

When considering the relationship between Moldova and Romania, the common historic past shared by the two countries needs to be taken into account. In the Middle Ages the territory of contemporary Moldova, along with a third of the territory of contemporary Romania, formed a single state called the Moldovan Principality. After the war between Russia and Turkey in 1806–12, the eastern part of the Moldovan Principality (Bessarabia), located between the Prut and Dniester Rivers, fell to the Russian Empire. The other part remained part of the Ottoman Empire. Since 1812 the territory of contemporary Moldova has been a part of the Russian Empire (1812–1918), of Romania (1918–40 and 1941–44), and the Soviet Union (1940–41 and 1944–91).

After the revolution in Romania in 1989 and the acquisition of independence by Moldova in 1991, both states moved towards a new relationship of being equal and independent states. Considering the special importance of this new relationship for citizens of both countries, a non-visa regime was introduced. But, when Romania joined the EU on 1 January 2007, Moldova became a neighbour of the EU, and according to EU regulations a visa regime was introduced for Moldovan citizens when crossing the Romanian border.

However, for the time being, political problems and mutual accusations between the governments of both countries hinder cooperation between Moldovan and Romanian enterprises as well as the development of mutual trust between entrepreneurs. Whilst the relationship between Moldova and the EU has been continually improving in recent years, the relationship between Moldova and Romania had been gradually deteriorating until mid-2009. After the Alliance for European Integration became the governing party in Moldova, the relationships between Moldova and Romania at the intergovernmental level improved significantly.

SMES IN MOLDOVA: CHARACTERISTICS AND DEVELOPMENT

SMEs play an important role in the Moldovan economy. In 2009, 43 700 enterprises, which amounted to 97.8 per cent of the total number of registered enterprises, were SMEs, employing 58.7 per cent of all employees and contributing 39.2 per cent of the total turnover to the national economy. SMEs were present in all sectors of the national economy, with the majority of them (41.2 per cent) involved in trade. Only 11.7 per cent operate in industry, another 6.9 per cent in transport and communication, 5.7 per cent in construction and 5.3 per cent in agriculture (NBS, 2010).

Moldovan SMEs face several serious problems. In particular, limited access to resources impedes their competitiveness and possibilities for growing the business, which is very important on external markets. One of the barriers they face is a severe lack of financial resources for purchasing and renewing production equipment. For example, the Government of Japan offered grants for purchasing production equipment to export-oriented Moldovan SMEs in rural areas. The total sum of requested grants amounted to more than US$15.5 million, exceeding the sum envisaged by the fifth tranche of the grant by nine times (Infotag, 2010).

Another problem impeding business development is related to skilled labour. As a negative consequence of the EU enlargement, the outflow of workers from Moldova has increased considerably. For years, citizens of Moldova have left the country, in search of better paid jobs, moving to both Eastern and Western countries. In 2007, 335 600 citizens left to work abroad, which is 8.2 per cent higher than in 2006. Labour migration to four EU countries (Italy, Portugal, Greece and Romania) amounted to 78 500 people, plus 221 000 to two NIS countries, namely Russia and Ukraine. In more detail, 210 800 Moldovans went to Russia, 62 300 to Italy, 10 700 to Turkey, 10 200 to Ukraine, 7400 to Portugal, 5200 to Greece, 4900 to Israel and 3600 to Romania. In the first months of 2009, in the context of the worldwide financial crisis, the number of persons declared by Moldovan households as travelling to other countries for work or at least the search for work was estimated to amount to 272 500 (NBS, 2009b). The ongoing outflow of workers results in a severe shortage of qualified personnel. Its impact on SMEs is aggravated by the fact that Moldovan SMEs, as elsewhere, prefer to hire their relatives and friends, even when they do not possess a sufficient level of skills and experience (Birca, 2005).

Cross-border cooperation is not possible without a mutual interest from both sides; and not surprisingly, perhaps, Moldovan entrepreneurs appear more interested in cooperation than their Romanian counterparts. Romanian entrepreneurs are interested in some of the opportunities provided by the relationships with Moldovan companies such as entering a new market with great potential (the NIS market), a cheap labour force, available production space at low cost and lower prices for input material. However, they also face barriers, amongst them the economic and political instability in Moldova, non-familiarity with the legislation, miscommunication, poor promotion of business in Moldovan neighbouring regions, lack of business ties, and, similar to Moldovan entrepreneurs, the lack of a qualified labour force.

The main needs of SMEs when trying to internationalize are related to management skills and well trained personnel who are ready to work with business partners on foreign markets. Therefore, access to information about potential foreign business partners, regulations, and other issues regarding the business environment on foreign markets are important, a lack of which can prevent SMEs from participating in international alliances and other international business networks (OECD, 2002, p. 74).

Also, formal requirements such as visa regimes may further impede cross-border cooperation as well as internal enterprise development. One of the risks to entrepreneurship development in border regions of Moldova could have been the tightening of the visa regime, which was expected to occur after Romania's accession to the EU (Smallbone and Li Meng, 2005). The tightening of the visa regime actually took place after 2007, when Romania joined the EU. Improving the capacity of SMEs and their ability to initiate and develop cross-border cooperation requires the implementation of appropriate policies in the countries involved in joint activities. Of particular importance is support for those SMEs that have effectively developed partnerships of mutual benefit for all partners (OECD, 2000). In this regard, the next section will take a closer look at Moldovan enterprises and their expectations regarding cross-border cooperation with Romania before and after Romania joined the EU.

THE IMPACT OF EU ENLARGEMENT ON MOLDOVAN SMES: SOME EMPIRICAL RESULTS

Methodology and Data

This section draws on results from three projects and several semi-structured interviews with entrepreneurs in Moldova, which were carried out between 2006 and 2009. Before Romania joined the EU, in 2006 and as part of a larger project concerned with cross-border cooperation in Ukraine,

Belarus and Moldova, we interviewed representatives of 40 SMEs, which participated in cross-border cooperation and which were based in Cahul and Edinet, the two Moldovan districts located next to the Romanian border (Welter et al., 2007). Also, 20 representatives of business support institutions were interviewed. The purpose was to identify factors that impact the development of cross-border cooperation in selected NIS regions and to assess the potential impact of the EU enlargement on entrepreneurship development in Ukraine, Belarus and Moldova.

Additionally, we draw on ten interviews with entrepreneurs involved in external economic activity, which were conducted at the end of 2007, one year after Romania joined the EU (Aculai, 2008). The aim was to identify to what extent the expectations of entrepreneurs, which dated back a year, had proved realistic. Furthermore we used the results of 28 interviews held during late 2008 and early 2009 with Moldovan SMEs in border regions, which were involved in exporting goods and services, or initiating the export, including two interviews with those who had ceased their engagement within the last or second last year prior to the interview (Aculai et al., 2009).

All enterprises that participated in this research are privately owned and represent small and medium businesses. The surveyed enterprises are involved in agriculture, production of mineral water, packing, bakery, textiles, road maintenance, as well as transportation services and trade. The enterprises which sell services are involved in businesses such as tourist services and transportation of goods. The cross-border business contacts between Moldovan and Romanian enterprises tend to be stable and sustainable. The only exception is the import and export of agricultural products, since these activities occasionally might attract random one-time providers and customers.

Export and import of goods is the leading type of cross-border business activities and partnerships that occur between Moldovan and foreign enterprises, in particular those based in Romania. More complex forms of cooperation, such as technology exchange, subcontracting, foreign investment or founding of joint ventures, are not widespread.

Some Moldovan enterprises engage in different types of cross-border activities that may complement each other. For example, an enterprise may be engaged in importing and/or exporting as well as providing management training to its business partner across the border. In other cases an enterprise may be involved in several cross-border types of activity which belong to the same area of business. For instance, it might export mineral water to Romania and import beer from Romania to Moldova.

Expectations of Moldovan Entrepreneurs before Romania's Accession to the EU

In 2006, entrepreneurs and business support institution representatives, whom we interviewed in 2006, differentiated between anticipated short-term and long-term effects of the EU enlargement on business activities. Most of the respondents expected the situation to initially worsen after Romania joined the EU, but at the same time expecting long-standing positive effects of Romania's integration into the EU. This opinion is exemplified by an entrepreneur residing in the Cahul district, who pointed out that the inclusion of Romania into the EU and thus, the emergence of a common border between Moldova and the EU, would over time have a positive impact on the Moldovan economy because the EU might be expected to have a vested interest in maintaining economic and social stability in its neighbouring countries. Within the framework of the EU Neighbourhood Policy and other EU programmes, which would also include Moldova, some funding is likely to be provided to sponsor the development of infrastructure. However in the interviewee's opinion, short-term obstacles to cross-border cooperation would emerge immediately after Romania joined the EU.

Entrepreneurs were apprehensive that visa regulations would become stricter as a consequence of the EU enlargement, which in fact happened. Before Romania joined the EU, Moldovan citizens did not need a visa to enter Romania. After Romania became an EU member, stricter rules regarding travel were indeed imposed. Moldovans cannot travel to Romania without obtaining a visa prior to their visit, which is nowadays a compli-cated and time-consuming process. Although Moldovan entrepreneurs acknowledge the intention of the EU to secure its external border and to control migration, they believe its current visa policies to be unnecessarily complex. After 2007 many entrepreneurs believed that this problem could be easily solved if the governments of the two countries were willing to do so, some entrepreneurs even viewing the issue as a deliberate response of both governments to political tensions between Moldova and Romania.

Also, after the Soviet Union broke down in 1991, many residents of Moldova emigrated, or went to work or study abroad. This also contributed to the development of international business partnerships between Moldovans who stayed in the country and those who left. Many labour migrants left their families behind in Moldova, therefore strong connections between Moldovans living in Moldova and abroad were maintained, which sometimes developed into business contacts. This can be illustrated by a story of a student from Moldova who went to Romania to study. Every time her parents visited her, they brought over some items to trade in Romania in order to cover their travel expenses. Over time the parents developed working relations with businesspeople from both Moldova and Romania, who placed with them the orders to deliver certain items. This kind of partnership proved financially beneficial for the family and soon became their family business.

When asked which changes they expected to take place in the business environment after Romania's EU membership, Moldovan entrepreneurs anticipated a sharp decrease of their businesses' competitiveness in the Romanian market. Before 2007, the competitiveness of Moldovan products was based on their low prices, resulting from the low labour costs in Moldova. Often, Moldovan SMEs could afford to set particularly low prices for the goods they produced and sold, because they were producing and trading (partly) in the shadow economy. However, even before Romania joined the EU, taxes, costs of raw materials and transportation in Romania increased, leading to an increase of the costs Moldovan entrepreneurs had to carry. For example, in an interview carried out in 2006, the interviewee mentioned that the ecological tax in Romania had increased 30 times from previous years, and a road tax was introduced, which resulted in increased transportation costs. Finally the cost of raw materials was also raised in order to adjust Romanian prices to the European level. All those changes had taken place within just a few years.

Furthermore, customs control operations at the Moldovan–Romanian border became stricter, restricting illegal cross-border activities. Given the fact that many Moldovan SMEs had been involved in the shadow sector of the economy and/or had drawn on illegally imported materials, this further resulted in increased costs for many Moldovan SMEs. It was reasonable to expect that the price competitiveness of Moldovan products in the Romanian market was to decline significantly in the coming years. On the other hand, SMEs which were located close to the border, that is, within 30 to 50 kilometres from the border line, hoped to be eligible for more favourable visa and customs regulations.

In addition, during the process of Romania's accession to the EU, in order to prepare the Romanian economy to meet the new EU standards, the Romanian government gradually introduced new quality standards for goods and new regulations for their import and export. Again, this impacted on Moldovan enterprises trading in the Romanian market as the entrepreneurs had to ensure that their products complied with those new and, in any case, more demanding requirements.

At the same time businesses from Western and Central Europe, which had a longer history of trading under market economy conditions, entered the Romanian market, thus contributing to fierce competition. As a result, many Moldovan entrepreneurs perceived business cooperation with Romanian partners as insecure and unprofitable, even before Romania officially entered the EU. SMEs were particularly concerned about this, since their competitiveness tended to be significantly lower in comparison to large enterprises, and they also tend to be more actively involved in the shadow economy.

Some SMEs, especially those which had contacts with relatively large Romanian enterprises (the international wholesale company, METRO, or the airport), hoped that EU enlargement would not affect them negatively. They counted on the strong contacts they maintained with their Romanian partners and on the fact that they were not engaged in the shadow sector. Moreover, the shared language and culture of Moldovans and Romanians was seen as beneficial for cross-border cooperation. For example, entrepreneurs who inhabit both sides of the Prut River, which separates Moldova from Romania, were likely to respond positively to offers of business cooperation initiated by citizens of the other country. Some of the entrepreneurs interviewed mentioned that even though economic benefits were the main reason for them considering cross-border cooperation, they were also willing to do business with people of the same ethnicity, thus indicating an important role for shared values originating from their joint history and culture. Some respondents also believed that the support they obtained from their Romanian partners was, to a large extent, due to the recognition of their shared ethnicity. Sometimes, however, ethnic and historical factors might have a negative effect: some Moldovans and Romanians felt suspicious towards their potential partners and feared misunderstanding and arrogance.

To summarize, the main anticipated positive effects of EU enlargement, as articulated by entrepreneurs prior to Romania's integration into the EU, were as follows: Moldova's new status as EU neighbour would result in new possibilities for the integration of Moldova into the EU. In particular, Moldovan enterprises could obtain better access to the European markets, also through their Romanian partners. Moreover, lower costs of goods and services in Moldova compared to Romania might attract new foreign partners to the country. Also, entrepreneurs expected new possibilities regarding accessing additional funds through EU programmes as well as new knowledge and management know-how through their Romanian partners. Finally, entrepreneurs were confident that business ethics among Moldovan entrepreneurs, especially among SME owners, would improve, partly because they would have to meet the new and rigid EU requirements when trading and selling in Romania. All in all, the respondents considered that any improvements in the political relationships between the Moldovan and Romanian governments would positively affect the decisions made by local authorities and, in turn, foster business cooperation between the two countries.

The Situation for Moldovan SMEs since Romania's EU Membership

In contrast to their expectations of the effects of Romania's EU membership, the interviews during 2007 to 2009 showed that the majority of the entrepreneurs indicated that they were affected negatively by the EU enlargement. They believed that the conditions allowing for effective business cooperation with their Romanian partners had worsened. Interviewees indicated the (anticipated) introduction of a strict visa regime as their most pressing problem. Under these regulations, Moldovan entrepreneurs experienced severe difficulties when travelling to Romania for meetings and negotiations. Entrepreneurs felt that they had to invest a considerable amount of time and money to arrange their trips to Romania. Furthermore, new visa regulations limited the opportunity for participation of Moldovan entrepreneurs in trade fairs and exhibitions in EU countries. Such exhibitions and trade fairs, however, were viewed by Moldovan entrepreneurs as a valuable resource for making business contacts and promoting their products abroad, and many interviewees mentioned their past positive experiences at such exhibitions and fairs.

Under these circumstances many people tried to find their own solutions to deal with visa problems. For example, a significant number of Moldovans have two citizenships: they are both Moldovan and Romanian citizens, which helps them to avoid problems with customs and visa offices as well as simplifying their business transactions in Romania. As early as 2005, many Moldovans had already applied for and were granted Romanian citizenship. Many Moldovan citizens also sought Romanian citizenship in order to be able to travel without visas to other EU member states and find better paid employment in those countries (Calac, 2005). Around 120 000 people have obtained dual citizenship, with many more in the process of obtaining it – almost one million (Savciuc, 2009).

In mid-2009, Moldovan entrepreneurs still believed that the strict visa regulations of the EU regarding Moldovans should and will eventually be softened. In their eyes, the first step to be taken should be the optimization of the application process, in order to make it more time-effective and less complicated; one possible solution refers to opening additional Romanian consulates in Moldova. Also, over the past two years both politicians and entrepreneurs raised the issue of extra allowances for businesses located within 30–50 kilometres from the border. However, until 2009 these issues were never fully addressed because of political tensions between the

Moldovan and Romanian governments. At present, Moldovan citizens living next to the Romanian border within 30 kilometres have been granted a simplified process of border crossing to Romania.

As anticipated by Moldovan entrepreneurs, in 2007 many Western European companies entered the Romanian market. These companies have more advanced technologies, higher levels of product quality and design and use more sophisticated methods of promoting sales than their Moldovan counterparts. Therefore many Moldovan companies had to leave the Romanian market unless they could attract foreign investors. At the same time, taxes and tariffs in Romania increased; therefore prices for Moldovan products were also raised, affecting their low price strategy, which often constituted their major competitive advantage. For example, such was the experience of a Moldovan company engaged in producing cereals. Until 2007, the company had successfully traded in Romanian markets. Their production was in demand due to its quality being equal and its prices being lower than those of competing goods produced in Romania. After Romania joined the EU, new products from other EU countries appeared on the Romanian market, which were sold in a similar price range, but were of higher quality, better design and more actively advertised than the Moldovan product. The managers of the Moldovan company actively tried to modify and renew their business cooperation with the Romanian partner, with whom they had a long-standing business relationship. Nevertheless, in 2008, the Romanian company went bankrupt and went out of business, because it could not cope with the increased competitiveness on the domestic market. The Moldovan enterprise managed to save the business by reducing the volume of sales on its domestic market.

Since Moldovan SMEs could not compete with businesses which were engaged in producing modern and high quality products and services, they tended to focus on narrow market niches in Romania. However, these niches left them vulnerable, as they had to cope with the accelerated modernization of many Romanian companies, which frequently were supported by their new Western European partners. For example, one Moldovan SME was involved in the maintenance and restoration of old machinery, which was manufactured in the Soviet Union and which was still in use by some Romanian and Moldovan SMEs. The managers of this enterprise planned to gradually reorient their business, in order to target the maintenance of newer brands of machinery. However, as EU membership forced Romanian enterprises to quickly modernize and adapt to Western technological standards, the Moldovan company lost its clients and consequently had to leave the Romanian market.

Entrepreneurs also pointed out indirect restrictions on their exports to the EU. For example, managers of a company producing equipment for wineries pointed out that their production would meet quality requirements of the EU, and their costs were lower than their competitors. However, in order to protect domestic markets of EU members, the EU imposed less favourable conditions on the import of equipment from non-EU countries. This prevented the Moldovan company from trading on EU markets and it furthermore forced them to leave the Romanian market after Romania joined the EU.

The general tendency of Romanian entrepreneurs to seek business cooperation primarily with Western European-based companies presents another threat to the development of business partnerships between Moldovan and Romanian companies. Even before the integration of Romania into the EU, Romanian companies tended to express a greater interest in establishing business contacts with their European colleagues than with Moldovan entrepreneurs. Such contacts were viewed by many Romanian enterprises as presenting greater opportunities for business development. The lack of interest Romanian entrepreneurs showed in establishing partnerships with Moldovan enterprises has always been an obstacle for a more active development of cross-border cooperation. In this regard, Romania's EU membership facilitated the possibilities for Romanian enterprises to develop contacts with European partners, to gain experience of trading in the context of advanced market economies and to receive access to EU funding.

In particular, the smaller businesses in Moldova stated that the conditions for doing business with Romanian partners had worsened. Larger companies within the SME sector, which had developed long-standing partnerships with their Romanian counterparts more often, were of the opinion that the changes after EU enlargement had a positive effect or even that their companies were not affected by EU enlargement at all. Instead, their expectations, namely that EU enlargement would provide them with new opportunities to enter European markets, proved to be realistic. Bigger Moldovan enterprises were able to establish new business partnerships with established partners from Romania and other EU countries. For example, a Moldovan company involved in tobacco production had only worked with one Romanian partner prior to Romania's integration into the EU. With the assistance of its Romanian partner, it was later incorporated into an international group of companies. As a result, the management of the Moldovan enterprise was able to modernize equipment and to increase the salaries of employees while sales and distribution as well as issues with the sales and distribution are now dealt with by the group management.

Another example is that of a Moldovan enterprise which developed successful partnerships with companies from Romania and Italy to which countries it exports workout clothing and fabrics. As a result of this partnership, the Moldovan company was able to purchase new machinery and to start trading on other European markets, which assured the stable growth of the company. The successful development of the company manifests itself in the growth of employment and modernization of machinery. For example, by 2007 the company was employing 92 people, compared to 11 people in 1999, while the old machinery produced in the Soviet Union had been completely replaced by up-to-date Italian and German equipment.

Thus, enterprise size influences the managers' perspective on cross-border cooperation between businesses based in Moldova and Romania. Large enterprises more often attract the interest of potential foreign investors and partners, while the smaller firms, even relatively successful ones, find it more difficult to meet the requirements and standards imposed by Romania. The limited access to information regarding those norms as well as the lack of training and consulting services contributes to the status quo.

Given the changes and difficulties in sustaining their business with Romania since its EU membership, Moldovan entrepreneurs have started to re-examine their market priorities. Agriculture and the processing industry account for the bulk of the Moldovan economy. The small domestic market, as well as a lack of modern technologies for processing, preserving and transporting perishable agricultural products, makes exports to neighbouring countries an urgent priority. Moldova's two neighbours, Romania and Ukraine, are both attractive markets for Moldovan entrepreneurs because of their larger domestic markets and higher levels of economic development. Also, the similarity of language, culture and ethnicity foster the development of cross-border economic activity with the Ukraine and Romania.

The Ukrainian market is a traditional one for Moldovan goods, where many of them are well known. At the same time, the Ukrainian market is a part of the huge NIS market, where demand for goods is not as saturated and diversified as in the EU. Demand for goods is quite similar for Moldovans and Ukrainians because both peoples once belonged to the same country, that is, the Soviet Union. Contacts from Soviet times still serve as a basis for some of today's business partnerships between Moldovan and Ukrainian entrepreneurs. But Moldovans generally lack confidence in the prospects for long-term, stable business cooperation with Ukrainians because of the uncertainties in the economic and political life of the Ukraine. In general, Moldovan businesses base their market choice between the Ukrainian or the Romanian markets on profit considerations, assisted by lower costs in the former market.

A Moldovan vineyard owner offers such an example. This entrepreneur has many years of agricultural experience and extensive contact with potential partners in both Romania and Ukraine who could enable export opportunities in their respective countries. When the first batch of Moldovan wine was ready for sale in 2005, the entrepreneur analysed market sales and other conditions in both nations. In 2005, he preferred to export to the Ukraine, because the export procedure at that time was simplified. Meanwhile, he is deliberately waiting to see how Romania's EU membership will change its requirements for wine imports. Currently, the entrepreneur is focusing on establishing a long-term contract with the Romanian partner.

CONCLUSIONS

SME development in Moldova faces significant challenges, including the limited access to finance, labour, information and training, all of which explains the relatively low competitiveness of SMEs. The small Moldovan market forces many Moldovan businesses to seek international business relations. In this regard, the shared language, history, culture and family ties between Moldovan and Romanian citizens may contribute to the potentially successful development of cross-border cooperation between SMEs in the border regions of Moldova and Romania, as well as to the economic and social development of these regions. When Moldovan entrepreneurs started to serve the Romanian market in 1990, the geographical proximity and soft border facilitated contacts with Romania in all spheres of life, business included. Nevertheless, before Romania joined the EU in January 2007, cross-border cooperation between Moldovan and Romanian enterprises had been developing relatively slowly. The forms of cooperation were often limited to exporting and importing goods, and rarely included the exchange of information, training and the establishment of joint ventures or other more substantial forms of cooperation. Moreover, after Romania joined the EU, the opportunities for cross-border cooperation between Moldovan and Romanian SMEs decreased further, mainly because of new and rigid visa and customs regulations, higher requirements for the quality of goods, and higher taxes in Romania. Many entrepreneurs therefore choose to wait, while some preferred to establish foreign contacts in other countries, first of all, in the other neighbouring country – Ukraine.

The empirical data illustrate that many Moldovan entrepreneurs, albeit recognizing short-term negative effects initially, had high hopes for a longer-term positive impact of Romania's EU membership. The interviewees assumed that the territorial and cultural proximity of the nations of

Moldova and Romania could further facilitate cross-border business cooperation. However, more than three years after Romania joined the EU, there appear to be fewer and fewer opportunities for Moldovan SMEs to cooperate with their Romanian partners.

After EU enlargement, those Moldovan SMEs that are involved in or seeking business partnerships with Romanian partners have experienced a greater need to access informational resources and to receive consulting services. In particular, Moldovan entrepreneurs expressed their need to obtain information regarding new legal regulations and standards at EU level, which were to affect their partnership with businesses from Romania. Furthermore, the interviewees indicated that they needed access to information, consulting and training services regarding possible opportunities to participate in EU projects. The interviewees indicated their willingness to explore the opportunities to team up with their Romanian business partners to participate in such projects. Thus, improving access to information and training could enable Moldovan SMEs to more actively seek business partnerships in Romania.

For example, the European Neighbourhood Policy and the programmes administered by the EU to support cross-border cooperation could potentially facilitate networking and business partnership between businesses, non-profit organizations and individuals of Moldova and Romania. Both Moldova and Romania participate in three Euroregions and their activity could serve as another resource to promote cross-border cooperation. These institutions provide opportunities for networking; however, business networking in particular is not emphasized. Along with cultural and environmental projects, it may be helpful to launch projects aimed at facilitating contacts between businesses in neighbouring countries.

The launching of EU programmes with the purpose of promoting cooperation between Moldovan and Romanian companies and/or business-oriented NGOs could also positively affect the present situation. Within recent years new EU-sponsored projects like, for example, the Joint Operational Program Romania–Ukraine–Moldova, which aims at promoting business partnerships across the borders, have been announced and publicly discussed. Nevertheless, by mid-2009 none of these projects had been launched. This has negatively affected the credibility of Western donors in the eyes of many Moldovan entrepreneurs, who now express doubts about the EU's commitment to assisting SMEs in the neighbouring countries.

The strained relationship between the Romanian and Moldovan governments in 2007 until mid-2009 created additional obstacles for the cooperation between SMEs in these two countries. The political relations between Moldova and Romania were complicated. The language, culture and history they share would make stronger cross-border ties seem natural and desirable. At the same time the strained relationship between the governments of the two countries diminished the opportunities for cross-border business cooperation, which in turn negatively impacted on Moldovan enterprises seeking to trade on the EU markets. The political crisis in Moldova in summer 2009 and the global financial crisis further affected the perspectives of Moldovan enterprises to effectively seek cross-border partnerships. Consequently, the decrease in business opportunities across the board affected the general performance of Moldovan SMEs. The improvement of political relations between Romania and Moldova that occurred after the elections in 2009 opened opportunities to improve economic cooperation between the two countries, including between Moldovan SMEs and their Romanian partners.

Successful cross-border cooperation between businesses also requires support from regional or local governments. Governmental officials should realize that cross-border cooperation is also beneficial for local communities in providing income possibilities and employment. Scholarly research, the input of international consultants and the media could provide a valuable contribution in raising the awareness of the benefits of such cooperation. Regional or local governments could cooperate more closely with business associations in order to have a better understanding of the challenges faced by those SMEs that seek to establish or develop cross-border cooperation. In order to improve the possibilities for cross-border cooperation of Moldovan SMEs, it is crucial that the respective governments of Moldova and Romania recognize the challenges faced by entrepreneurs and address the situation.

REFERENCES

Aculai, E. (2008), *External Economic Cooperation of Moldovan Enterprises*, Chisinau, Moldova: Institute of Economy, Finance and Statistics.

Aculai, E., A. Bulgac, N. Vinogradova, A. Novac and T. Colesnicova (2009), *Grounding the Mechanism of Supporting SMEs Exporting Goods and Services they Produce*, Chisinau, Moldova: Institute of Economy, Finance and Statistics.

ADEPT and EXPERT-GROUP (2008), 'Moldova and the EU in the context of the ENP-Realization of the Action Plan EU–Moldova (February 2005–January 2008)', available at: http://www.e-democracy.md/publications/realizarea-pauem, accessed 11 May 2009.

Birca, A. (2005), 'Why people do not like small and medium-sized organizations', *Economica*, **XIII**(1), 34–6.

Calac, D. (2005), 'How will the EU Enlargement turn for Moldova?', *Logoss-press*, **8**, 8.

EC (2004), 'EU-Moldova ENP Action Plan, European Commission and the Republic of Moldova', available at: http://ec.europa.eu/world/enp/pdf/action_plans/moldova_enp_ap_final_en.pdf, accessed 26 March 2011.

GRM (2008), 'Report of the Government of the Republic of Moldova on the implementation of the EU–Moldova Action Plan (February 2005–February 2008)', available at: http://www.mfa.gov.md/img/docs/raport-final-capitolul-2_1.doc, accessed 26 March 2011.

Infotag (2010), 'Over 100 Moldovan SME compete for Japanese grant', available at: http://economie.moldova.org/news/over-100-moldovan-sme-compete-for-japanese-grant-206819-eng.html, accessed 15 April 2010.

NBS (2009a), 'Exports by countries 1997–2009', National Bureau of Statistics of the Republic of Moldova, available at: http://www.statistica.md/public/files/serii_de_timp/comert_exterior/serii_anuale/eng/2_eng.xls, accessed 26 March 2011.

NBS (2009b), 'Labour force in the Republic of Moldova: employment and unemployment in 1st quarter 2009', National Bureau of Statistics of the Republic of Moldova, available at: http://www.statistica.md/newsview.php?l=ro&idc=168&id=2607, accessed 21 May 2009.

NBS (2010), 'Main indicators of small and medium enterprise activity in 2009', National Bureau of Statistics of the Republic of Moldova, available at: http://www.statistica.md/pageview.php?l=ro&idc=371&id=2494, accessed 26 March 2011.

OECD (2000), 'Enhancing the competitiveness of SMEs in the global economy: Strategies and policies', available at: http://www.oecd.org/document/49/0,3746,en_2649_34197_1866225_1_1_1_1,00.html, accessed 26 March 2011.

OECD (2002), *OECD Small and Medium Enterprise Outlook*, Paris: OECD.

Popescu, N. (2008), 'The Voronin–Smirnov meeting in the shadow of the EU', available at: http://www.azi.md, accessed 24 June 2008.

Savciuc, A. (2009), 'Romanian citizenship and Bessarabians', available at: http://andreisavciuc.wordpress.com/2009/08/26/cetatenia-romana-si-basarabenii/, accessed 26 March 2011.

Smallbone, D. and Y. Li Meng (2005), 'Effects of EU enlargement on entrepreneurship and institutional development in border regions', draft report, Small Business Research Centre (SBRC), Kingston University, UK.

Welter, F., D. Smallbone, E. Aculai, N. Isakova and A. Slonimski (2007), 'Cross-border co-operations in Belarus, Moldova and the Ukraine and EU enlargement: summary report', Siegen: PRO KMU, available at: http://www.prokmu.de, accessed 12 November 2007.

7. Cross-border cooperation and innovation in SMEs in western Ukraine

Nina Isakova, Vitalii Gryga and Olha Krasovska

INTRODUCTION

Increasing competition in the global market means that innovation and internationalization are of vital concern to all enterprises. In border regions cross-border cooperation offers many potential advantages for small and medium enterprises (SMEs). Promotion of innovation activity as grounds for competitiveness of businesses is one of these advantages; it is of particular value to transition economies suffering, among other deficiencies, from a low level of innovation in SMEs.

Castellacci et al. (2005) undertook a comprehensive review of modern trends in innovation studies. With regard to innovation in SMEs, a comparative evaluation of nearly 40 different innovation policy tools in 11 European regions is discussed in Asheim et al. (2003). Aidis and Welter (2008a; 2008b) identify a number of peculiarities of innovation practices among SMEs operating in unfavourable, transitional business environments.

The enlargement of the European Union, and European Commission policies related to it, have given new impetus to studies of cross-border cooperation between nations, regions, institutions and individuals, and particularly to research focusing on 'new' borders within Europe and those with new neighbours of the EU. Researchers of cross-border cooperation (CBC) in Ukraine have studied Ukrainian state relations with its neighbours, but also border trade and scholarly exchange (Clem and Popson, 2000; Van Houtum and Scott, 2005; Scott, 2006; Williams and Balaz, 2002).

As yet, little has been published on the relationships between cross-border cooperation and innovation in SMEs in a transition environment. Hence, this chapter is intended to contribute to our understanding of the processes affecting entrepreneurial development in a transitional context, with CBC as a factor aiding innovation among enterprises, because it gives them an opportunity to access resources and knowledge from partners in better developed neighbouring regions.

In this context, this chapter is concerned with cross-border cooperation between SMEs in Ukraine and their counterparts in the new members of the enlarged European Union, and its impact on innovation in SMEs. It is based on selected results from a two-year research project, which investigated issues related to the development of entrepreneurship in border regions, cross-border cooperation and EU enlargement.

The chapter starts with an overview of CBC research and practice from the late 1990s. This is followed by Ukrainian aspirations and achievements in private entrepreneurship development and innovation. Discussion of the core theme is based on evidence from in-depth interviews with entrepreneurs from Lviv, Volyn and Transcarpathia oblasts[1] carried out by the authors in 2006. The chapter finishes with our conclusions.

ENLARGEMENT OF THE EU AND NEW OPPORTUNITIES FOR UKRAINIAN ENTERPRISES IN BORDER REGIONS

Cross-border cooperation by various economic agents is increasingly attracting the attention of policy makers, as well as researchers. The literature on cross-border cooperation among new neighbours of the EU is rich in publications on its different aspects (Andrusevich, 2009; Uiboupin, 2007; Welter et al., 2007a; Hamann and Holsbo, 2006; Scott, 2006; Van Houtum and Scott, 2005; Huber, 2003; Perkmann, 2003; 2002; OECD, 2001; Smallbone, 2000; Blatter and Clement, 2000; Clem and Popson, 2000). For example, Huber (2003) provides a typology of inter-business cooperation which distinguishes between the role played by different forms of transaction costs and the importance of building and maintaining trust. He distinguishes three forms of cooperation: cooperation based on (majority and minority) ownership, where principal–agent problems are most important; incentive contracts (such as franchising and licensing), in which incentives are provided for in the contract; and business relationships, which are not based on formal contracts and where trust is therefore comparatively more important.

Cooperation between border regions is a tradition within other European countries, but in post-socialist states it only became possible after 1989 in Central and Eastern Europe and after 1991 in the former Soviet republics.

The new geopolitical situation has activated both formal and informal relations between individuals, institutions and enterprises. Periphery border regions can make use of cross-border business cooperation to foster regional development through the growth of international trade and technology transfer (Uiboupin, 2007).

Regional governments in the border regions of transition countries, through cooperation with their counterparts in neighbouring states, have an opportunity to benefit from EU policies promoting the development of border regions. The issue was one of the themes in the Bologna Charter, which itself emerged from a June 2000 OECD meeting of ministers responsible for SMEs and industry in Italy. The process of EU enlargement has only amplified the significance of research related to cross-border cooperation and partnerships between enterprises in transition countries, EU-accession states and new EU members. Among other important effects, CBC is looked upon as a means to facilitate access to foreign markets, as well as to technology and managerial know-how (OECD, 2001).

INTERREG, the PHARE Programme and the ENP Instrument were initiated by the EU with the purpose of levering the development of economies in the new regions of the enlarged Europe, and to foster cooperation (European Commission, 2003). The ENPI Cross-Border Cooperation Programme is to be implemented between 2007–13 on the borders of current EU member states with Ukraine, which is eligible for three land-border programmes, namely: Poland/Belarus/Ukraine; Hungary/Slovakia/Romania/Ukraine; Romania/Moldova/Ukraine. These have four priority support areas (Andrusevich, 2009):

1. economic and social development;
2. enhancement of environmental qualities;
3. increase of border efficiency;
4. support of people-to-people cooperation.

Direct (formal) border connections between Ukraine and Poland, Slovakia and Hungary were started in 2004 and with Romania in 2007. Ukraine has signed a number of agreements with EU countries and a Ukraine–EU action plan, which includes the simplification of visa procedures. In May 2005 Ukraine became a candidate member of the EU. The INTERREG, TACIS and PHARE Programmes have contributed to the development of the Ukrainian border oblasts (Welter et al., 2007a). It is argued that small-scale border oblasts have particularly flourished due to their increasingly relevant role as implementation units for European regional policy on multi-level governance. European regional policy is implemented, among other means, through institutional development of the Euro regions which are argued to be of particular relevance to this purpose (Perkmann, 2003). The Ukrainian border oblasts belong to four Euroregions (Bug, Lower Danube, Carpathian and Prut) together with the corresponding provinces in Poland, Romania, Slovakia, Hungary, Moldova and Belarus. However, Euroregions are mainly a top-down experiment, and entrepreneurs know little about these opportunities and do not benefit from them (Welter et al., 2007b).

Becoming part of a wider Europe is a priority for Ukraine: EU enlargement creates new possibilities, but also problems in the framework of the 'neighbourhood' policy as each of the neighbouring countries has unique objectives when dealing with the EU. Discussing the consequences of EU enlargement for border regions, Smallbone and Li Meng (2005) suggest distinguishing between direct and indirect effects, plus short-term and long-term effects, remarking on the possibility of other dynamic influences.

Research by Van Winden et al. (2007) on cross-border activities in five cities led to the formulation of three categories of cities that want to become more competitive in the knowledge-based economy as follows: 'the contribution of cross-border activities to the regional knowledge-based economy', 'strategic orientation', and 'cross-border institutions and policy processes'. An emphasis on networks consisting of nodes and linkages and a new partnership approach is suggested by the writers to be a fruitful area for research and policy making on CBC in a knowledge economy (Van Winden et al., 2007).

Research results and observations by the authors in the western Ukrainian border oblasts lead to the conclusion that the enlargement of the European Union does not always exert a positive influence on entrepreneurship and innovation development, and this is particularly true for smaller companies (Welter et al., 2007b). In this context, we will describe those cases in which the new geopolitical situation has resulted in strengthened domestic enterprise and encouraged innovation in border regions.

ENTREPRENEURSHIP IN UKRAINE'S TRANSITION ECONOMY

In Ukraine, entrepreneurship represents a means of increasing the range of domestic products and services, of creating an effective competitive environment, stimulating innovation, reviving the entrepreneurial initiative of the population, creating new jobs, increasing flexibility in the employment system, and strengthening regional economies (Vaschenko et al., 2009). SMEs constitute an integral part of domestic entrepreneurship and are expected to speed up structural changes in the economy and increase efficiency in the use of national resources.

In Ukraine, small businesses include sole proprietors ('entrepreneurs' or 'physical persons' in terms of Ukrainian legislation) and small enterprises (legal entities). According to Item 63 of the 2009 version of the Economic Code of Ukraine,[2] small enterprises (regardless of sector) are those which employ no more than 50 people, and with a gross income of under 70 million UAH[3] per annum (fixed at 500 000 EUR per annum until 2009); large enterprises are those with employment exceeding 250 people and a gross income exceeding 100 million UAH; other enterprises fall into the category of medium enterprises.

Since the nation obtained independence in 1991, the Ukrainian SME sector has gradually developed regardless of the slow pace of economic reform and questionable commitment among officials in the early years of transformation (Smallbone and Welter, 2008). The introduction of a simplified system of taxation and accounting for small enterprises, deregulation, and reforms in permit systems from the late 1990s to early 2000s have all contributed to positive growth in the small business sector (Table 7.1).

Table 7.1   Characteristics of small enterprises development in Ukraine

Year	No. of small enterprises	No. of small enterprises per 10 000 inhabitants	No. of small enterprises' hired employees, thousand people	% of small enterprises' hired employees in total employment	% of small enterprises in total volume of products (services)
2000	217 930	44	1709.8	15.1	8.1
2001	233 607	48	1807.6	17.1	7.1
2002	253 791	53	1918.5	18.9	6.7
2003	272 741	57	2034.2	20.9	6.6
2004	283 398	60	1928.0	20.2	5.3
2005	295 109	63	1834.2	19.6	5.5
2006	307 398	66	1746.0	19.0	4.8
2007	324 000	70	1674.2	18.4	4.4

Source: Osaulenko (2008).

Ukrainian entrepreneurship as a socio-economic phenomenon has developed in the conditions of a transition economy, facing the inevitable constraints imposed by deficiencies in legislation and other market institutions. It has been repeatedly revealed by surveys of business owners and managers that the viability of SMEs is hampered by tax pressure, administrative barriers, limited access to external finance, and management and manpower deficiencies (Smallbone et al., 2001; IFC, 2005; 2007). Although generally admitted to be a positive feature for economic development, Ukraine's recent WTO accession (on 16 May 2008) may have created additional obstacles for smaller enterprises by changing the nature of competition in the country (Vaschenko et al., 2009).

The aforementioned barriers have pushed some entrepreneurs into the shadow sector of the national economy, which, according to different methods of evaluation, constitutes between 40 and 70 per cent of economic activity. For instance, by the internationally acknowledged DYMIMIC approach (Bajada and Schneider, 2005), in 2006 the shadow sector of the economy amounted to 56.8 per cent (Vaschenko et al., 2009).

Excessive regional concentration of sources of finance and business has led to wide regional variations in business development, particularly between the capital (Kiev) and the rest of the country. Such variations may be caused by differences in economic structure, demand conditions and institutional arrangements, which in turn can have an effect on the attitude of the population towards entrepreneurship (Smallbone and Welter, 2008; Smallbone et al., 2001).

Since 2000 the State Committee of Ukraine on Regulation Policy and Entrepreneurship (SCURPE) has started to rate oblasts (applying 52 indicators) according to the levels of entrepreneurial development and support for small business. These ratings are looked upon as a policy instrument to encourage regional authorities to pay more attention to this issue. Four groups of oblasts are identified, namely: leaders, followers, core group and outsiders. The border oblasts of Lviv and Volyn are in the core group, occupying 17th and 18th places, and Transcarpathia oblast is among the outsiders, occupying the last place, 27th (SCURPE, 2008).

Growth in the commitment of regional authorities to foster small business and entrepreneurship development, which is noticeable in many oblasts, is producing little effect, primarily because of a deficiency in funding. For example, the National Programme of Small Entrepreneurship Development in Ukraine between 2007 and 2008 received from the state budget 1 per cent of the sum needed for its implementation (Vaschenko et al., 2009). In terms of numbers, Ukrainian experts evaluate the scale of small business development as one approaching similar indicators in European countries (Lyapin, 2003). At the same time, it is generally acknowledged that the qualitative characteristics of Ukrainian small enterprises – and hence their contribution to economic growth, regional development, employment and innovation – are still far behind those of the world's best examples (IFC, 2007; Isakova, 2008; Vaschenko et al., 2009). Developing innovation is one of the challenges for domestic enterprises in both the high-tech and low-tech sectors.

INNOVATION: VITAL IN THE KNOWLEDGE ECONOMY AND A CHALLENGE FOR UKRAINIAN ENTERPRISES

In the contemporary knowledge economy the competitiveness of enterprises depends on their innovative ability and technology (Brown and Ulijn, 2004). Innovation is no longer seen as the exclusive domain of technological leaders. The latter remain crucial for international competitiveness, but at the same time sustainable economic growth requires innovative approaches in all the spheres – knowledge-based services, organization of business, marketing and so on. In a knowledge-based economy innovation in low- and medium-technology firms is no less important than that in high-technology enterprises for the sake of a better balance in industrial policy (Hirsch-Kleinsen and Jacobson, 2008).

To this end, companies need to cooperate with different actors – suppliers and users of new technologies, public research institutes and other organizations (Castellacci et al., 2005). They need to have access to knowledge, and intensify innovation strategies, which are based not just on internal innovation (which might be difficult, especially for small enterprises), but also using the strategies described as 'open innovation'. In a world of widely distributed knowledge, companies are advised not to rely entirely on their own resources, but should also access processes or inventions from other companies (Chesbrough, 2003).

The impact of firms' technological capabilities and wider environmental characteristics on the overall growth of SMEs was studied by Hashi and Krasniqi (2008), who compared three advanced Central Eastern European countries (Poland, Hungary and the Czech Republic) with three laggard countries in South Eastern Europe (Albania, Macedonia, and Serbia and Montenegro). This international research proved that technological capability is directly related to the ability of firms to use new processes, produce new products, develop new organizational structures conducive to growth, and network in external economies.

Developing an innovation-driven economy is crucial for Ukraine's competitiveness if it aims to gain a competitive advantage which is potentially more sustainable than that based mainly on price (Porter, 1990). At present, the number of industrial enterprises which have innovation costs is comparatively small (Table 7.2).

Table 7.2   Innovation activities of industrial enterprises by type of innovation

	2005		2006		2007	
	No.	%*	No.	%	No.	%
Enterprises which had innovation costs (spent money on innovation), including:	1193	11.9	1118	11.2	1472	14.2
Research and development	317	3.2	293	2.9	429	4.1
Purchase of new technologies	113	1.1	98	1.0	120	1.2
Purchase of machines, equipment, devices and assets related to introduction of innovations	549	5.5	510	5.1	898	8.7
Production design and other types of activities to introduce new products, new methods of production	378	3.8	353	3.5	–	–
Marketing, advertising**	336	3.3	292	2.9	–	–

Notes:
* Per cent in total number of industrial enterprises.
** Since 2007 indicator transferred to other costs.

Source: Kalachova (2008).

A low level of innovation can be observed in industrial enterprises belonging to all types of business, ownership structures and sizes, but innovative enterprises tend to be larger on average (Isakova, 2008). In 2007, innovation was pursued by 14.2 per cent of industrial enterprises and the most frequently-mentioned type of innovation was purchase of equipment and software, which accounted for 75 per cent of all types of innovation and 68.9 per cent of innovation costs in industrial enterprises (Derzhkomstat, 2009).

A pilot survey of innovation in enterprises was held in 2006 in five sample regions of Ukraine (Kiev city, the Crimean Autonomous Republic, Donetsk oblast, Kharkiv oblast and Chernivtsy oblast). Chernivtsy oblast is a border province adjoining Romania. Not surprisingly, the peripheral Chernivtsy appeared to be the least innovative of all the regions in the survey (Derzhkomstat, 2009).

There is no simple answer to the question of why Ukrainian enterprises are not innovating. A deficiency of finance is the most frequent response to be encountered in survey results. This is a serious obstacle of course, but from a broader perspective of national or regional innovation systems it is obvious that finance is not the only reason. Ukraine possesses great research and development (R&D) potential in absolute numbers. For instance, in 2007, official statistics included 1404 research institutions employing 155 500 people, including 78 800 researchers. Research institutions involved in engineering R&D comprise 49.4 per cent of the entire science field (Derzhkomstat, 2009). A feature inherited from the Soviet period is that the national innovation system is lacking in efficiency, productivity and successful implementation of research results in practice (Josephson and Egorov, 2002). A lack of R&D funding is a major problem for Ukraine's national innovation system; for example, in 2008, the share of R&D expenditure in GDP was 0.8 per cent (Derzhkomstat, 2009).

The national and regional innovation systems appear unbalanced and lacking in strong links between innovation producers–R&D institutes and innovation users–enterprises (in terms of the linear model of innovation development), thus failing to create innovative milieus in the regions to facilitate innovation in SMEs. Domestic R&D institutions are an important, but by no means the exclusive, source of innovation for SME. In such conditions, companies should be encouraged to be more active in seeking cooperation with various factors, including enterprises in neighbouring countries, on the basis that cooperation with business partners is known to contribute to innovation within enterprises. Innovation cooperation allows enterprises to access knowledge and technology that they would be unable to access on their own. There is also great potential for synergies in cooperation as partners learn from each other (OECD, 2005). Previous research has shown that cooperation of enterprises in the field of innovation was a characteristic of Polish firms, that reported the introduction of product and/or process innovations. Most typically such cooperation occurred within the supply chain. Polish SMEs were less inclined to cooperate with technology transfer institutions (Strychalska-Rudzewicz, 2007). In Sweden 40 per cent of companies conducting innovation activities during 2006 to 2008 reported having a cooperative partner. Almost 80 per cent of all enterprises with innovation activities in Sweden cooperate with suppliers of equipment, materials, components or software, followed by customers (70 per cent) and other enterprises in the sector (63 per cent). In Denmark, the share of innovative enterprises with innovation cooperation increased from 12 per cent in 2007 to 19.1 per cent in 2008, including 13.2 per cent in low-technology industries, 24.7 per cent in medium-technology industries and 33.9 per cent in high-technology industries.

The creation of an environment favourable to SME cooperation, particularly in the field of cross-border cooperation, is one of the objectives of the European Commission's Entrepreneurship and Innovation Programme, which the Commission established to support innovation and SMEs in the EU (EIP, 2009). CBC with innovative partners in more developed economies facilitates access to information relevant to SME innovation, new technologies, equipment and markets, thus compensating for shortages of innovation resources at the firm and country level. In Slovenia, for instance, the contribution of EU business partners to innovation was found to be higher than that of Slovenian business partners (Jaklic et al., 2008).

Bearing this in mind, it is potentially advantageous for enterprises in peripheral border regions of less-developed countries to make use of the benefits of their geographical proximity to Western business partners, and to make use of opportunities for cross-border cooperation. By these means, deficiencies in the regional innovation systems of western Ukrainian border regions could to some extent be compensated for by cooperating with neighbouring countries, and by learning the latter's innovative business practices.

IMPACT OF CROSS-BORDER COOPERATION ON INNOVATION IN SMES: SOME EMPIRICAL RESULTS

Methodology and Data

Discussion of the core theme of this chapter is based on selected results from a project focused on the relationship between the development of entrepreneurship in border regions in Ukraine, Moldova and Belarus, cross-border cooperation and EU enlargement. In Ukraine, this research programme has included the evaluation of opportunities for cross-border cooperation in three oblasts which border new members of the European

Union (Poland, Hungary, Slovakia and Romania), and an assessment of potential consequences of CBC and EU enlargement for the development of entrepreneurship (Welter et al., 2007a). The project used in-depth interviews with representatives of public and private institutes, households and enterprises in border regions in Ukraine, Moldova and Belarus. In Ukraine 120 interviews were conducted within the project, including 10 with institutions involved in support of cross-border cooperation and entrepreneurship development, 10 with households, and 20 interviews with entrepreneurs in each of the three case oblasts.

The empirical data used in this chapter are based on 60 in-depth interviews[4] with owners and managers of enterprises which were involved in CBC. Enterprises were chosen by researchers at random, through observation of small-scale trading activities at markets and border crossing points and through assistance from business associations and business service providers. These enterprises were selected to represent different sizes, sectors and age groups (Welter et al., 2007b).

Literature on innovation in SMEs provides researchers with a variety of typologies of innovation (Garcia and Calantone, 2002). The concept of innovation that is used in the chapter is intentionally broad: *any change in an entrepreneurial context that is introduced with the aim of improving business performance or, in the initial phase, to allow for evolution of the business, including production of new (or modified) products and services; introduction of new technologies; purchase of new equipment; plus introduction of new organizational decisions and management approaches.*

Cross-Border Cooperation and Innovation in Western Ukrainian SMEs

Since 1991, Ukrainian enterprises in western border regions have had the opportunity of using cross-border cooperation to introduce innovations into their businesses. The existence of more advanced market reforms in western border regions made it possible for entrepreneurs in countries such as Hungary, Poland, Slovakia and Romania to make more progress in adapting to and developing a more Western style of doing business. They were also able to develop business management skills by learning from their business contacts in mature market economies. Although not the only means of accessing business knowledge and skills, cross-border cooperation certainly facilitated it for entrepreneurial people in border regions, providing them with an advantage over the rest of their country.

The geographical proximity of economies with higher levels of private entrepreneurship in many cases helped both nascent and mature entrepreneurs to develop new business ideas, sources of supply and markets.

Although at early stages of transition Ukrainian cross-border entrepreneurship was mostly characterized by small-scale shuttle trading, gradually some of the traders turned to more sophisticated types of businesses, having accumulated business knowledge, skills and capital.

The case studies included a variety of enterprises involved in different types of cross-border entrepreneurial cooperation, varying in terms of the length of inter-business cooperation (equity or non-equity based), with purchaser/supplier relationships at one extreme and joint ventures with enterprises of different sizes at the other (Weaver, 2000; Smallbone, 2000). In the sample, there were no innovative or technologically advanced SMEs operating in high-tech industries, but enterprises in low-tech industries can be argued to also possess these qualities (Sandven, 1996) and to be innovative to some extent.

With the purpose of finding out the association between CBC activity of enterprises and their innovation practices, qualitative information from 60 cases was analysed and the nature and extent of innovation in the sample evaluated. The innovation activity in case study enterprises was identified and evaluated on the basis of 'general profile of the business'; 'nature and type of cross-border entrepreneurial activities'; 'motives for engaging in CBC activities' (e.g. purchase of new equipment or technology); 'use of new information and communication technologies' and 'learning outcomes'.

In terms of innovation, SMEs under analysis serve as examples typical for transition economies, in which small enterprises are innovative only at a national or regional level. The importance of such innovation lies in the fact that by introducing new products and services onto the domestic market, SMEs demonstrate that the flexibility of small organizations allows them to alter a national economy; the input of new ideas and processes can result in far-reaching changes (Smallbone and Welter, 2008).

Considering the economic situation in transition countries on both sides of the western Ukrainian border in the late 1990s and early 2000s, with market reform still under way, regional economies underperforming, and regional innovation systems distressed, it is not surprising that in general the level of innovation in case studies is rather low. Cases of more successful CBC and subsequent innovation depended on the relatively higher levels of development in regions in Poland, Hungary and Slovakia, cultural affinity and the existence of a shared history; language issues, ethnic ties and the ability of entrepreneurs to draw on social capital (Smallbone and Li Meng, 2005). Based on the details given above, the following three main categories of SME innovativeness were identified by the authors:

1. the 'new products' group;
2. the 'new services' group;
3. the marginal group of enterprises with no innovation apparent.

In order to understand these categories of innovativeness, it is necessary to give further clarification. The 'new products' group includes cases where SMEs developed products new to the home region or the enterprise. In all cases the introduction of new products was made possible thanks to the purchase of new (for the company) equipment and technologies, and the transfer of know-how from their CBC partners. There were cases when leasing was the means to acquire new equipment.

The 'new services' group of enterprises included those providing services new to the region. The importance of this type of innovative enterprise should be emphasized, as the service and trade sectors were less developed than industry in Ukraine's command planned economy, and were monopolized by the state as in the rest of the Soviet Union (Aslund, 1995). Thus, innovative companies in services and trade have contributed to transformation of the structure of the economy. In addition, SMEs which introduced 'new services' to businesses have contributed to a positive change in the development of entrepreneurship in the region. With regard to businesses engaged in trade: they were innovative in the way they were managing their operations, and this was particularly evident among firms established in the 1990s. They learned how to do business from their counterparts in Poland and other neighbouring countries, they studied consumer demand in the home region and abroad, and they responded appropriately. Wholesale traders contributed to innovation in other businesses by importing and selling on modern equipment, materials and the like. This type of SME brought changes to the nature of supply and demand in the region.

The third group of SMEs were classed as 'marginal' because almost no trace of innovation, or aspiration among entrepreneurs to innovate, could be found. Nevertheless, entrepreneurs were able to acquire basic business knowledge and skills and to introduce change into their business management methods through their CBC contacts. Table 7.3 presents an overview of the nature and extent of innovation in the whole sample group.

Table 7.3   SMEs involved in CBC by innovation and business type

Type of business	Type of innovation		
	New product	New service	No innovation
Manufacturing	L3, L6, L9, L13, L14, L15, L17, L20, T1, T2, T4, T5, T8, T11, T14, T15, V2, V6, V8, V9, V10, V16, V17, V20		
Consumer-oriented services		L2, L6, L8, L10, L16, T3, T7, T18, V4, V11, V12, V14, V18, V21	L1, L18, L19, T16, V1, V19
Business-oriented services		L4, L5, L7, L11, L12, V3, V5, V13, T12, T13, T17, T19, T20	T10, V7, V15
Nascent (less than 0.5 year)	T11, T15	T7, V18	
New (0.5–3 years)	L6, L13, V9, V10	L4, L5, T12, T17, V13, V21	T10, T16
Established (4–10 years)	L3, L9, L14, T2, T4, T5, T8, T14, V20	L2, L11, L12, V3, V11, V14, T13, T18, T20	L18, V7
Mature (11 years and more)	L15, L17, L20, T1, V2, V6, V8, V16, V17	L7, L8, L10, L16, T3, T19, V4, V5, V12	L1, L19, V1, V15, V19
Micro (1–9 empl.)	L6, L13, L14, T1, T2, V10	L5, L8, L10, L16, T12, T20, V12, V13, V18, V21	L1, L18, T10, T16, V1
Small (10–49 empl.)	L3, L17, L20, T4, T15	L2, L11, L12, T3, T7, T13, T18, V3, V14	L19, V7, V19
Medium (50–249 empl.)	L9, L15, T5, T8, T11, T14, V2, V6, V8, V9, V16, V17, V20	L4, L7, T17, T19, V4, V5, V11	V15

Note: L – Lviv oblast; T – Transcarpathia oblast; V – Volyn oblast.

Source: Authors.

Innovation was pursued by enterprises regardless of the size and age of companies; as to the sector, all manufacturing SMEs demonstrated some level of innovation, while non-innovative companies were mainly found among consumer-oriented and business-oriented services. Deficiency of capital is cited as one of the major reasons for a low level of innovation among SMEs in Ukraine, which is why it is interesting to consider those cases which had access to foreign capital from business partners. With regard to equity, the cross-border cooperation of most enterprises that demonstrated innovation was based on a non-equity purchaser/supplier relationship. Nevertheless there were 13 cases with equity-based CBC in the form of (former) joint ventures, franchises and an affiliate of a Polish company. Some of these enterprises had just started cooperation with foreign business partners at the time of our interviews, in 2006. For instance, there were two nascent joint ventures in Transcarpathia oblast; one was to start a refuse processing plant and the other a prepared meals plant (both new types of production for Ukraine).

The case of the prepared meals plant demonstrates the role of equity-based CBC in product innovation. It was a new enterprise, established just a few months before the interview, with the main activity being the manufacture of prepared meals and other food products, and their sale through its own retail network. The business idea resulted from the owner's visits to neighbouring countries, where he was first acquainted with the prepared meals products. He then did his own research on the availability of the product in Transcarpathia, concluding that there was a gap in the market in his home region. The next step was to establish contacts with a Hungarian producer, and to reach an agreement on franchising in Uzhgorod (Transcarpathia). The Hungarian business partner was interested in cooperation because of the lower level of labour costs and lower regulatory standards for food products in Ukraine. With these two factors inhibiting the Hungarian business partner from entering Western European markets, he concentrated on developing business in Ukraine. A Hungarian–Ukrainian joint venture was registered and a special agreement on leasing equipment signed.

Some businesses in the equity-based CBC group had ended their joint venture operations for different reasons and registered as Ukrainian companies. For instance, a furniture manufacturer in Lviv oblast had been a Polish–Ukrainian joint venture involved in the export of Polish-made furniture to Ukraine. Although the Ukrainian owner was disappointed with his Polish business partner, the experience of cooperation allowed him to accumulate information about the industry in Poland, and the Polish supply and demand market. At the time of the interview in 2006 the company was producing its own furniture, had built markets in Poland and other European countries, and was continuing non-equity-based cross-border cooperation with other Polish enterprises.

Another case of a former joint venture is a limited liability company with about 150 employees, engaged in manufacturing and installation of metal and plastic windows and doors. In 1996 it was registered as a Polish–Ukrainian joint venture. The Polish business partner, who was running a similar business in his home market, decided to expand into the neighbouring Volyn oblast of Ukraine, where the market for his products appeared more promising than in Poland. The Polish business partner organized the production site, advised on the purchase of equipment and supervised the overall business management and training of staff. For personal reasons (bad health) he later had to quit the joint venture, which consequently became a Ukrainian company. This unfortunate circumstance, however, did not put an end to the cross-border cooperation experience of the business. Close partnerships continued with Polish companies, in particular with those in the nearby Lublin region. Learning from the Polish business partners had allowed the company to maintain and develop markets for its innovative products and services, not only in its home region of Volyn but also in Lviv, Rivne, Khmelnitsky, Kiev, Ivano-Frankivsk and Zhytomir.

In the cases of joint ventures, entrepreneurs were primarily interested in new equipment and technologies, which was an indication that in such cases foreign investment helped to develop process innovation among enterprises situated in Ukrainian border regions. Foreign investment was attracted to one Lviv business, which started as a cafe with a snooker room, and in 2006 was becoming a fully-developed snooker club. For this purpose, Polish investment was again being used for the construction of a new building and purchase of facilities necessary to develop this new type of entertainment venue. Security systems, wood-processing equipment and plastic bottle production lines were other cases in which foreign investment through joint ventures was used to develop innovative products and services.

Innovation in the non-equity-based CBC group was demonstrated by a Lviv company founded in 1997, with 35 employees by the time of the interview in 2006. Visits to Poland in the early 1990s were one of the inspirations for the business idea. Since the very beginning the company was involved in CBC with Polish trade and manufacturing firms and in international cooperation with producers of a wide range of goods in other countries. The firm is one of the leading producers of souvenirs and gift products in Ukraine: it buys a variety of those types of goods from business partners abroad and prints images and inscriptions on a variety of surfaces using modern technology. Gradually the firm's management has succeeded in establishing business partnerships with the largest suppliers of souvenir products in Poland, Germany and elsewhere. The clients in the Ukrainian market include both local companies and the offices of international firms, which also commission small consignments for export. To develop their export activity is one of the company's long-term objectives. With regard to innovation, the company has purchased modern equipment for thermal pressing, which expands the ability of printing machines to add images to products, and provides for the highest quality and stability of images. In-house quality control is organized with the aim of ensuring the highest quality of production. The company is constantly implementing new technologies, improving quality and enlarging its scope of printing techniques.

Information built up from case studies on the evolution of CBC, the profile of entrepreneurs, motives for developing cross-border entrepreneurial activities, and individual learning have led to the understanding that although many entrepreneurs have intentionally made decisions to introduce new products or services, others never (formally) planned to make their businesses innovative. Cases in which entrepreneurs were looking for cross-border partners in order to purchase or lease equipment, or to develop new products or services for their home regions, can be referred to as 'deliberate innovators' cases. At the other extreme, there are small-scale traders who were pushed by necessity to go to Poland to look for markets for their goods. Even in such 'accidental' cases, individuals were learning 'new' business practices and official and unofficial regulations and norms in business.

'Deliberate' cooperation was initiated by a dentist in Uzhgorod (Transcarpathia oblast) in an attempt to bring up-to-date dental equipment and materials to Ukraine with the ultimate aim of introducing innovation to dentistry. He met his future business partners at trade exhibitions in Hungary and the Czech Republic, and started CBC with small-scale purchases of equipment and materials. At the time of the interview the private enterprise was continuing to purchase equipment from abroad, together with its installation and maintenance. The respondent was looking forward to using CBC potential to develop his enterprise into a wholesale trading company, which could introduce new dental supplies to Ukraine.

There is evidence from the case studies that some companies with new products and services were 'accidental' innovators in the initial stage of business development. The owners of cargo transportation companies serve as examples of 'accidental' innovators: they had to introduce innovations whilst complying with EU emission standards for goods vehicles. In this regard it may be useful for further discussion to differentiate between 'deliberate' and 'accidental' innovators in border regions that are in transition. An increase in the number of 'deliberate' innovators might be among the entrepreneurship policy objectives designed to foster regional innovation.

CONCLUSIONS

SMEs in the Ukrainian transition context have a role in enlarging the range of domestic products and services, creating an effective competitive environment, stimulating innovation, reviving entrepreneurial initiative among the population, creating new jobs, increasing the flexibility of the employment system and strengthening regional economies. Ukrainian SMEs have to operate under major constraints related to deficiencies in legislation and other market institutions; these in turn create barriers to doing business, including tax pressure, administrative barriers, limited access to external finance, and management and manpower deficiencies.

The level of innovation, which is an imperative in a knowledge society within a globalized system, is rather low in Ukrainian SMEs due to scarcity of internal capital and other resources, lack of venture capital in the country and limited cooperative links with new knowledge producers. In this context, SMEs in peripheral border regions, with the intention of improving their performance and growing by means of innovation, can make use of the opportunity presented by their geographical proximity to borders, with potential access to CBC and Western business partners. By these means, deficiencies in the regional innovation systems of western Ukrainian border regions can to some extent be compensated for by cooperation with SMEs in neighbouring countries and by learning innovative business practices.

The case studies included a number of enterprises involved in different types of cross-border entrepreneurial cooperation in terms of life span agreements and whether or not there was equity involvement. There were more enterprises with experience of participating in short-term and non-equity-based CBC. The case study evidence illustrates that the new geopolitical situation in Europe has resulted in strengthened domestic enterprise and has pushed forward innovation in peripheral border regions.

Personal and collective learning was repeatedly acknowledged by entrepreneurs to be an important factor in driving successful change and innovation in the entrepreneurial activities of SMEs in border regions. In the case of joint ventures, entrepreneurs were primarily interested in new equipment and technologies, an indication that foreign investment helped to develop (process) innovation among companies in Ukrainian border regions. Based on the information on the motives for CBC, two types of entrepreneurial innovators were identified: 'deliberate' and 'accidental' innovators. In this context, an increase in the number of 'deliberate' innovators should be among the entrepreneurship policy objectives which are designed to foster regional innovation in SMEs.

It was revealed that cross-border cooperation by western Ukrainian SMEs definitely had a positive effect on the development of entrepreneurship and on innovation practices. In this context, EU programmes should (attempt to) strengthen the component of SME-based CBC with states like Ukraine to facilitate the building of innovative capabilities of SMEs. However, further development of the existing EU-supported schemes of 'regional open innovation platforms', 'cross-border innovation centres', and 'cross-border innovation corridors'[5] would only be effective if a more innovation-friendly institutional environment were created and a generally improved business climate in transition countries installed. To this end an increase in the level of innovation and entrepreneurship development in border regions requires a joined-up policy approach in such spheres as business, innovation and cross-border cooperation. Selected results from this international project carried out in Ukraine have made it apparent that the interrelation between CBC and innovation among enterprises in a transition context needs further research and careful analysis.

NOTES

1. The oblast is the territory administrative unit in Ukraine.
2. See http://zakon.rada.gov.ua/.
3. Following the world financial crisis of 2008 the exchange rates were subject to fluctuation. In 2009: 1 Euro (EUR) = 10 to 12 Hryvnia (UAH).
4. Interviews with owners/managers of SMEs were held by the authors in February–July 2006.
5. Information is available at: http://www.eudimensions.eu/ and http://www/finrusinno.ru/.

REFERENCES

Aidis, R. and F. Welter (eds) (2008a), *The Cutting Edge: Innovation and Entrepreneurship in New Europe*, Cheltenham, UK and Northampton, MA, USA: Edward Elgar.

Aidis, R. and F. Welter (eds) (2008b), *Innovation and Entrepreneurship: Successful Start-ups and Businesses in Emerging Economies*, Cheltenham, UK and Northampton, MA, USA: Edward Elgar.

Andrusevich, N. (ed.) (2009), 'Assessment of the EU–Ukraine Action Plan implementation: environment and sustainable development', Lviv: Resource and Analysis Centre 'Society and Environment'.

Asheim, B., A. Isaksen, C. Nauwelers and F. Todling (eds) (2003), *Regional Innovation Policy for Small–Medium Enterprises*, Cheltenham, UK and Northampton, MA, USA: Edward Elgar.

Aslund, A. (1995), *How Russia Became a Market Economy*, Washington, DC: Brookings Institution.

Bajada, C. and F. Schneider (eds) (2005), *Size, Causes and Consequences of the Underground Economy: An International Perspective*, Aldershot, UK: Ashgate.

Blatter, J. and N. Clement (2000), 'Cross-border cooperation in Europe: historical development, institutionalization, and contrasts with North America', *Journal of Borderlands Studies*, **15**(1), 15–53.

Brown, T.E. and J. Ulijn (eds) (2004), *Innovation, Entrepreneurship and Culture: The Interaction between Technology, Progress and Economic Growth*, Cheltenham, UK and Northampton, MA, USA: Edward Elgar.

Castellacci, F., S. Grodal, S. Mendonca and M. Wibe (2005), 'Advances and challenges in innovation studies', *Journal of Economic Issues*, **39**(1), 91–122.

Chesbrough, H.W. (2003), *Open Innovation: The New Imperative for Creating and Profiting from Technology*, Boston, MA: Harvard Business School Press.

Clem, J. and N. Popson (eds) (2000), *Ukraine and its Western Neighbours*, East European Studies conference proceedings, Washington: Woodrow Wilson Centre.

Derzhkomstat (2009), Official Site of the State Committee of Statistics of Ukraine, available at: http://www.ukrstat.gov.ua/, accessed 10 July 2009.

EIP (2009), 'Entrepreneurship and Innovation Programme', available at: http://www.eubusiness.com/topics/sme/cip, accessed 19 April 2010.

European Commission (2003), 'Wider Europe – neighbourhood: a new framework for relations with our eastern and southern neighbours', Communication from the Commission to the Council and the European Parliament, Brussels: Commission of the European Communities.

Garcia, R. and R. Calantone (2002), 'A critical look at technological innovation typology and innovativeness terminology: a literature review', *Journal of Product Innovation Management*, **19**(2), 110–32.

Hamann, K.E.H. and A.M. Holsbo (2006), 'How to succeed as an SME in the internal market: innovation strategies for cross-border business', available at: http://www.eurofound.europa.eu/emcc/content/source/eu06025a.htm, accessed 7 August 2009.

Hashi, I. and B. Krasniqi (2008), 'Entrepreneurship and SME growth: evidence from advanced and laggard transition economies', available at: http://ssrn.com/abstract=1125130, accessed 15 June 2009.

Hirsch-Kleinsen, H. and D. Jacobson (2008), *Innovation in Low-tech Firms and Industries*, Cheltenham, UK and Northampton, MA, USA: Edward Elgar.

Huber, P. (2003), 'On the determinants of cross-border cooperation of Austrian firms with Central and Eastern European partners', *Regional Studies*, **37**(9), 947–55.

IFC (2005), 'Business environment in Ukraine', Kiev: International Finance Corporation.

IFC (2007), 'Business environment in Ukraine', Kiev: International Finance Corporation.

Isakova, N. (2008), 'Integrating cutting-edge chemical knowledge and entrepreneurial drive: the case of new substances in Ukraine', in R. Aidis and F. Welter (eds), *Innovation and Entrepreneurship: Successful Start-ups and Businesses in Emerging Economies*, Cheltenham, UK and Northampton, MA, USA: Edward Elgar, pp. 105–24.

Jaklic, A., J.P. Damijan and M. Rojec (2008), 'Innovation cooperation and innovation activity of Slovenian enterprises', LICOS Centre for Institutions and Economic Performance Discussion Paper no. 201/2008, available at: http://ssrn.com/abstract=1107204, accessed 23 July 2009.

Josephson, P. and I. Egorov (2002), 'Ukraine's declining scientific research establishment', *Problems of Post-Communism*, **4**, 43–51.

Kalachova, I. (ed.) (2008), *Science and Innovation Activity in Ukraine, 2007. Statistics Collection*, Kiev: State Committee of Statistics of Ukraine.

Lyapin, D. (ed.) (2003), *Doctrine of Private Initiative*, Kiev: Institute of Competitive Society.

OECD (2001), 'Cross-border co-operation for enterprise and investment promotion in the Northwest region of the Russian Federation', paper presented at a meeting in St Petersburg, June.

OECD (2005), *The Measurement of Scientific and Technological Activities: Guidelines for Collecting and Interpreting Innovation Data: Oslo Manual*, 3rd edn, Paris: OECD.

Osaulenko, O. (ed.) (2008), *Statistical Yearbook of Ukraine 2007* (in Ukrainian), Kiev: State Committee of Statistics of Ukraine.

Perkmann, M. (2002), 'Euroregions: institutional entrepreneurship in the European Union', in M. Perkmann and N.L. Sum (eds), *Globalization, Regionalization and Cross-border Regions*, Basingstoke, UK and New York: Palgrave MacMillan, pp. 103–24.

Perkmann, M. (2003), 'Cross-border regions in Europe: significance and drivers of regional cross-border co-operation', *European Urban and Regional Studies*, **10**(2), 153–71.

Porter, M.E. (1990), *The Competitive Advantage of Nations*, New York: Free Press.

Sandven, T. (1996), 'Typologies of innovation in small and medium-sized enterprises in Norway', STEP Report Series no. 199604, available at: http://www.step.no/reports/Y1996/0496.pdf, accessed 3 August 2009.

Scott, J.W. (ed.) (2006), *EU Enlargement, Region Building and Shifting Borders of Inclusion and Exclusion*, Border Regions Series, Aldershot, UK: Ashgate.

SCURPE (2008), 'Rating of development and support of small entrepreneurship at the local level in 2007', available at: http://www.dkrp.gov.ua/control/uk/publish/, accessed 12 August 2009.

Smallbone D. (2000), 'Enhancing the competitiveness of SMEs in transition economies and developing countries in the global economy and their partnerships with SMEs of OECD countries: strategies and policies', background paper for the Bologna Conference for Ministers responsible for SMEs and Industry Ministers, Bologna, Italy, June.

Smallbone, D. and Y. Li Meng (2005), 'Effects of EU enlargement on entrepreneurship and institutional development in border regions', draft report, Small Business Research Centre (SBRC) Report, Kingston University, UK.

Smallbone, D. and F. Welter (2008), *Entrepreneurship and Small Business Development in Post-socialist Economies*, London: Routledge.

Smallbone, D., F. Welter, N. Isakova and A. Slonimski (2001), 'SMEs and economic development in Ukraine and Belarus: some policy perspectives', *MOCT-MOST: Economic Policy in Transition Economies*, **11**(3), 252–74.

Strychalska-Rudzewicz, A. (2007), 'Cooperation of Enterprises in the Area of Innovative Activity', paper presented at the 6th International Conference on Computer Information Systems and Industrial Management Applications, available at: http://www.computer.org/portal/web/csdl/doi/10.1109/CISIM.2007.24, accessed 20 March 2010.

Uiboupin, J. (2007), 'Cross-border cooperation and economic development in border regions of western Ukraine', Electronic Publications of Pan-European Institute, available at: http://www.tse.fi/pei/pub, accessed 10 August 2009.

Van Houtum, H. and J. Scott (2005), 'Good practices and situational ethics of cross-border cooperation', Policy Paper, Berlin and Nijmegen: EXLINEA.

Van Winden, W., A.H.J. Otgaar, C. Berger and C.J.M. Speller (2007), *Cross-border Cooperation for Knowledge-based Development: Towards a Roadmap*, Rotterdam: Euricur.

Vaschenko, K.O. et al. (2009), 'On the state and perspectives of development of entrepreneurship in Ukraine' (in Ukrainian), National Report, Kiev: Derzhkompidpriemnitstva.

Weaver, M. (2000), 'Strategic alliances as vehicles for international growth', in D. Sexton and H. Landström (eds), *Handbook of Entrepreneurship*, Oxford and Malden, MA: Blackwell, pp. 387–407.

Welter, F., D. Smallbone, E. Aculai, N. Isakova and A. Slonimski (2007a), 'Cross-border partnerships in Belarus, Moldova and Ukraine and the consequences of EU enlargement: state of the art literature review', Beiträge zur KMU-Forschung 3, Siegen: PRO KMU.

Welter, F., D. Smallbone, E. Aculai, N. Isakova and A. Slonimski (2007b), 'Cross-border cooperations in Belarus, Moldova and the Ukraine and EU enlargement', Summary Report for INTAS 04-79-6991, Siegen: PRO KMU.

Williams, A. and V. Balaz (2002) 'International petty trading: changing practices in Trans-Carpathian Ukraine', *International Journal of Urban and Regional Research*, **26**(2), 323–42.

8. Cross-border entrepreneurial cooperation at the household level: Belarus and EU countries

Anton Slonimski, Anna Pobol,
Olga Linchevskaya and Marina Slonimska

INTRODUCTION

Being on a geographical and economic frontier between the countries of the European Union (EU) and the Commonwealth of Independent States (CIS), during its fifteen years of sovereign development Belarus has formulated objectives of its external economic policy that are to a large extent oriented towards the countries of its western border. Some new member states of the EU, such as Poland, Lithuania and Latvia, have become strategic partners for Belarus in terms of cross-border cooperation (CBC). Cross-border trade with Lithuania has steadily intensified during 1999–2004, with Latvia during 1997–2004, and with Poland during 2000–2004, especially at the level of regions bordering these countries, such as Brest, Vitebsk and Grodno. For example, the greatest volumes of export–import transactions are with Lithuania and Poland in the Grodno region. The negative trade balance of the Brest region with its border countries zone is generated mainly by the excess of import deliveries from Poland above export (Belitsky and Rudenkov, 2005, pp. 41–5; Litviniuk, 2009, p. 182).

However, these data reflect only the official statistics. No petty traders' cross-border transactions have been taken into account in the official statistics, although the informal economic activity did flourish during the transition period. It has been argued in scientific circles that informal entrepreneurial activities can be a seedbed for new enterprises (for example Smallbone and Welter, 2006). However, the existing body of literature studying the CBC in the post-Soviet countries is overwhelmingly oriented towards actors such as businesses and institutions (Chubrik et al., 2008; Erlovskih, 2005; Sidorchuk, 2007). We have tried to supplement the existing picture of CBC by interviewing (besides SMEs and institutions) the households involved in such activities (Slonimski and Slonimska, 2006; Welter et al., 2008). This chapter is concerned with entrepreneurial activity of Belarusian households in cross-border cooperation.

We refer to cross-border cooperation of households as a basic, historically and logically primary type of international partnership. 'Even if there were no contacts at the level of government, the contacts between simple people would stay' (Grodno regional government official). At the same time, contrary to the common perception of households' shuttle trade as one of the most primitive types of business organization, our study shows that this phenomenon is complex, based on the developed nature of the forms of cross-border cooperation described later in the chapter. The aims of the chapter are to investigate: (i) the forms and characteristics of households' CBC; (ii) the factors influencing the selection by household of different CBC forms; (iii) the factors driving the development of these forms into more institutionalized activities; and (iv) the impact of households' CBC on households themselves and on the region.

RESEARCH METHODS AND DATA SOURCES

Methods of Data Collection

A total of 30 in-depth face-to-face interviews were carried out in three out of six regions of Belarus – Brest, Grodno and Vitebsk (ten in each region). The interviews were conducted on a semi-structured basis, using a topic guide. Household respondents were identified by the researchers at random, through observation of petty trading activities. More specifically, households were identified in three ways:

1. By observing the *ways* petty traders use *to cross the border* (the railway stations at the border crossing points, the bus and shuttle bus stations, the motor border crossing, trains and cheap airlines).
2. By investigating the *spots* where the petty traders *sell* their goods, for example by asking local people where one could buy cheap goods usually brought from the neighbouring countries (for example markets on both sides of a border, bazaars, hotels, tourist zones, ferryboats). In addition, newspapers, announcement boards and online forums for *advertisements* were checked; this gave an idea of the extent to which the cross-border activity is continuous. Application of this method required a preliminary basic knowledge of the petty-traded goods structure. The method of 'approaching the goods, not people', also enabled the sector diversity of the sample to be achieved.

3.   Using researchers' *own networks* for establishing contacts and initiating trust-based communication. The familiarity of Polish and Lithuanian colleagues of the interviewers with the foreign partners of
Belarusian 'shuttle traders' (potential respondents) contributed to
trust-building between researchers and interviewees. In interviews
with casually chosen respondents, the communication between a man
as an interviewer and a woman as a respondent has proved to be
psychologically the best for trust-building (Brest Household 1, Brest
Household 2, Brest Household 3, Brest Household 5, Brest Household 8, Brest Household 10 in Table 8.1).

Case Study Regions

The regions were selected to include two western border regions (Brest
region, bordering with Poland and Ukraine, and Grodno region, bordering
with Poland and Lithuania), and one eastern (Vitebsk region, bordering
with Latvia, Lithuania and Russia) (Table 8.1). These regions have opened
up to commercial activity of the population relatively recently, and hence
provided a possibility to observe the process of the households' cross-
border activity development, in a variety of both newly emerged and mature
businesses of newcomers and more experienced travellers, in both traditional and newly discovered market niches, under continuously changing
institutional conditions.

Brest region
The choice of household respondents in the region was based on the
region's administrative centre, namely Brest and two Polish cities: Terespol
and Biała Podlaska. The interviewers met the respondents randomly on the
Polish side of the border in the local markets, stations and in cross-border
trains (Brest Household 1, Brest Household 2, Brest Household 3, Brest
Household 5, Brest Household 10 in Table 8.1). In order to get acquainted
and to establish confidence with the respondents, the researchers offered
help to potential respondents in cargo transportation and in crossing the
Polish–Belarusian border with the double permitted quantity of goods. A
variety of methods were used by the researchers to get into conversation
with potential respondents, such as asking respondents for consultation as
'start-ups' in petty trading. In order to conduct interviews on the Belarusian
side of the Polish border the interviewer casually chose potential respondents among women who addressed him at the station in Brest asking for
help to transport alcohol and tobacco products across the border (Brest
Household 8). In other cases (Brest Household 4, Brest Household 7, Brest
Household 9), the interviewer already had a contact with the respondents,

established through a common acquaintance, such as a neighbour of the respondent, a relative of the interviewer (Brest Household 4), or colleagues of the interviewer (Brest Household 9).

Grodno region

The choice of households for interviews was preconditioned by the character of external economic linkages of the Grodno region households. The administrative centre of the studied region, the city of Grodno, is situated rather close (about 80 kilometres) to the administrative centre of the Podlaskie region in Poland, the city of Bialystok, which during the last 10–15 years has turned into the largest logistical centre for 'shuttle traders' from many post-Soviet states of Eastern Europe, particularly Belarus, Ukraine, Russia, Lithuania and Latvia. Even according to official statistics, 25 per cent of the population in the Grodno region are Polish, and many families have close relatives in Poland. Potential respondents were sought predominantly at the Belarusian border railway stations and markets (Grodno Household 3, Grodno Household 4, Grodno Household 8, Grodno Household 9, Grodno Household 10). Polish colleagues of the interviewer in Bialystok assisted in looking for respondents at the Polish wholesale–retail markets and shops (Grodno Household 1, Grodno Household 2, Grodno Household 7), and Lithuanian colleagues, at the automobile market in the city of Vilnius (Grodno Household 6). In addition, a contact was established through one respondent (Grodno Household 2) with another (Grodno Household 7), because they have kinship relationships and cooperate with each other during the shuttle business trips abroad. Finally, the method of identifying a respondent through his/her close relative in Grodno (Grodno Household 7) was also used.

Vitebsk region

This region borders two countries: the new EU members, Lithuania and Latvia, which were part of the former USSR until 1991. The distance from the Polish border to Vitebsk region is about 200 kilometres, which affects the structure of cross-border trade. However, several respondents engaged in CBC with Poland have been selected for research, taking into account the historical and the present active economic relationships of households in the Vitebsk region with Poland (Vitebsk Household 1, Vitebsk Household 2, Vitebsk Household 4, Vitebsk Household 6, Vitebsk Household 7). Friendly connections of interviewers in the region were used to find potential respondents in eight out of ten cases. Additionally, two respondents were found in the Vilnius market (Lithuania) with the help of Lithuanian colleagues.

Table 8.1 Characteristics of the surveyed household respondents

No. of case study	Sex	Age	Occupation	Education	Experience in business	Business	Countries	Data on partners
Brest region								
Brest H1	Female	62	Pensioner (formerly a school teacher)	Higher education	10	Resale of clothes received from the partner – a seamstress in Poland	Poland	50-year-old woman, a seamstress at home, met in a market (Poland)
Brest H2	Female	60	Pensioner (formerly a music teacher in kindergarten)	Secondary special (musical school)	5	Illegal work as a housekeeper and nurse for children of Polish partner; search for clients in Belarus for sale of refrigerating machinery	Poland	40-year-old man, businessman – builder, operational experience of 15 years, distant relative
Brest H3	Female	60	Pensioner (formerly a nurse)	Secondary special (pedagogical school)	20	Illegal work as a housekeeper and nurse for an invalid woman in her Polish partner family; trade of Polish medical products (Pampers) through the relatives in Belarus and announcements in newspapers	Poland	50-year-old man, the owner of a drugstore, acquaintance through the girlfriend of the respondent

No. of case study	Sex	Age	Occupation	Education	Experience in business	Business	Countries	Data on partners
Brest H4	Male	40	Worker in a state enterprise	Secondary	15	Resale in Belarus of imported domestic house slippers; resale of waterproof shoe glue and accessories, sewing-shoe thread to a Polish partner (shoemaker)	Poland	60-year-old man, the owner of a fine shoe workshop, met in a market in Poland
Brest H5	Female	35	Unemployed (formerly an employee in a private enterprise which was liquidated)	Secondary	15	Wholesale purchases in Poland (meat products by trade brigades) and resales in markets of Belarus	Poland	Owners and sellers in Polish shops, met at purchases
Brest H6	Male	33	Engineer at a state enterprise	Higher (university)	10	Purchases of unlabelled gold products in Poland, transport to Belarus, labelling (illegal labels to resemble Russian manufacturing) and sale	Poland	50-year-old man, the owner of a jewellery workshop, met through a colleague of the respondent on shuttle business
Brest H7	Male	40	Engineer at a state enterprise	Higher	10	Resale of souvenir production obtained in Polish markets and wholesale warehouses with the help of the wife who is an individual entrepreneur	Poland	Private (individual) sellers in the Polish markets and wholesale warehouses, no constant partners

ID	Gender	Age	Occupation	Education	Years	Activity	Country	Notes
Brest H8	Female	57	Pensioner (formerly railway employee)	Secondary	10	Illegal export of large volumes of spirit for selling in Poland	Poland	Sale in Poland to wholesale buyers, no constant partners, purchase of goods from constant supplier
Brest H9	Male	52	Pensioner (formerly a military officer)	Higher	6	Export of diesel fuel in tank of his own car and sale in Poland	Poland	In several Polish villages 3–4 known clients, acquaintances at sales
Brest H10	Female	59	Pensioner (formerly a teacher in a building school)	Secondary special (building college)	15	Purchase of children's second-hand clothes in Poland and sales in Brest	Poland	A relative (cousin), pensioner, about 70 years old
Grodno region								
Grodno H1	Female	50	Manager in a polyclinic	Higher	10	Resale of florist's goods (garlands, beads, tapes, rings, flowers, etc.) from Poland	Poland	40-year-old woman, higher education (agriculturist), owns a shop of wedding accessories (15 years)
Grodno H2	Male	29	Master at a state factory	Higher (technical)	7	Resale of children's pushchairs for twins from Poland	Poland	Woman, higher linguistic education, co-owner of a trading business (shop)

No. of case study	Sex	Age	Occupation	Education	Experience in business	Business	Countries	Data on partners
Grodno H3	Female	40	Kindergarten nurse and seller at a market (both are part-time jobs)	No data	6	Resale of seasonings and dry mixes from Poland (the husband also sells diesel fuel in Poland and buys auto accessories for sale in Grodno)	Poland	No constant partners
Grodno H4	Female	30	Seller	Higher (economic)	9	Resale of washing liquids from Poland and Russia, brought in for 'personal use'	Poland Russia	40-year-old man in Poland, a distant relative, no constant partners in Russia
Grodno H5	Male	50	Pensioner (formerly a policeman)	Higher (pedagogical)	15	Resale of diesel fuel in Poland and Lithuania	Poland Lithuania	Constant customers in both countries
Grodno H6	Male	42	Engineer	Secondary special (studies in high school)	5	Resale of cars purchased in Lithuania	Lithuania	A seller from the Lithuanian automobile market
Grodno H7	Female	55	Pensioner (formerly a radiologist)	Secondary special	15	Resale of electrical goods and plastic products from Poland	Poland	1) A seller of electrical goods; 2) a seller of plastic products.
Grodno H8	Male/female (2 respondents)	58 (the husband) 55 (the wife)	Unemployed (former factory worker) Unemployed	Higher (technical)	10	Resale of bathing accessories from Poland	Poland	No constant partners (purchases in a market)

ID	Gender	Age	Employment	Education		Activity	Country	Notes
Grodno H9	Female	35	Unemployed (formerly worked in communications)	Higher	6	Resale of knitted caps brought from Poland	Poland	Wide contacts with many sellers in Polish shops (sales and wholesale bases)
Grodno H10	Female	55 (mother) 30 (daughter) 30 (daughter)	Pensioner Employed Employed	No data Higher Higher	6	Resale of cornices brought from Poland	Poland	No constant partners (goods are bought in shops)
Vitebsk region								
Vitebsk H1	Male	35	Engineer in a computer servicing firm	Higher	7	Purchase of mobile phones on demand through a constant partner in Poland; purchase of tourist equipment in Poland and resale in Belarus	Poland	Owner of a mobile phone shop
Vitebsk H2	Male	50	Engineer (car repairs)	Higher	15	Resale of diesel fuel in Poland and Lithuania through his relatives and acquaintances; purchase in Poland and Lithuania of building materials, foodstuffs, assistance in automobile purchases in Lithuania	Poland Lithuania	Polish relatives for car business: colleagues in Lithuania

No. of case study	Sex	Age	Occupation	Education	Experience in business	Business	Countries	Data on partners
Vitebsk H3	Female	65	Pensioner (formerly a librarian)	Higher	10	Purchase of 'second-hand clothes' in Lithuania with the help of his constant partner and resale in Belarus; import of medicines to Lithuania and sale through the sister	Lithuania	Relative (sister)
Vitebsk H4	Female	54	Cartographer (a private firm)	Higher	10	Trade of artificial flowers in Belarus from a wholesale warehouse in Poland with the constant partner	Poland	Owner of a business selling artificial flowers and other attributes
Vitebsk H5	Male	59	Pensioner (formerly a military pilot), also works as a security guard in bank	Higher	11	Assistance in automobile purchase in Lithuania and additional security services	Lithuania	No constant partners, purchases made through casual sellers at the car market
Vitebsk H6	Male	48	Sports instructor (formerly an electronics engineer)	Higher	5	Purchase of tourist equipment in Poland through constant partner and resale in Belarus	Poland	No constant partners, advisers: Polish colleagues on sports

Vitebsk H7	Female	38	Children's needlework teacher (formerly a technologist of weaver's manufacture)	Higher	5	Sale in Poland of tapestries of her own production	Poland	Owners of shops of art products, no constant partners
Vitebsk H8	Male	63	Pensioner	Higher	15	Export of diesel fuel in own car tank to Latvia and Lithuania and its resale through his relatives and acquaintances	Latvia Lithuania	Relative (son) and fellow workers of the respondent
Vitebsk H9	Female	66	Pensioner (formerly a commodity researcher)	Secondary (trading college)	15	Purchase of 'second-hand clothes' in Poland through the constant partner and resale in Belarus	Lithuania	Relative (daughter) and Lithuanian sellers
Vitebsk	Female	65	Pensioner (formerly a teacher)	Higher	15	Export and resale of medicines in Lithuania	Lithuania	Relatives (family of the sister)

Source: Own interviews.

CROSS BORDER ENTREPRENEURIAL ACTIVITY AT THE HOUSEHOLD LEVEL

Characteristics of the Households involved in CBC

Large-scale expansion of the household shuttle trade has developed for the majority of respondents because of sharply reduced incomes in their main place of work, because of factory closures and mass redundancies as a result of the disintegration of the USSR (Table 8.2). Initially, trade was carried out with Poland where there had been a sharp jump in prices as a result of shock therapy. Subsequently, as the economy of Poland strengthened, the range of commodities trade broadened and prices declined as a result of increasing labour productivity associated with the modernization of manufacturing. In addition, the direction of trade was reversed. The structural and cyclical unemployment in both Belarus and neighbouring countries encouraged petty trading during the years after the disintegration of the USSR. In Poland, enterprises were losing contracts, and the expansion of the EU was associated with restrictions on agricultural activities, which forced the inhabitants of rural areas to look for alternative employment.

> Petty trade exists because of hopelessness – people have no chance to receive a job at home.

> Cross-border cooperation is a *lifesaver* for many households from Brest region, for pensioners and many unemployed people. (Brest Household 10)

> Cross-border petty trade provides to a respondent an opportunity to support the existence of herself and her family in conditions of small wages typical for the region comparing with the capital city. (Grodno Household 3)

> The border 'feeds' half of the local community: those keeping the guard (customs inspectors, boundary guards) and those crossing the border. (Vitebsk Household 2)

Respondents demonstrated a variety of personal characteristics, although certain patterns can be identified. For example, approximately two-thirds of the 30 interviewees were women; two-thirds were educated to tertiary level; the majority were over 50 years old; almost half were formally retired from work.

> Cooperation in its current form was formed after the respondent retired on pension at 55 when the Polish relative has suggested the respondent to work and live in their house as a nurse. (Brest Household 2)

Cross-border cooperation allows the respondent to receive a monthly income exceeding his monthly officer pension by three to four times (US$250). A part of the revenue generated must be spent on the inevitable costs accompanying the business. The income from the business contributes about half (50 per cent) of the total monthly income of his family. (Brest Household 9)

It would appear that the enforcement of new border regimes associated with EU enlargement has led to an increase in the average age of those involved in petty trading. This is reflected in the age structure of petty traders interviewed in all three regions, with the majority being more than 45 years old. Many people in this age group have no alternative employment or income possibilities; those who only traded occasionally, looked for more profitable possibilities to earn an income once the new border regulations rendered simple trading activities more difficult and time-consuming. However, relatively few respondents were unemployed; in other words, many petty traders also had a supposedly full-time job. The profile of cross-border traders in the Belarusian context shows that individuals involved in this particular form of entrepreneurial activity comprise a broad cross-section of the population. They cannot be characterized as predominantly unemployed people, and/or those without education. The position of respondents in their families is often that of a major earner or his/her helper.

Forms of Cross-Border Petty Trading

The basic types *of households' cross-border activity* in all cases studied involved petty trading across the border (such as clothes, meat products, gold jewellery, souvenirs, diesel fuel, vodka and cigarettes). Sometimes, such trade is complemented by services rendered across and on the other side of the border, such as a nurse and housekeeper in a Polish family (Brest Household 2), assistance in purchasing automobiles in Lithuania (Vitebsk Household 2), security services (Vitebsk Household 5). Respondents are involved in the export and import of a wide *range of goods* and delivering them to the consumer market (see Table 8.1). It should be noted that the subjects of trade presented in the case studies are typical of cross-border petty trade as a whole.

Usually each petty trader is specialized in a main good that he/she knows a lot about, such as mobile phones, diesel fuel, clothes, tourist equipment and medicines. However, almost all respondents have vodka and cigarettes on departure to Poland, Lithuania and Latvia. In the process of toughening the customs requirements and restrictions on the volume and assortment of imported and exported goods, many households have had to stop importing some goods from Poland that were in demand, such as home appliances and building materials.

Table 8.2   Characteristics of the Belarusian households

No.	Characteristics (parameters)	Household data
I. Age and sex		
1.	In the pension age women older than 55, men older than 60 and other pensioners (for example, former military and working in harmful working conditions)	33 answers (100%) (3 relatives of respondent were taken into consideration too) 15 persons (46%) F = 11, M = 4 the oldest = 66 years old
2.	Middle-aged respondents (31–55-year-old women, 31–60-year-old men)	14 persons (42%)
3.	Youth (30 years old and younger)	4 persons (12%) F = 3, M = 1 the youngest = 20 years old
4.	Average age of respondents	49 years old
5.	Sex of respondents: • female • male	21 persons (64%) 12 persons (36%)
II. Education		
1.	Higher	29 answers (100%) 21 (73%)
2.	Specialized secondary (college etc.)	5 (17%)
3.	Secondary	3 (10%)
III. The countries involved in cross-border cooperation		
	Border with:	35 answers
1.	Poland	24
2.	Lithuania	8
3.	Latvia	1
4.	Ukraine	1
5.	Russia	1

No.	Characteristics (parameters)	Household data

IV. Cross-border cooperation and partnership

No.	Characteristics (parameters)	Household data
1.	Length of cross-border cooperation (experience of cross-border business)	30 answers 100%)
	● under 5 years;	4 persons (13%)
	● 6–10 years;	16 persons (54%)
	● 11–15 years;	9 persons (30%)
	● more then 15 years.	1 person (3%)
2.	The average experience of cross-border business, years	10
3.	The time of the last partnership	25 answers (100%)
	● under 3 years;	8 persons (32%)
	● 4–5 years;	7 persons (28%)
	● 6–10 years;	5 persons (20%)
	● 11–15 years;	5 persons (20%)
	● more than 15 years	–
4.	Partnership with foreign relatives	8 cases from 30 interviews (Brest = 2, Vitebsk = 5, Grodno = 1)
5.	Involvement of other household members in cross-border cooperation	23 cases from 30 interviews (77%)

Source: Authors.

As for the regional distribution of goods, alcoholic drinks, cigarettes, gasoline and diesel fuel are exported to Poland, Lithuania and Latvia, and certain types of medicines are more often exported to Lithuania and Latvia. The foodstuff, clothing, building materials and the other consumer goods (such as 'second-hand' clothes from Europe, tourist equipment, artificial flowers and mobile phones) are exported from Poland, cars from Lithuania. The stages of development of this type of cross-border trade typically include: first, finding out which goods there is a demand for in the border country and in Belarus, by talking to acquaintances and relatives or by means of personal trip; secondly, a trip to Poland/Lithuania to investigate; thirdly, through the sale and purchase of goods; fourthly, crossing the border where the customs duties can be raised from the goods; fifthly, sale of goods in Belarus in official trading territories of the markets or through a network of personal contacts. The *specific types of cooperation* pursued include buying and reselling goods, delivering the goods of other people, rendering services on crossing the border and information exchange to traders.

Terespol and Biała Podlaska are the most visited towns for the purpose of cross-border trade by inhabitants of the Brest region. Conditions for the successful realization of cross-border trade are created there. There are many wholesale warehouses, hypermarkets and a large marketplace. Respondents buy goods at the markets, in the wholesale shops (*gurtowni*):

> There are some constant places of purchase of the goods and hence the familiar sellers in wholesale shops. In the market the respondent buys goods from various private persons depending on the order placed by his wife. (Brest Household 7)

It is common for cross-border traders to have Polish or Lithuanian partners with whom they became acquainted in the market, or on the recommendation of some relatives:

> Some Lithuanian friends provide orders to the respondent, as a childhood friend who is engaged in car repair and lives near the border; or the former colleague who lives in Mariampole. (Vitebsk Household 5)

Restrictions and Risks

Until recently, the main restrictions on petty trading have been quotas on the transport of goods. In each category of good, there is a limit on how much can be transported over the border duty free (that is, two or three pieces with a total weight of 50 kg per person). Goods within these quotas are declared to be transported for private consumption, and petty traders travel as tourists. Because of these restrictions, alternative schemes of petty trading activity organization have arisen, including a circuit of redistribution of transported goods between colleagues, and concealment of goods in specially equipped automobiles and on the body of traders. Possible negative scenarios include the confiscation of goods by officers, bribes and extortions.

> The main barriers lay in the custom rules and interpretations of them, which are often not logical. For example, the limitation of weight of allowable imported goods per one person leads to the situations that two to three people have to transport the articles which weigh more, in parts, after disassembling them. (Grodno Household 1)

> The respondent imports sports equipment from Poland. In order to solve the problem of customs restrictions on weight of the imported goods, she goes by car to Bialystok with the whole family (the husband and two children, 20 and 16 years old). (Vitebsk Household 6)

Some difficulties have arisen as a result of the tightening of customs rules on both sides of the Polish and Belarusian border:

> The main barrier is the customs rules (limitations) and the 'lawlessness of the customs officers at the border' (bribes, confiscation of things which the customs officers liked, extortion etc.). (Grodno Household 2)

Another restriction is a low solvency of mass demand in Belarus, which forces traders to look for cheaper goods to buy, not from companies but at wholesale markets. The latter do not issue invoices and are not certified by tax offices. Moreover, in the case of more sophisticated and solvent demand, the requirements for a variety of goods on the market *make it necessary* for traders to contact many companies for very small quantities of a good from each. This means that traders have to approach the border with invoices from many firms for these small lots. Even if the petty traders would like to register the transported goods as wares, this would hardly be realistic, because customs officers would not be willing to register hundreds and thousands of small invoices each day. For the majority of respondents, cross-border trading involves various risks, most of which are concentrated at the moment of crossing the border and can be managed in many sophisticated ways.

> In order to earn some income, the respondent started weaving tapestries, which she sold through art shops in Belarus, at the same time going on regular trips to Poland, organized by her church. Initially, she took some of her tapestry with her as gifts, but she soon discovered that there was an opportunity to sell her goods through art galleries in Poland. The risk consists in that products can be detained on border as products of arts. As a rule, they go in a group of 6 to 8 people on a minibus and have the documents on religious character of travel with them. Customs services in that case arrange almost no examination. Accordingly, problems with customs do not arise. (Vitebsk Household 7)

The activity when goods are purchased is completely legal, and sales are legal in the territory of Belarus up to 60 days per year. But there is a risk of being fined for illegal transportation of cigarettes, spirits, meat products and gold ware above the norm for personal use. Putting labels on these goods (as if they were manufactured in Russia) is also illegal. Forbidden entrepreneurial activity is punishable by imprisonment from three to eight years. In addition, all respondents hide the income they earn when inspected for tax, which is an additional source of risk. Cross-border trade is also connected with health risks for respondents (trips by train, bus, frequent stressful situations).

An important factor is a heavy physical load (the trips take place at night sitting in the bus; it's necessary to stay without sleep for a long time in stressful periods of the customs inspection on the border). The main behavioural lesson is that business trips and alcohol are incompatible. Some colleagues of the respondent on 'shuttle' business not only have left business, but died from the large amounts of alcohol they started to consume for relaxation after stressful trips. (Vitebsk Household 1)

One of the probable risks of spirit transportation on a body is its high inflammability. There was a well-known occasion, when once during spirit-transporters' smoking there was a break of a package with spirit and an ignition. As a result of ignition of other packages the woman received very strong burns resulting in death. (Brest Household 8)

Trips in the traders' own car for the purpose of selling diesel fuel are dangerous as the respondent can become a victim of swindlers, robbers, or become involved in an accident. To minimize these risks, auto traders prefer to go abroad in the company of friends and colleagues.

In cross-border trading, one needs to know many unwritten rules of behaviour in risk situations. For example, the respondent tries to take the safest route during the daytime, and usually goes with two or three of his colleagues. The rule 'it's better to have 100 friends than 100 roubles' helps a lot. (Grodno Household 5)

On the opinion of a respondent being an intermediary at purchase of cars in Mariampole [a town in Lithuania], main risks in his CBC include: (1) the risk of armed assault on the way to the market (when the money for purchase is brought in cash); (2) the risk of having an accident on the way back. (Vitebsk Household 5)

Relations with Partners in CBC

Family networks
Most often petty trade is a family business with a flexible distribution of responsibilities.

Types of partnership within a family include: help from family members with the transportation of goods across the border and sales in the market; retail distribution of the imported goods among their acquaintances and friends; 'infrastructural support', though provision of space from the workplace of the spouse and/or children. The place of official employment of the spouse/children often provides a degree of 'infrastructural support' for shuttle business by:

1.   changing the numbers of mobile phones in order to evade detection by tax bodies;

2. minimizing transport charges and insurance;
3. solving problems connected with illegal purchase of the goods at customs and border services.

Family networks that include expatriates are the basis of many cross-border cooperation activities. Relatives from neighbouring countries sometimes render help by providing money and labour, offering advice on markets and infrastructure, and providing further contacts in shuttle trading.

> The main employment of the respondent in Poland is child and house care of the Polish partner for a certain payment and gifts. The Polish partners are the respondent's distant relatives, and visiting them is the reason of her trip declared to Polish authorities. (Brest Household 2)

> The respondent lives in a small Belarusian city located 60 km from Daugavpils in Latvia and 40 km from Zarasaj in Lithuania. The family network extends across the borders of three countries, involving a mix of different nationalities. The respondent, his wife and his sons are all involved in cross-border trading activities. (Vitebsk Household 8)

Links in the cross-border supply chain

Cross-border petty trading is not necessarily a sporadic activity carried out by individuals. Often it is organized in larger chains that include non-family as well as family members. A distinct division of roles can be observed within these networks, based on the property status of their participants and the corresponding size of turnover controlled by them. One can distinguish the following functional roles:

1. *Agents:* typically Belarusians, who have been sent to or previously settled down in the border regions of Poland. Their functions include the organization of the supply of goods from the Polish side, consultation and networking. Notably, no such 'agent' can be identified on the Belarusian side for Poland.
2. *Business owners:* people with accumulated initial capital to pass on to the next stage of entrepreneurship (such as small shops with an aesthetic outlook in the prestige areas of the city).
3. *Transporters:* their main function is to assist larger traders by undertaking the transport of their goods across the border. Transporters unite in informal brigades to cross the border, guided by distinct leaders. They assist each other in the distribution of transported goods in order to keep within legal quotas.
4. *Retailers:* local inhabitants whose duties are to sell the goods at the marketplace.

5.   *Managers:* people who hire the transporters and retailers in the chain
       of buying/reselling of goods.

A change in the distribution of roles among the members engaged in CBC
might occur through narrower specialization in some cases and a shift of
responsibilities to newcomers, depending on the experience and capital
accumulated by participants.

> As the respondent's daughter works in a chemicals firm in the Grodno region
> [near Vilnius, Lithuania], she has access to cheap traditional medicines from
> Russia, Ukraine and Belarus, which are popular among elder people in Lithu-
> ania, but not legally importable in most cases. They establish an original
> 'division of labour' when the respondent's daughter provides purchase of the
> goods, the respondent transports the goods to Lithuania, and respondent's elder
> sister who is married and lives in Vilnius sells the goods herself and with help of
> a neighbour. (Vitebsk Household 3)

Foreign partnerships

Many respondents buy goods from regular foreign partners, rather than in
the markets, most often from wholesale suppliers. Respondents contact
their foreign partners through personal meetings, phone calls (including
mobiles) and emails. There is practically no language barrier with Polish
partners, since there are Polish TV and radio channels freely accessible to
people in the Grodno and Brest region and 'showing more interesting
cartoons and films than those of national channels':

> In the beginning, 15 years ago the respondent practically didn't know Polish.
> However he has quickly enough mastered the colloquial Polish. The partner
> speaks Russian a little; he learned language in secondary school and through
> communication in the market. (Brest Household 4)

Agreements with partners are typically informal, confidential, and based on
verbal arrangements rather than a formal contract. Trust 'comes with time',
being based on long-term acquaintance, which is often connected with the
present or past professional activity or family relations. Commonly, CBC is
a secondary function in addition to the contact with friends and relatives.
Such a situation excludes conscious fraud during the cooperation.

> The respondent has neither agreements nor contracts with her partners from
> Poland. She pays her purchases in cash. Sometimes she exchanges small
> presents with partners, especially with her cousin. She considers good, friendly,
> confidential relations in her business to be very important. (Brest Household 10)

The work with a constant Polish partner is built on the full trust of the parties. The partner has a good reputation in Poland and this facilitates her business. This is also an example for Belarusians. No guarantees other than oral agreements are available to both Polish and Belarusian partners. (Grodno Household 1)

Many respondents indicated that they received some concessions from their Polish partners, such as delayed payment or the possibility to return goods in some cases. Guarantees in such partnerships are based on decency rather than the law and precise fulfilment of verbal arrangements. In addition, small presents to each other are common.

The Polish partner sometimes gives some goods without payment (i.e. with delay of payment and with an opportunity of return). In addition, she may take payment in Euro or US dollars, which is favourable since there are no losses on exchange in Belarus and Poland. (Vitebsk Household 1).

Polish partners like little presents and small services (for example, using mobile phone to call to another purchaser, etc.), words of gratitude, the offer of a cigarette. Besides the respondent frequently sells them, with a small benefit for himself, his 'duty-free' bottle of vodka (additional 0.5 litre allowed for transport only to inhabitants of a border zone [within 30 kilometres]). (Brest Household 9)

The basic risks in communication with foreign partners arise when conditions of access to the goods are illegal; when respondents do not observe the rules of transportation of the goods across the border (concealed goods taken over the established norm in order to avoid paying the customs charges); and when large sums of cash have been involved (for example in the purchase of a car). In these cases, trusting partners is important. Cases of deceit on the part of foreign partners were not emphasized by respondents, which suggests they are not common. They only referred to the importance of their own vigilance in the case of purchasing goods, in order to avoid spoilage.

Types of Cooperative Relations

Depending on the nature of the goods involved, various types of cooperation with foreign partners can be formed in order to carry out operations most effectively (Table 8.3). For instance, in Grodno Household 3, Grodno Household 8, Grodno Household 9 and Grodno Household 10, the objects of trade were seasonings and dry mixes, bathing accessories (sponges, slippers, etc.), knitted hats and curtain tracks. These are typical factory-produced consumer goods that are readily available in Polish shops, so there is no need for a regular partner to supply them. In addition, when the purpose is to minimize the risks of unsuccessful sales in the Belarusian

Table 8.3   Typology of household partnerships by the type of traded good

Object of trade	Mass consumption consumer goods of typical factory manufacture	Goods are available in every shop. The purpose of shuttles is to minimize the risks of unsuccessful sales in the Belarusian market by the maximal expansion of the range relative to demand available in the Belarusian market, causing them to contact many sellers.
Type of partnership	No constant partners Transactions with occasional traders	
Nature of collaboration	Information exchange	
Object of trade	Goods available on free sale, but at the specialized sellers	The need for transportation costs minimization naturally narrows the circle of potential partners in the region; the positive attitude and readiness for additional services determine the final choice of the partner.
Type of partnership	Several constant partners in the short run	
Nature of collaboration	Training, transfer of knowledge and know-how, credit relations	
Object of trade	Goods, availability of which is limited	Respondents enjoyed advantages in purchasing goods on the most favourable conditions. CBC was based on strong confidential contacts.
Type of partnership	One constant partner in the long run	
Nature of collaboration	Provision of access to the goods, and the consultancy help in choice of goods against remuneration	

Source: Authors.

market by maximizing the variety of goods for which there is an effective demand in Belarus, petty traders contact a large number of sellers rather than a single one, and they are thus able to change partners easily.

Grodno Household 1, Grodno Household 2 and Grodno Household 7 represent the goods accessible for free sale, but only from specialized sellers (such as florists, sellers of babies' pushchairs for twins, sellers of electronic goods). Since one of the conditions of shuttle activity is the minimization of transport costs, the circle of potential sellers is usually small and the benign attitude and cheerful free-of-charge consultation of sellers finally determines which sellers the respondents cooperate with on a regular basis. As a result of this established communication, foreign partners are often willing to supply goods on credit or to buy any goods ordered by phone, prepared beforehand and paid for only on the customer's arrival.

In two cases, the circuit of cross-border cooperation was determined by the fact that access to the goods had been limited and respondents enjoyed advantages in purchasing them on the most favourable terms (Grodno Household 5 and Grodno Household 6). In the first case, high-quality diesel fuel, which was not available in bulk, was bought by the respondent from a familiar railway employee in Belarus for the purpose of resale in Poland at a higher price. In the second case, the respondent, a seller of used cars, with help from a contact in Lithuania, obtained access to cars transported from Germany before they were available on the open market, which allowed him to choose cars which were in the best condition. In these cases, cross-border cooperation was based on strong confidential contacts and included the provision of access to goods and advice on the choice of goods. Both kinds of services have been employed by the respondent.

THE ROLE OF HOUSEHOLDS' CROSS-BORDER ENTREPRENEURIAL ACTIVITIES IN THE NATIONAL ECONOMY

Factors influencing Households' CBC

Analysis of the empirical data suggests that the following factors influence the business-oriented cross-border cooperation of Belarusian households. At the *micro level*: the petty traders' previous business experience; vocational training of respondents and members of their families, colleagues and foreign business-partners; connections with relatives in neighbouring countries; knowledge of languages of neighbouring countries, culture and customs of their population, close mentality of respondents and their foreign partners; high educational level; knowledge of legislation, customs and other rules; availability of spare time; connections for the purchase, sale and transportation of goods across the border, allowing people to become accustomed to and familiar with the environment (shuttle trade brings people together); access to information and communication technologies (Internet, mobile phones). At the *macro level*, the conditions for this type of CBC to develop include: difference in prices, quality and range of products and services (on occasion a scarcity of particular products and some services), such as babies' pushchairs for twins (Grodno Household 2); new opportunities on the markets in neighbouring countries (Bialystok and Mariampole as the original logistical centres of Eastern Europe); close proximity to a border, resulting in low cost of transport and a high frequency of trips; the presence of consulates in frontier regions increases efficiency regarding the receipt of visas and access to other consular procedures; development of activity of Euroregions in adjacent territories (the simplified border transitions, days of national culture, good neighbourhood and other actions develop the relations of citizens).

Influence of EU Enlargement on Cross-Border Cooperation Development

EU enlargement has negatively affected the border business and co-operation links of households in Belarus. Factors affecting cross-border cooperation in this way include: the establishment of visa procedures between Belarus and Poland, instead of the previous voucher system and other simplified schemes of border crossing; requirements for insurance and the need to have a certain sum of money per day of travel; rigid health regulations; the prohibition of importing meat and dairy products from Poland; prohibition of export of natural plants and saplings because of phytocontrol; tightening of customs regulations and ambiguity in their application. Following the accession of the Baltic States and Poland to the EU, customs rules and formalities have become significant barriers for households involved in shuttle trade across the border. EU enlargement has even contributed to a significant change in the age profile of the shuttle traders. Those that have remained 'in the business' are those for whom the structural crisis in Belarus has left no alternative ways of earning a living. The effects of legalizing the business have not had a significant impact because most people who had managed to accumulate sufficient capital for larger-scale operation had already done so earlier.

At the same time, EU enlargement has been a favourable factor for the development of agro-tourism business in Belarus (for example guest houses in rural areas), because it has enabled access to European funds within the framework of special programmes. However, since the time of the last EU enlargement, the situation for CBC has not improved. Schengen zone enlargement has depressed the cross-border cooperation of households and individual entrepreneurs. The reasons are that visas are expensive and it is impossible to obtain a long-term visa. The number of cross-border electric trains (from Brest or Grodno) has been reduced because of non-profitability. The option of adding carriages to long-distance trains is now under consideration.

As a result, households search for new forms of CBC to overcome the new barriers. For example, entrepreneurs working in different commodity groups, and having an annual visa for 90 days of stay in Poland, gather in a single minibus for a day-trip to Poland, which is a way to save visa days compared to the two days needed when travelling by train. In addition, entrepreneurs help each other to take more goods by sharing quotas.

Effects of Cross-Border Cooperation for Households

The importance of cross-border trade for the majority of responding households is considerable, as such business provides a comfortable life for several families and their members covering several generations, including aged parents. The specific benefits include: self-employment for able-bodied members of families (including the unemployed and pensioners); new and supplementary kinds of activity; increase of material well-being of families; development of business ideas and skills, including partnerships and business schemes; opportunities for the initial accumulation of the finance needed to open a legal business; accumulation of social capital by overcoming the psychological barriers and appropriating the cross-cultural negotiation and conflict management skills; information on the markets of neighbouring countries – new members of EU; connections and recommendations of colleagues on business or their support; an opportunity to increase social status.

At the same time, it should be acknowledged that the shuttle trade of households can sometimes be harmful and risky, as previously explained. But it does provide traders with a job, an opportunity to realize entrepreneurial capacities and to accumulate initial capital; it can also lead to traders losing professional qualifications gained in their earlier sphere of activity (for example school teachers, biologists, musicians, physicians).

Economic Effects of Household CBC

For *end users*, shuttle business provides an expansion of the variety of products and services available, freeing them from the necessity to go to Poland for purchases. It is possible to save on overhead costs and the stock of supplies held and sometimes to make an individual order for the supply of particular types of products.

Positive spillover effects can also be identified on *other participants in the market*. One is the exchange of information about possibilities of improving the conditions of life and about the shifts in social and economic organization; the other is an opportunity to involve additional clients thanks to the increased product variety (strategy of associative and timesaving sales).

For the *region* (Table 8.4), shuttle business is an efficient mechanism for reducing the social tension in conditions where there is a shortage of employment opportunities and where the population is struggling against

Table 8.4   Households' CBC effects on the border regions' development

Time horizon	Positive benefits/contribution	Costs/negative effects/threats
Contemporary	Learning of market economy laws among the population of the region, to get entrepreneurship activity skills Maintenance of employment Means of struggle against poverty and impoverishment of the population, improvement of the financial position of the population of a region Supply the poor population with economic goods	Excessive competition for the domestic manufacturer, production decrease Outflow of capital abroad Uncontrolled import of poor quality goods at higher prices or in unsanitary conditions (meat products) Uncontrolled export of cheaper Belarusian goods (vodka, cigarettes, fuel, medicine) Evasion of taxes Outflow of qualified personnel from industrial sphere and broken destinies of people, forced to trade instead of working in their professions
Future	Development of businesses integrated into a cross-border market in the region due to accumulation of capital and experience of international cooperation Increase competitiveness of the border areas due to gaining of skills in identification of niches, flexible reaction to the market, and manufacturing of new products Restoration of the destroyed communications and networks of cooperation with the neighbouring countries	'Costs of missed opportunities' Long-term economic development from non-use of people's qualifications while shuttle trading 'Failure' in transfer of know-how because of lack of continuity of workers in education, culture, science and complex manufacturing Emigration of initiative and enterprising people in the case of finding more effective employment abroad

Source: Authors.

poverty. It is also a chance for the region to benefit from the endeavours and personal initiative of its citizens, through the creation of new, small firms which are already embedded in the interregional logistical structure.

However, the research also reveals that the *potential of household CBC* in contributing to entrepreneurship development and regional development through shuttle trade differs between regions. For instance, in the Vitebsk region, CBC is focused on Russia, due to geographical proximity to the Russian border. However, shopping for an individual's own needs in the

Vitebsk region is done by making trips to Poland, which has no border with the region, but rather borders with Lithuania and Latvia.

There are also *negative effects* of the long-term involvement of people in shuttle trade and tight barriers to the initial accumulation of capital (which delays the process of transition of shuttle trade into institutionalized business), including the cases of personal degradation of people (a loss of professional qualification, increased alcohol consumption, appropriation of obscene language due to severe survival conditions).

For *inhabitants*, participation in CBC at both institutional and personal levels gives them the opportunity to receive first-hand information about what is happening in the EU and how neighbouring countries are developing. Cross-border measures foster contacts between Belarusians as well, leading to the emergence of *cooperation networks inside the country*.

CONCLUSIONS AND IMPLICATIONS

Cross-border cooperation in the western regions of Belarus with Poland, Latvia and Lithuania has deep roots in the history of the region, characterized by soft borders with these countries, language similarities, and maintained links between the populations. These factors have enabled the population to make a quick start in cross-border entrepreneurial activity as soon as political conditions allowed. They also serve as an additional, high-value asset for today's cross-border business activity involving households, and hopefully for sustainable CBC in the future.

Currently the cross-border entrepreneurial activity of households in Belarus is characterized by a wide variety of forms, well-thought-out organizational mechanisms and developed networks of people, both in the domestic country and abroad, with defined roles and functions that are flexible enough to adapt to changing external conditions. The determining factor of the form, degree and depth of collaboration of households with foreign partners is the type of the good traded: the form of collaboration selected should be the one that is the most efficient for that type of good. However, when a market niche for the good is found, turnover grows and, in successful cases, where traders aspire to grow their enterprise, the households succeed in achieving the required primary capital accumulation to progress to the level of an institutionalized private firm. It should be recognized, however, that the forms of cooperation may change at this stage (for example a wholesale business requires constant representatives on the other side of the border), but the earlier established cross-border contacts help to organize the business on a new level.

Cross-border entrepreneurial activity of households has proved to be a significant phenomenon with a multifaceted influence on people's fates and regions' developmental trajectories. However, its importance for the social and economic development of the region or country is not based on the variety of cross-border cooperation forms, but rather on, first, the number of links in the chain of trade cooperation and the content of role functions of each link. In conditions of overregulation, many links emerge simply because of the necessity to overcome high barriers. Moreover, many schemes of 'collaboration' are worked out only as a mechanism to provide some immunity against the overwhelming bureaucracy and conditions which hamper the initial accumulation of capital. The second characteristic refers to the dynamics of the forms and features of cooperation. The transition to more complex forms of entrepreneurship is important from the viewpoint of the (size and quality of) *value added*, since this will affect its contribution to economic development, but also from the viewpoint of the humanization of activity to counter the degradation of people which petty trade can cause.

The policy implications of the analysis include a need to eliminate the overwhelming bureaucracy, the barriers preventing the population from discovering and exploiting new market niches, and the initial negative attitude towards petty traders from state bodies and customs officers. EU expansion caused a significant change in the conditions for households' cross-border cooperation in Belarus, leading to a change in the forms of CBC. This new stage of cross-border cooperation of households deserves further scholarly attention.

REFERENCES

Belitsky, M.E. and V.M. Rudenkov (eds) (2005), *Cross-border Trade of Belarus*, Minsk: Pravo i economika.
Chubrik, A., I. Pelipas and E. Rakova (eds) (2008), *Belarusian Business in 2007: Condition, Tendencies, Perspectives* (in Russian), Minsk: IPM.
Elovskih, V.V. (2005), *The Role of Small Business in the Belarusian Economy*, Minsk: Logvinov.
Litviniuk, A. (2009), *Transborder and European Regional Cooperation* (in Russian), Minsk: BSPU.
Sidorchuk, I. (ed.) (2007), *Local Government in Belarus* (in Russian), Minsk: Tonpik.
Slonimski, A. and M. Slonimska (2006), 'Regional peculiarities of business activity of the population of Belarus' (in Ukrainian), *Regional Economy*, **2**, 195–203.
Smallbone, D. and F. Welter (2006), 'Conceptualising entrepreneurship in a transition context', *International Journal of Entrepreneurship and Small Business*, **3**(2), 190–206.

Welter, F., D. Smallbone, S. Slonimski and M. Slonimska (2008), 'Internationalization of SMEs in Belarus', in L.-P. Dana, I.M. Welpe, M. Han and V. Ratten (eds), *Handbook of Research on European Business and Entrepreneurship: Towards a Theory of Internationalization*, Cheltenham, UK and Northampton, MA, USA: Edward Elgar, pp. 57–76.

PART IV

Policy Perspectives

9. Cluster development and cluster policies in EU border regions

Peter Zashev

INTRODUCTION

A regional cluster (see Enright, 2000; 1996) is an industrial cluster in which member firms are in close geographical proximity to each other. The most general definition of an industry cluster is 'geographical concentrations of industries that gain performance advantages through co-location' (Doeringer and Terkla, 1995). These advantages include, for example, access to specialized human resources and suppliers, knowledge spillovers, pressure for higher performance in head-to-head competition, and learning from the close interaction with specialized customers and suppliers. Beyond the basic definition, however, there is little consensus on how to define an industry cluster. Clusters may differ in many dimensions: the type of products and services they produce, the locational dynamics they are subjected to, their stage of development, and the business environment that surrounds them, to name a few.

A cluster is represented by a local production system that is embedded in a local social system. Each affects the ability of a cluster to produce synergy. The most effective clusters, which are animated or 'working', are relatively complete systems with specialized support and considerable social capital. Latent clusters may have the production system elements but lack the social system necessary to diffuse information and innovation and facilitate business deals. Potential clusters have incomplete production and social systems but have the basic ingredients to be developed as systems (Rosenfeld, 1997). Lastly, proponents of industry clusters claim that the clusters that include industries across several sectors are more adaptable to change, and can better withstand downturns in the economic cycle (Doeringer and Terkla, 1995; Rosenfeld, 1997).

Cluster policies have an increasingly important role to play in the academic analysis and policy making related to regional economic development, although there seems to be a substantial gap between the academic debate and policy actions on the ground. In academia there is a significant research stream trying to qualify and quantify clusters (Rosenfeld, 1996, 1997; Doeringer and Terkla, 1995; Jacobs and DeMan, 1996; Pedersen, 1997; Hill and Brennan, 2000), to analyse the factors that contribute to their development and success (Doeringer and Terkla, 1995; Rosenfeld, 1997; Pouder and John, 1996; Woodward, 2005), as well as the internal and external linkages of the companies forming a cluster (Rosenfeld, 1997). Very few of these studies aim to compare more than one region based on empirical data collected from various stakeholders in the process, such as companies, organizations and authorities.

In most EU member states, border regions are perceived as part of the periphery that is less developed than the core regions. On one hand, such a development level is hardly conducive to cluster development, but on the other hand, the border should be, and must be, observed as an opportunity instead of an obstacle. The border means a difference in incomes, prices, industrial structures, cultures and tastes. Such differences generate opportunities such as: (i) each side may find its own potential competitive advantage; and (ii) mutual learning can turn the regions into bridges between the entire countries.

This chapter reviews the problems involved in cluster development and policy making in border regions to identify key problem areas and offer a concrete set of measures that enable cluster development with an optimal balance of resources, efforts and expected results.

The chapter's empirical evidence is based on more than 180 interviews with key informants among regional authorities, business support organizations and local experts and on more than 250 interviews with entrepreneurs and managers from companies operating in different border regions, drawn from Bulgaria, Greece, Serbia, Germany, Poland and Finland. These regions varied in their level of industrial development, administrative capacities and experience in cross-border cooperation. The chapter's concluding part summarizes the key findings but also suggests several ways to optimize cluster policies as to better fit their overall rationale, namely regional economic development.

CLUSTER DEVELOPMENT AS A POLICY INSTRUMENT

Following the popularization of clusters by Michael Porter in the early 1990s, several scholars and many policy makers have targeted the possibility of using cluster theories as a tool for designing better economic policies, to boost either national competitiveness or regional economic development.

The opportunity to use clustering as a means for improving targeting efforts in economic development activities was referred to by Anderson in 1994. The study concluded that industry cluster approach can be a more effective analytical tool than traditional industry segmentation methods in understanding the dynamics of a region and identifying strategies for attracting, retaining, growing, and establishing industry in a region.

By identifying clusters, and understanding specific needs (that is, infrastructure or workforce needs) of the industries within the clusters, policy makers can build on the existing strengths in the region and provide more appropriate assistance to businesses. This is in contrast to many current policies, which direct resources at the industries the region hopes to attract, regardless of whether the existing environment is conducive to the development of these industries (Doeringer and Terkla, 1995).

Woodward (2005) summarizes Porter's cluster strategy as opposing the concept of industrial targeting as follows:

1.   Support the development of all clusters, not choose among them.
2.   Strengthen established and promising clusters rather than attempt to generate entirely new ones.
3.   Top-down government strategies should not guide development. Cluster initiatives are advanced by the private sector, with government as facilitator.

Cluster theories have become increasingly popular in policy making (Roelandt and den Hertog, 1999; Forslida and Midelfart, 2005) or as tools for industrial analysis (Becattini, 2002). Various policies and policy makers in the field of small and medium-sized enterprises (SMEs) also regard cluster theories as an instrument in building policies for SMEs' support and regional development, illustrated by several EU reports (Enterprise DG, 2003). According to them, cluster policy should be about empowerment, that is, helping communities to help themselves. This means putting in place favourable framework conditions for cluster development: promoting a climate of trust and confidence, fostering regional appropriation and identity, smart and interactive connections and knowledge valorization, and, as a result, preventing and avoiding transfixing people, firms and the community, thanks to social capital.

In a global economic environment where one may witness the constantly shifting nature of business patterns, clustering theories and strategies could be the source for an effective economic development strategy. Economic development policies that target individual firms or industries are arguably no longer the most viable option for many regions. Cluster theories certainly have a place in studying the competitive potential of regions in general, and cross-border regions in particular. A starting point could be to elaborate what makes the difference between national regions and cross-border regions. Evidently it is the existence of a national border, but a border should be interpreted in its widest possible definition – not only as an obstacle for the free flow of goods, services and labour force but also as a linguistic, cultural and social divide between regions.

These obstacles significantly modify the strategies needed to enable and stimulate the development of business networks in general and clusters in particular. While in the context of cross-border regions the identification of potential clusters could be handled using established methods, their nurturing and development is affected by the border divide in its wider definition.

One of the main shortcomings inherent in a focus on cluster development is that the likelihood of success will vary between regions – regions in general, and cross-border regions in particular. A prerequisite to developing a cluster is the identification of regional competitive advantage based on one or many factors such as labour force characteristics, unique regional attributes, the availability and quality of public and private infrastructure, and proximity to both input and product markets. Industrialization efforts must identify the targeted industry/firms and provide the services and infrastructure necessary to ensure that these businesses remain successful. Thus, the designing of an industry cluster programme requires an extensive understanding of the region and its economic processes (Barkley, 2001).

One problematic issue is the competence of public officials to either identify regional competitive advantage, select 'good' industries/firms to target, or to design programmes to assist specific sectors. Regional competitive advantage changes over time in response to new technologies, tastes and institutions. It is a leap of faith to assume that state and local development authorities appreciate regional, national and international economic processes well enough to assess regional competitive advantage accurately. In addition, the selection of specific targets for industry clusters is problematic because projections of industry-wide growth prospects are notoriously unreliable. Growth prospects change over time in response to market forces, and individual firms within an industry may exhibit employment and sales trends counter to that of the industry as a whole (Barkley, 2001).

Research on industry clusters is remarkably consistent in its description of the institutional environment required to nurture and support clusters (ibid.). Many economists are not optimistic that appropriate institutional arrangements will emerge, because cooperative behaviour is limited by incomplete information, opportunistic behaviour and committed assets. These researchers conclude that a consensus for promoting economic development will occur only when the total gains are expected to be very large, when the distribution of the benefits and costs is quite clear, and when the community can reach agreement on helping those who might be harmed (ibid.). In the context of cross-border regions this issue is particularly important, as trust between communities and business actors may be in short supply.

To justify cluster development efforts, some seeds of a cluster should have already passed a market test. Various prerequisites exist that determine whether or not a cluster emerges and, if so, where (see, for example, Brenner, 2000; Brenner and Fornahl, 2002). These include market conditions, technologies, the ongoing globalization process, industry- or region-specific characteristics such as infrastructure, the organization of the regional innovation process (Cooke, 2002) and differences in regional business culture (Saxenian, 1994). Cluster development initiatives should embrace the pursuit of competitive advantage and specialization rather than simply imitate successful clusters in other locations. This requires building on local sources of uniqueness. By identifying clusters, and understanding the specific policy support needs (that is, infrastructure or workforce needs) of the industries within the clusters, policy makers can build on the existing strengths in the region and provide more appropriate assistance to businesses. It is in this context that experts should identify the industries in which 'both sides of the border' have their greatest competitive advantage. These 'driver industries' may have spillover effects on suppliers and customers located in the same region to form industry clusters. A specific question that arises in the case of cross-border regions is the degree to which the border may diminish these spillover effects. The long-term goals of sustaining the economic vitality of a region can only be achieved through a continuing process in which the clusters themselves become players in contributing to their own growth and supporting continuing improvements in the foundations that support them.

Both formal and informal networking are a very important part of cluster development. Informal networks are established by means of personal contacts, and usually function alongside formal decision paths and institutions. While outsiders find these networks difficult to identify, they can lead to a dramatic reorganization of traditional and accepted power structures. Formal networks, on the other hand, do not present a challenge in the same way to old established power structures. They are often created by agreements that are soundly based in established institutions. Unlike informal networks, these agreements and the composition of formal networks are often well documented.

The importance and the role of social infrastructure in defining industry clusters is another common pattern identified in the literature. Rosenfeld (1996) argues that information flows are essential in an effective industry cluster. However, an information flow will not be possible in the absence of a developed social infrastructure. Therefore a cluster may be in place, but its successful development, or at least its efficiency, will be highly dependent on social interaction, trust and a shared vision.

CLUSTER FORMATION AND DEVELOPMENT IN CROSS-BORDER REGIONS

As cluster studies are rarely combined with studies of cross-border cooperation, there is significant potential in reviewing and analysing the specific circumstances and obstacles for cluster development in cross-border regions. One notable exception is the in-depth analysis and spatial planning activities in the Oresund region between Denmark and Sweden (Hospers, 2004; Jensen and Richardson, 2004; Maskell and Törnqvist, 1999; Sornn-Friese and Sorensen, 2005; The Öresund Committee, 2006).

However, the formation of clusters in cross-border regions may create a new and enlarged arena for local rivalry. By enabling the sharing of experiences and ideas, the firms, institutions and individuals alike will almost certainly boost their general level of competitiveness. The role of local rivalry is particularly important in the context of learning by firms watching each other within a market. Best practices set by someone who shares the same environment and faces the same challenges are invariably more visible and create more direct pressure to catch up, than 'miracles' achieved by actors in far-away places.

However, for all this to occur, and for tangible and competitive cross-border clusters to appear, the biggest effort should be to diminish the visibility and the overall impact of the border as such. A border, as discussed above, is comprised of much more than physical barriers. That is why the applicability of cluster theories and strategies in cross-border regions may depend on the knowledge and thorough analysis of ways of bringing together all the stakeholders involved in this process at every level: institutional, entrepreneurial, cultural, linguistic, academic and so on. Such an approach may require solid skills in cross-cultural communications, as well as knowledge about the institutional and economic structures across the border. In the absence of such skills and knowledge organizing, co-opting and coordinating joint initiatives, company networks and projects may prove impossible.

Developed by the author, Figure 9.1 shows the sequence and key steps in developing some regional competitive advantage or idea into a fully operational cluster. While the first two steps could be regarded as preconditions that must be present on the ground, the latter two could be considered as actions. The absence of critical mass or size as a precondition can be

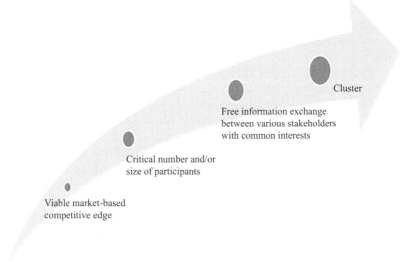

Source: Author.

Figure 9.1   From a market-based competitive advantage to an operational cluster

compensated by a powerful market-based idea that may itself generate the rapid generation of many and sizeable participants.

Viable Market-Based Competitive Edge

The first step is to verify the presence of market demand. Cluster building and development is rich with examples that show the artificial belief of authorities that regional development money may substitute for or generate the missing market demand (Bresnahan et al., 2001; Clar et al., 2008). The temptation is especially strong in the context of the EU enlargement and the development funds targeted at new member states. As a result an unproductive cooperation could occur between authorities and companies that is not targeted at fostering the entrepreneurial advantage of a region but instead aims to build a virtual one, which explains the need to apply for funds.

Within the case study regions, Tornio–Haparanda provides an example of managing to build an operational cluster based only on a competitive, market-based idea. The idea came after the regional authorities managed to convince and lure IKEA to open a shop in the region less than two years ago. The estimated number of visitors is an impressive 1.2 million per year, which is a significant number by the standards of these sparsely populated regions. The authorities skilfully recognized the opportunity offered by this inflow of people and decided to stimulate the development of bigger shopping opportunities. That was done by planning and finding an investor for the thirteenth biggest shopping mall in Finland to be accomplished in 2009. The shopping mall contributed to stimulating entrepreneurial activities by offering commercial premises for various shops, restaurants, cafeterias and other services. This was followed by an open discussion of how to make the people coming for shopping stay longer in the area and what services (hotels, restaurants and so on) were needed to make this happen. A key element was the open mode of operation, in which the authorities discuss opportunities with entrepreneurs from both sides of the border. The level of determination certainly suggested that the end result would be successful. It is important to emphasize that the fundamentals were interpreted correctly, namely that the cluster will be built around actual market demand created by an existing inflow of people with sufficient purchasing power.

Again it should be stressed that actions were preceded by a discussion in which all interested entrepreneurs were able to participate and make suggestions and comments. Undoubtedly IKEA made the necessary market research needed to choose Haparanda as an investment site, but it was Haparanda's authorities that worked hard to turn IKEA's attention to it. Furthermore it was Tornio's authorities who recognized the opportunity and developed the idea of building a shopping mall on the border, in close cooperation with the Swedish authorities, as well as with entrepreneurs. This is clearly an example of a proactive policy-making approach that worked well, first, because it followed and built on existing demand instead of trying to create it artificially, and secondly, because it managed to get all stakeholders discussing the concrete opportunities and needed actions.

That contrasts with south-east Estonia where policy makers are seeking to promote cluster development in agro-tourism and crafts, although neither are presently supported by sufficient demand in terms of number of visitors. In such cases perhaps it is too early to speak about clusters, but rather about the need to promote the region and make sure that the growing number of visitors is matched by a growing number of services to be offered. Thus one may say that there is a potentially latent cluster in search for demand, but it is not possible to argue that this is a cluster in the classical sense.

Critical Number/Size of Participants

An existing market-based opportunity must be backed by the presence of resources, which includes stakeholders interested in and capable of working together in utilizing the identified opportunity. It is of critical importance that the number of players is realistically estimated in order to ensure there is a sufficient amount of players (companies, organizations, entrepreneurs and so on) present and interested in taking part. However, the existing literature says little about that quantitative aspect of cluster identification. One idea is to measure the size and importance of a given industry measured in terms of number of companies or their share in regional employment or Gross Regional Product.

A good example of how size is perceived to matter is the way an entrepreneur from south-east Estonia describes his vision of clustering activities: *'When a bus breaks down, then we take the passengers. And if we have not capacity to fulfil orders, then another firm helps'* (South-east Estonia Enterprise 4). The local authorities there clearly state that 'There are mostly small enterprises in the region, which are not very actively cooperating. A problem is also that enterprises in the region are rather micro and small enterprises and they lack both human and financial resources to contribute to cooperation.' Another illustration about the importance of *critical mass* comes from Poland, where in the region of Biała Podlaska on the premises of the former furniture factory a concentration of small furniture companies are located (11 enterprises), together with a few other logistics companies. However as (i) they are not functionally interrelated; (ii) there are not many of them; and (iii) none of them is considerably big, it is difficult to see a possible cluster formation.

The qualitative dimension is also a serious issue in cluster identification. In the interviews conducted in the CBCED project, many entrepreneurs mistakenly take any *sell–buy* business-to-business (B2B) interaction for clustering activity. It is the case that simple B2B interaction may sometimes evolve further when different companies realize the benefits of various forms of broader cooperation: 'There are cases of cooperation with other companies located in Görlitz in the form of helping each other out with material and special makings. This form of collaboration cannot be called a cluster' (Görlitz Enterprise 2), or 'a flexible type of clusters, in which the partners are only trying to negotiate all together with the suppliers for a better price' (Serres Enterprise 15). Similarly, the empirical evidence suggests that there are no 'clusters' in the classical understanding as:

> Geographic concentrations of interconnected companies and institutions in a particular field. Clusters encompass an array of linked industries and other entities important to competition. They include, for example, suppliers of specialized inputs such as components, machinery and services, and providers of specialized infrastructure. Clusters also often extend downstream to channels and customers and laterally to manufacturers of complementary products and to

companies in industries related by skills, technology, or common inputs. Finally, many clusters include governmental and other institutions – such as universities, standards-setting agencies, think tanks, vocational training providers, and trade associations – that provide specialized training, education, information, research, and technical support. (Porter, 1998)

Instead, the cases identified in the study regions are more like loose regional networks of enterprises with similar interests than a functionally inter-related cluster. This includes a purchasing group with common methods of negotiating the prices of purchased goods, logistics, possibilities of shipping small quantities and negotiations of prices of purchased cars and prices of cell phone operators (Biała Podlaska Enterprise 1), or subletting customers in cases where firms have insufficient capacity (Hochfranken Enterprise 5). Another issue is that in some regions, enterprises are almost entirely micro and small enterprises, lacking both human and financial resources to contribute to cooperation. Slightly larger enterprises already cooperate on a national level (South-east Estonia).

Free Information Exchange between Various Stakeholders with Common Interests

The empirical data collected from the EU border regions in the CBCED project suggests that nothing helps a cluster form and develop more than a free and open information exchange between stakeholders interested in the success of their companies and their region. Not surprisingly, perhaps, from the point of view of the entrepreneurs the success of their industry in general is somewhat less important and appreciated less than the success of their own company. This must be taken into account when developing a strategy to get entrepreneurs on board in an information-sharing process aimed at establishing a framework for cluster formation and development. Understanding and taking into account the individual interests of participating entrepreneurs is an essential requirement in developing a successful strategy or cluster development.

The need for considering the above-mentioned is demonstrated well in a key informant report from eastern Estonia:

> Cooperation between enterprises is at the moment still on the level of meetings and discussions. The entrepreneurs are not yet ready to engage in deeper cooperation. But discussions about the need of cooperation have developed ways of thinking and understanding of the need to cooperate, especially when going to foreign market.

The lack of information exchange may be due to a passive attitude on the part of the authorities or overly sceptical entrepreneurs. This is described by a key informant from the Bulgarian region of Petrich as follows:

> Despite geographical concentration of clothing companies, utilization of common technology, utilization of common set of workforce skills, their activities are not linked. Usually relations (where existing) are limited and informal, based on friendships. For example an entrepreneur helps other to solve accidental problem. This kind of relations does not produce business benefits on regular base. Another type of relations is connected with exchange of information but these seemed to be not important practice. (Bulgarian entrepreneur Key informant)

At the same time, in another Bulgarian region, Kyustendil, the need for information exchange is already understood and informants say that:

> The existence of cluster-like form of organization has been identified. It comprises about thirty firms from the tailoring branch in the south-west part of Bulgaria. The formation of this cluster began when a branch organization of textile manufacturers was founded. This organization is created to defend its members' interests and it also makes it possible for complex orders to be taken. The idea is for firms to have better opportunities for cooperation and help each other with the realization of their production. (Kyustendil Chamber of Commerce)

One reason for a sceptical attitude on the part of entrepreneurs may be cultural, which emphasizes individual rather than collective values. For example, a Greek informant from the Florina region explained that 'local entrepreneurs (or those involved in agricultural production) do not share a sense of community, but instead prefer to act in an isolated, personal and "traditional manner"'. Another source in the Serres region in Greece suggested that 'the practice of cooperation is considered by most key informants as not embedded in the Greek mentality; enterprises activating in the same sector tend to view each other as competitors only, which simultaneously rules out any potential for cooperation'.

With respect to sharing information it seems that individual values rather than a spirit of cooperation can be found almost everywhere across the case study regions in six countries. In Estonia, for example, '(...) the Estonian mentality, which doesn't allow information to be shared easily and cooperation to be made unless there is immediate profit' (South-east Estonia Enterprise 17). Similarly, in Finland, it was reported that:

> The only constraint for collaboration is that as many of the enterprises work in the same sector, some are afraid that too much collaboration could tighten the

competition, but in my view the Russian markets are so extensive and continue to grow at such a speed that there is a market for all of us. (South Karelia Enterprise 2)

At the same time, some entrepreneurs do understand that sharing information and working together brings potential benefits for all. For example, another entrepreneur in the same Finnish region of South Karelia says: 'the best member benefit is that we get to know how other people have dealt with their problems and information exchange' (South Karelia Enterprise 11). A fellow entrepreneur from the same region added:

> The Club which unites enterprises in the region who are interested in doing business in Russia/CBC has only Finnish companies, small, medium and large. The club offers a medium through which entrepreneurs can exchange information and experiences. Some of the members are vertically linked with each other, but we look for synergies and have a complementary/horizontal relationship with the other members. Discussions with colleagues from different firms are very useful; hearing someone else's thought on the matters always teaches you something new. And I think it is also interesting to tell about our experiences to this forum because someone can benefit from our knowledge. (South Karelia Enterprise 14)

A similar initiative aiming to promote a spirit of cooperation exists in the German Hochfranken region, where a company:

> has organized a kind of 'regulars' table of knowledge', on whose occasion the foremen of the companies meet in one of the factories and exchange knowledge on the working level. The participants talk about the problems each of them had and how they have solved them. Such meetings are intended to take place four times a year. The participating companies do not compete but are able to learn from each other. (Hochfranken Enterprise 9)

Another example was found in Bulgaria, where 'in the framework of Expert group, established by the Bulgarian Ministry of Labour and Social Policy and the Bulgarian Association of Textile and Clothing (BATEC) the Expert group members discuss problems of light industry in their meetings aimed at common exchange of information' (Petrich Enterprise 3). Such top-down initiatives can be important, especially in regions where the companies are small and not united by some professional association, chamber of commerce or similar organization. However, bringing companies together into a group with common interests is not enough. What is equally important is to activate its participants to exchange information freely, which requires negotiating skills and an ability to cut corners and actively communicate the benefits. Otherwise, there is a danger that the experience of a Greek entrepreneur becomes widespread: 'We participate in a network of tourist firms called "Association of Tourist Agencies", but it's practically inactive, because we can't reach an agreement and jointly promote our common interests' (Serres Enterprise 13). Or as an interviewee in Germany reported 'the company has loose contacts with other companies located in the region intended to make use of joined and existing marketing channels and platforms but this has not worked out due to differing strategies of the companies' (Hochfranken Enterprise 6).

However, when successful, a strategy that convinces companies to actively participate in an information exchange network can bring co-operation to a higher level. A South Karelian entrepreneur commented:

> Yes. We collaborate quite a lot with companies who also serve accommodation services; we have meetings etc. in which we discuss matters relating to our businesses. It is both problem solving and information exchange. The companies in this cluster are all in the same line of business as we, tourism: accommodation services, cruise organizers and companies which organize activities for tourists. We do not all participate in all the activities. The companies are of different sizes, some are large hotels others small micro entrepreneurs. (South Karelia Enterprise 9)

A fellow entrepreneur from the Finnish region of Tornio added: 'We try to market each other's services to our contacts if we cannot help the customer ourselves. The services the companies offer are complementary' (Tornio Enterprise 11). Such an evolution of interaction between enterprises, from information exchange towards closer cooperation, was also identified in the Polish region of Zgorzelec, where a local entrepreneur commented 'Cooperation with carpentry companies from Zgorzelec in the scope of: customers exchange, setting the prices on the same level, exchange of information about companies that do not pay, informing customers in Zgorzelec about companies which produce good doors, windows, stairs etc.' (Zgorzelec Enterprise 12).

Forming a Cluster

As described above, once companies are linked through information exchange some start to develop closer interaction in various complementing fields, which is when one may say that a loose cluster is forming. As previously explained, a loose cluster consists of companies that are com-petitive as individual companies, but who express a demand for some form of cooperation. Both individual companies and their industry field are competitive. Further development of the cluster focuses on a deepening of their cooperation inside the cluster and the external promotion of its interests.

The concrete activities that follow information exchange to contribute to the development of the cluster may vary. For example, they may take the form of the introduction of a 'purchasing group, methods of negotiating the prices of purchased goods, logistics, possibilities of shipping small quantities, negotiations of prices of purchased cars and prices of cell phone operators, marketing, brand building' (Biała Podlaska Enterprise 1). Similarly, a Greek interviewee spoke of 'a flexible type of clusters, in which the partners are only trying to negotiate all together with the suppliers for a better price. Together they are able to get better prices, than every single firm could achieve separately' (Serres Enterprise 15).

Alternatively, further cooperation may be occasional as in 'the IT network of Upper Lusatia. The latter includes about 450 companies, with ca. 830 employees only in Görlitz. The companies specialize and collaborate occasionally and project related' (Görlitz Enterprise 15). Such occasional cooperation also happens in the case of tourism companies in Greek regions, resulting in cross-border cooperation networks in the tourism sector between firms from Bulgaria and Greece; there are several Greek firms cooperating with numerous tourism agencies and hotels from the other side of the borders. It appears to be a dynamic cooperation, which could evolve into a cluster formation in the future.

A pragmatic way to develop cooperation within a cluster is through subcontracting: 'In case of capacity overload, the company sublets orders or exchanges production capacities occasionally without a specific contract. While there was formerly rather competition, the companies complement one another now' (Hochfranken Enterprise 5). Similar examples can be found in Greece, where one entrepreneur reported that:

> In the less flexible type of cluster, the partners work together for a specific project. This type of cluster gives them greater power to negotiate and also allows them to complete the project on time. This is very important since many companies are not capable to complete a project on time, therefore in many cases they end up paying fines. (Serres Enterprise 15)

In some cases, entrepreneurs emphasized a common sense of belonging to a group or to a territory, as a unifying factor behind cluster creation and development. This is illustrated with a case from Ida Viru in north-east Estonia:

> We can see as a cluster the group of enterprises here on the port territory, which include the port, terminals, enterprise for producing electricity and another one

for managing the real estate of the port, also business incubator. This is a group of enterprises residing in one territory, who are very closely connected to each other. We have specialized and thanks to that created this kind of synergy. (Ida Viru Enterprise 14)

Belonging to a region, together with a willingness to develop it further, was a factor contributing to cooperation in some regions. For example, in south-east Estonia, it was reported that: 'A benefit has been first of all that they have started to realize that in tourism it is important to sell a region, it is necessary to sell also the neighbour and neighbour's neighbour and it is necessary to know what he is doing' (South-east Estonia Enterprise 1).

Another unifying factor could be a common objective, such as attracting Russian customers in South Karelia:

together with 3–5 other tourism entrepreneurs/companies we try to attract more Russian customers. We have designed and marketed some packages for them that include the cruise, accommodation in cabins or at the Imatra Spa. I am very interested in developing this cluster further – I think it benefits all the members. We could design new, different packages – that to me would seem the best way of developing our business. (South Karelia Enterprise 5)

The Cross-Border Status as an Advantage in Cluster Development

It is often assumed that a border region location hinders growth. In many cases, that is correct, when years of effective border controls, linguistic, cultural and historical differences have a negative effect on the opportunities for cooperation across the border. But on the positive side, cross-border status can represent an opportunity. It may bring additional demand as market structures on both sides of the border may be different. It may offer greater volume by adding to the number of companies, consumers and suppliers. Increased cross-border cooperation can offer access to a key gravitational centre for a future cluster in the form of large institutions such as a university, company or hospital.

In such circumstances, increased cross-border cooperation can contribute to the development of potential clusters by adding what is missing in both quantitative and qualitative terms. It may be in the form of higher number of participating enterprises contributing to the concentration achieving critical mass in the industry in question. Regional authorities can reduce the negative influence of the border and induce active cooperation and networking among companies, organizations and entrepreneurs.

The formation of a cluster does not automatically guarantee its success and consequently the prosperity of the region it operates in. The empirical investigation of study regions in the CBCED project identified a number of factors affecting the development of clusters and their contribution to regional development. Five of the studied regions have significant textile industries, with some form of cluster development, albeit weak in some cases. The problem is to define the development potential of these industry clusters, since the answer is important to policy makers seeking to decide how much effort and resources should be invested in encouraging their development.

However, the textiles industry is in decline across Europe. The industry is perceived to be a victim of globalization in that being labour intensive, it tends to migrate to low-wage locations. That can be illustrated with reference to the cross-border operations of the Greek textile companies who used labour in Bulgaria, then in Macedonia and more recently in Albania. Eastern Estonia experienced similar problems as the textile industry was growing at the beginning of the 1990s while it is shrinking at present. The problem for policy makers is whether or not a textiles cluster should be supported and developed even if it is clear that it is a short-term opportunity. Based on the example of Greek textiles companies, it may be argued that their activity in a mature industry gives little chance to develop further and grow, hence, policy makers should seek for alternatives. On the other hand, these companies are able to focus on specific activities, for example logistics and management, while relocating the labour-intensive parts of their business to locations further east (for example Ukraine, China). This may enable them to grow although they will almost certainly need support. Instead of 'abandoning' this cluster, policy makers could assist its adaptation to geographical shift, given its significant role for the regional economies. This dimension could also be included in the life cycle theory of clusters (Menzel and Fornahl, 2009). The model is based on two key processes: the first is that the emergence, growth, decline and renewal of the cluster depend on the technological heterogeneity of firms within it; the second is that firms have a larger relative absorptive capacity, when they are in the same location, and thus localized learning changes heterogeneity. A similar argument can be extended to the porcelain cluster in Hochfranken. It is a mature industry that does not have visible chances to develop further and grow.

Of course these questions also deal with the perception of timing. For instance the textiles cluster may well have five to ten years before completely losing its competitive edge. For the authorities, the five- to ten-year period should be used to identify another competitive advantage of the region, with a view to develop it into a competitive cluster. For this reason, it is important to be aware of the cluster's life stage.

The empirical data enabled us to investigate the concept of the over-dominant cluster, illustrated by the forestry cluster in South Karelia. Forestry has been the main business in South Karelia for almost 100 years, where the business is dominated by three companies. The majority of employment in South Karelia is either in forestry or in the supporting activities, such as services, research and logistics. Almost all key officials pointed to the cluster as the main reason for a low level of entrepreneurship in South Karelia. The cluster is simultaneously a reason of regional pride and a cause of concern. Pride due to its size, international fame and importance for the region; and concern about its overwhelming importance and, as mentioned above, its stage in the life cycle.

Several factors contribute to the vulnerability of what may seem a solid and well-grounded cluster. The most important factor is that wood-based products in South Karelia are to a large extent dependent on imported raw materials from neighbouring Russia. As Russia recently changed its export duties for raw wood, the foundations of the forestry cluster were deeply shaken. In combination with a (perhaps) temporary decline in paper prices, the industry is losing competitiveness. If the region had a more diversified economic structure it would have been easier to offset the consequences. The lesson to be learned is that the authorities should have tried to diversify earlier before the recent problems in the forestry cluster. Furthermore, it is important to analyse and choose the industry fields and company groupings that need assistance. The big forestry companies have both the financial and the human resources to develop and grow without much external assistance, but this is not the case with smaller enterprises.

CONCLUSIONS

The empirical analysis strongly suggests several key factors that contribute to coherent and target-based cluster development. In the development of new clusters the most important point is to properly evaluate their chances and general market viability. Often such an evaluation should not be exclusively in the hands of public regional authorities, as the competition for regional development funds may tempt them to see clusters where none exist or where there is very little potential for their development. As mentioned above, to justify cluster development efforts, the main parameters of a cluster should have already passed a market test. Cluster development initiatives need to embrace the pursuit of competitive advantage and specialization rather than simply imitate successful clusters in other locations. This requires building on local sources of uniqueness.

By identifying clusters, and understanding the specific needs (that is, infrastructure, labour skills and so on) of the enterprises within the clusters, policy makers can build on existing strengths in a region and provide more appropriate assistance to businesses. It is in this context that experts should identify the industries in which 'both sides of the border' have their greatest competitive advantage. But what if there are not enough companies, as in south-east Estonia or the general economic development is not high as in the Kystendil region or in Biała Podlaska? Can these regions also argue in favour of developing cluster policies and supporting them financially? Or perhaps it is better to review and re-evaluate their competitive advantages and see what can be developed and how. Regional development does not always necessarily need to be based on clusters.

For those regions that have loose networks of companies in single or complementary fields, an important question is how and what is needed to stimulate the formation of cluster development and growth. The most important conclusion based on the empirical data is that the most important condition is to unite entrepreneurs behind common goals, communicating these goals and creating a free information exchange between companies, policy makers and entrepreneurs. It is precisely the inability of entrepreneurs to outgrow the rivalries and the inability of the authorities to communicate the opportunities that seems to be the biggest obstacle preventing company groupings or loose networks from starting to cooperate more intensively for their own good and the good of the region.

There seem to be several reasons for the process of cluster development being slow in case study regions. One is the passive role of regional authorities and business support organizations. Another is the lack of interaction between companies and entrepreneurs on one side and the authorities on the other side. Finally, the empirical data confirms that companies need external push and incentives to cooperate more intensively, be it in promoting their business directly or indirectly through promoting the region. The collected data seems to confirm the positive correlation between business organization membership and business support services offered to the formation of clusters/loose clusters or at least a more intensive information exchange. The positive relationship between business organization membership and cluster formation is explained by the networking opportunities that membership offers, together with a sense of belonging.

It is very important to keep an expert level, independent evaluation on the development potential of particular clusters. The expansion of the Greek textiles clusters into Bulgaria first and then to Macedonia is a good illustration. As salaries go up it is only a question of time before a cluster based on cheap labour costs may start experiencing a rapid decline. The relevant question for policy makers is: does it pay to support it and what levels of support are appropriate and adequate? The same is valid also for regions with traditional clusters, such as South Karelia (forestry) and Hochfranken (porcelain). In these cases, the cluster may be in decline due to external factors such as the Russian wood export excise or not adapting to the globalization trend, as in Germany. The authorities must be knowledgeable about the development potential of their cluster and its abilities to adapt in constantly (and rapidly) changing business landscapes. Four to five years may not be long in terms of long-term competitiveness but at a regional level this can give the authorities enough time to check for other regional advantages and start diverting attention and resources from the present cluster to alternatives.

The empirical data suggests that authorities should be willing and able to help the clusters that have the best match between support needs and expected output. For example, the forestry cluster in South Karelia and the metallurgical cluster in the Tornio region are powerful and rich enough not to be in need of regional aid and assistance. In these cases the role of policy makers is more advisory and monitoring. On the other hand, tourism or wine producing in northern Greece, or Hochfranken automobile components need harnessing, attention and resources.

In such cases, it is for the regional authorities and business support organizations to decide where and how resources should be mobilized. One vital part of any strategy is to set clear priorities that are accepted by most levels of administration and more importantly have the full support of the entrepreneurs. That is not what happened in Hochfranken where regional experts indicated that the cluster policy was not accepted by the enterprises of the region because they had not been involved from the start. This again underlines the key importance of designing support policies and measures in close cooperation between policy makers, entrepreneurs and companies involved. A target-oriented approach could involve interviewing them as part of the policy design and planned implementation.

Some of the study regions demonstrate that clusters can become over-dominant and thus in a way 'suffocate' entrepreneurial development in a region. A typical case is the forestry cluster in South Karelia. It has historical roots and an overwhelming presence in the region that, according to most interviewees, has some significant negative effect for entre-preneurship development. There are two dangers in this respect. The obvious one is that the labour force is attracted to the security provided by big companies while local SMEs are attracted to the security and stability of being subcontractors to the big companies. Thus instead of generating entrepreneurial vigour the big companies can diminish it. The second danger is that regional authorities are much less keen to promote entre-preneurship as it is not greatly needed. A strong case for policy intervention is a need for diversification of the competitive advantages of the region and checking to see if efforts and resources could be better channelled into promising areas such as tourism or high-tech (in the case of South Karelia).

These could be considered as the main findings regarding clusters across their entire lifespan, starting with their identification through their harnessing, development and growth, and finishing with their decline or sometimes overly dominant position. The findings point to some substantial differences between theories and practice. The cluster theories presented above emphasize 'ideal' cases in which companies cooperate and find a common ground and public authorities skilfully stimulate these processes through various means.

In reality companies are less willing to cooperate than policy makers often assume. Often, serious push is needed to find common interests and goals and to communicate them to the various stakeholders. In the real world authorities are sometimes willing to find clusters where none exist, as this may increase their chances to receive additional regional development funds. The generation of open and frank dialogue between companies and authorities and the provision of more specialized business support services can positively affect cluster development.

REFERENCES

Anderson, G. (1994), 'Industry clustering for economic development', *Economic Development Review*, **12**, 26–32.

Barkley, D.L. (2001), 'Advantages and disadvantages of targeting industry clusters', Regional Economic Development Research Laboratory (REDRL) Research Report 09-2001-01, Clemson, SC: Clemson University.

Becattini, J. (2002), 'Industrial sectors and industrial districts: tools for industrial analysis', *European Planning Studies*, **10**(4), 483–93.

Brenner, T. (2000), 'The evolution of localised industrial clusters: identifying the processes of self-organisation', Papers on Economics and Evolution 0011, Jena, Germany: Max Planck Institute.

Brenner, T. and D. Fornahl (2002), 'Politische Möglichkeiten und Maßnahmen zur Erzeugung branchenspezifischer Cluster', Jena, Germany: Max Planck Institute for Research into Economic Systems.

Bresnahan, T., A. Gambardella and A.L. Saxenian (2001), '"Old economy inputs" for "new economy" outcomes: cluster formation in the New Silicon Valleys', *Industrial and Corporate Change*, **10**(4), 835–60.

Clar, G., B. Sautter and S.H. Hafner-Zimmermann (2008), 'Strategic cluster development: applying strategic policy intelligence to create a joint research agenda', Background paper for the CReATE project, available at: http://www.lets-create.eu/fileadmin/_create/downloads/del-1-2_cluster-background-paper_revised_final.pdf, accessed 10 May 2010.

Cooke, P. (2002), *Knowledge Economies: Clusters, Learning and Cooperative Advantage*, London: Routledge.

Doeringer, P.B. and D.G. Terkla (1995), 'Business strategy and cross-industry clusters', *Economic Development Quarterly*, **9**(3), 225–37.

Enright, M.J. (1996), 'Regional clusters and economic development: a research agenda', in U.H. Staber, N.H. Schaefer and B. Sharma (eds), *Business Networks: Prospects for Regional Development*, Berlin: Walter de Gruyter, pp. 190–214.

Enright, M.J. (2000), 'Survey on the characterization of regional clusters: initial results', working paper, Institute of Economic Policy and Business Strategy, Hong Kong: University of Hong Kong.

Enterprise DG (2003), 'Report on European seminar on cluster policy', Copenhagen, 10 June, available at: http://www.franceclusters.fr/docs/copenhag.pdf, accessed 14 June 2010.

Forslida, R. and K.H. Midelfart (2005), 'Internationalisation, industrial policy and clusters', *Journal of International Economics*, **66**, 197–213.

Hill, E.W. and J.F. Brennan (2000), 'A methodology for identifying the drivers of industrial clusters: the foundation of regional competitive advantage', *Economic Development Quarterly*, **14**, 65–96.

Hospers, G.J. (2004), 'Place marketing in Europe. The branding of the Oresund region', *Intereconomics*, **39**(5), 271–9.

Jacobs, D. and A.P. De Man (1996), 'Clusters, industrial policy and firm strategy: a menu approach', *Technology Analysis and Strategic Management*, **8**(4), 425–37.

Jensen, O.B. and T. Richardson (2004), 'Constructing a transnational mobility region. On the Oresund region and its role in the new European Union spatial policy', in S. von Dosenrode (ed.), *The Nordic Regions and the European Union*, Aldershot, UK: Ashgate, pp. 139–58.

Maskell, P. and G. Törnqvist (1999), *Building a Cross-border Learning Region. Emergence of the North European Oresund Region*, Copenhagen: Copenhagen Business School Press.

Menzel, M.P. and D. Fornahl (2009), 'Cluster life cycles – dimensions and rationales of cluster evolution', *Industrial and Corporate Change*, **19**(1), 205–38.

Öresund Committee, The (2006), *Annual Report 2005*, Copenhagen: The Öresund Committee.

Pedersen, P. (1997), 'Clusters of enterprises within systems of production and distribution', in M.P. van Dijk and R. Rabellotti (eds), *Enterprise Clusters and Networks in Developing Countries*, London: Frank Cass.

Porter, M. (1998), 'Clusters and the new economics of competition', *Harvard Business Review*, November–December.

Pouder, R. and C. John (1996), 'Hot spots and blind spots: geographical clusters of firms and innovation', *The Academy of Management Review*, **21**(4), 1192–225.

Roelandt, T.J.A. and P. den Hertog (1999), 'Cluster analysis and cluster-based policy making in OECD countries: an introduction to the theme', in OECD (ed.), *Boosting Innovation: The Cluster Approach*, Paris: OECD, pp. 9–27.

Rosenfeld, S. (1996), *Overachievers, Business Clusters that Work: Prospects for Regional Development*, Chapel Hill, NC: Regional Technology Strategies.

Rosenfeld, S. (1997), 'Bringing business clusters into the mainstream of economic development', *European Planning Studies*, **5**(1), 3–23.

Saxenian, A. (1994), *Regional Advantage – Culture and Competition in Silicon Valley and Route 128*, Cambridge, MA and London: Harvard University Press.
Sornn-Friese, H. and J.S. Sorensen (2005), 'Linkage lock-in and regional economic development: the case of the Oresund medi-tech plastics industry', *Entrepreneurship and Regional Development*, **17**(4), 267–91.
Woodward, D. (2005), 'Porter's cluster strategy versus industrial targeting', available at: http://www.nercrd.psu.edu/Industry_Targeting/ResearchPapersand Slides/IndCluster.Woodward.pdf, accessed 1 October 2006.

10. Governance structures and practices in cross-border cooperation: similarities and differences between Polish regions

Anna Rogut and Bogdan Piasecki

INTRODUCTION

At the end of the twentieth century, many regions became independent entities in economic terms (Macleod and Jones, 2007). Although they still remain part of national systems they have become economic actors (Capello and Nijkamp, 2009; Gualini, 2006), which rise to the position of primary participants in the global scene. This involves:

> a twin process whereby, firstly, institutional/regulatory arrangements shift from the national scale both upwards to supra-national or global scales and downwards to the scale of the individual body or to local, urban or regional configurations; and, secondly, economic activities and inter-firm networks are becoming simultaneously more localised/regionalised and transnational. (Swyngedouw, 2004, p. 26)

Their main asset in this regard is territorial capital – a combination of unique resources establishing territorial externalities (Capello et al., 2009; Capello et al., 2008; Davoudi et al., 2008; Athey et al., 2007; Sotarauta, 2004; Danson, 2003; Ki, 2001; OECD, 2001). Territorial capital, along with the non-local[1] (Lagendijk and Oinas, 2005), provides the basis for the development of territorial competitive advantages, which are of critical importance for the type, nature and direction of cross-border cooperation. Its efficiency is the derivative of the effectiveness of the mechanism coordinating interactions between political and administrative actors and their broader societal environment (Mehde, 2006). This mechanism is territorial governance defined as a process of vertical and horizontal coordination (Héritier, 2002) 'to promote territorial development at the local-regional level through the sustainable exploitation of territorial capital, in order to reconstitute, at supra-local levels (i.e. the European level), territorial fragmentation by boosting voluntary forms of transnational cooperation and by referring to the principle of subsidiarity at subnational level' (Davoudi et al., 2008, p. 37).

Territorial governance defined as above has been shaped by numerous factors, the most important ones being national constitutional and political contexts, mobilization around regional identities and the Europeanization of regional policy (Newman, 2000). This results in substantial differences in the shape of territorial governance, even in a unitary country, such as Poland. This issue becomes even more complicated in the case of cross-border governance (Popescu, 2008; Yang, 2006; de Vries and Priemus, 2003). Hence, the aim of this chapter is to outline the diversity of governance structures and practices in Poland (in the first part) and to present their impact on the scale, intensity, nature, and effects of cross-border cooperation (in the second part). Empirically, the chapter is based on results from the CBCED[2] project implemented in two contrasting Polish regions: Zgorzelec and Biała Podlaska (case study regions), which differ not only in terms of geographical location but also in terms of historical, cultural, social and economic aspects, which influence the mechanisms of domestic institutional and policy change (European Commission, 2007). The chapter starts with a brief description of these case study regions and ends with short conclusions.

CASE STUDY REGIONS: DESCRIPTION

The regions of Biała Podlaska and Zgorzelec are located at opposite ends of Poland.

Biała Podlaska is situated in the central-eastern part and borders with Belarus. The border was established after World War II by the Yalta treaty, according to which part of the territory that previously belonged to Poland was given to Belarus and incorporated into the Soviet Union. The framework for Polish–Belarusian institutional cross-border cooperation was formed by the Declaration of Good Neighbourhood, Mutual Understanding and Cooperation between the Republic of Poland and Belarus (signed in 1991), the Treaty of Good Neighbourhood and Cooperation (signed in 1992) and a number of other agreements related to border clearances, tourism development, education, and the transit of goods, signed in the following years.[3] Biała Podlaska, with approximately 113 975 inhabitants, is at present one of the poorest counties in Poland. The county is a typically rural one; agriculture is the basis of the county's economy, providing employment to over 60 per cent of working people and also giving rise to the food and meat processing industry. Other developing sectors in the county are: wood (mainly construction carpentry and furniture), metal, manufacture of building materials, clothing and transportation. For the purpose of developing entrepreneurship and to improve the investment attractiveness of the county, a Duty-Free Area in Małaszewicze was created. At the same time, in the Belarusian region of Brest, a Free Economic Zone was established, offering exceptionally beneficial conditions for foreign investments. From 1975 to 1999, the city of Biała Podlaska fulfilled the function of the capital city of the former Biała Podlaska Province, which provided a strong development impulse to the city. After the 1999 administrative reform, the Biała Podlaska Province became part of the present Lublin Province, and the city of Biała Podlaska was relegated to the role of a county seat and, according to our empirical studies, this has had significant consequences for cross-border cooperation (Box 10.1).

BOX 10.1   MARGINALIZATION OF BIAŁA PODLASKA

'It was much better at the beginning of the 1990s. At present, the governor is banned from Brest. The Province Governor's office was moved to Lublin, and Ukraine has become fashionable. We are trying to make up for it, but the Marshals do not want to get engaged. It is a pity, as it is the main trade route, better than Ukraine. We didn't do much with Ukraine; after the big victory of the Orange Revolution the situation has reversed. Lublin is naturally closer to Ukraine and we are left alone with the national border which is more and more dividing.' (Key informant, Communal Office of Terespol)

A different situation is observed in Zgorzelec, located on the western border of Poland with Germany and the Czech Republic (soft border). Its location has undoubtedly been an advantage for cross-border activity, especially since the beginning of the 1990s when a contract of cooperation based on partnership between the cities of Zgorzelec and Görlitz on the German side was signed (1991). The same year, an association called Europa-Haus Görlitz e.V. was created as a platform of cultural cooperation for both cities. Europa-Haus Görlitz participated in a number of civic and institutional initiatives on either side of the Nysa River, and was transformed into a Polish–German institute for the coordination of cross-border issues. In December 1993, working groups, temporary project groups, and a coordination committee were appointed under another partnership contract. Cooperation further intensified in 1995 with the establishment of the Municipal Coordination Commission, which was transformed in 2002 into the Regional Coordination Commission for Niederschlesischer Ober-lausitzkreis and the Zgorzelec County. In 1996, the authorities of Görlitz and Zgorzelec issued a common declaration of the cities of Zgorzelec and Görlitz as well as a draft appendix to the Contract of Cooperation Based on Partnership. The next step was to form a common municipal body named Europe-City Zgorzelec/Görlitz (1998), a cross-border association of communes. In 2006, the cooperation with Görlitz was extended to mutual help in the event of catastrophes, natural disasters and serious accidents. One of the recently signed agreements (September 2006) is concerned with building bridges on the Lusatian Nysa River designed for pedestrian and bicycle traffic (the city of Rothenberg–Toporów/the commune of Pieńsk–Deschka/ the commune of Neißeaue–the city of Pieńsk). Some cross-border cooperation goes beyond Polish–German contacts, involving tripartite cooperation (Poland, Germany and the Czech Republic) and broader international cooperation.[4] At the moment, Zgorzelec has a population of approximately 95 000. Its economy is fairly diversified, covering manufacturing, construction, energy suppliers, and both market and non-market services. Additionally, the attractive natural environment makes the region a potentially good centre for tourism and recreation. The county has a number of locational advantages, including a good transportation network. However, foreign investors prefer counties neighbouring Zgorzelec, such as Kamienna Góra and Wałbrzych, where Special Economic Areas offer them numerous privileges and allowances.

DETERMINANTS OF REGIONAL GOVERNANCE STRUCTURES AND PRACTICES

Poland is a country with a relatively high level of decentralization of the tasks of public administration, which is a positive outcome of the 1990 and 1999 political reforms that established three levels of territorial units: self-governing provinces, counties and communes. The self-government authorities of these units are elected in direct elections. The elected legislative bodies (province, county and commune parliaments) in turn appoint executive bodies: province, county and commune boards. These three levels of self-government are not subordinated hierarchically to one another but rather complement each other; their responsibilities do not overlap, and the province authorities do not supervise county or commune self-governments. The self-government authorities notwithstanding, the Polish government's territorial administration also operates in the provinces and is represented by province governors (*voivodes*). Thus, at the province level, a certain dualism may be observed with respect to public administration, which triggers turf wars and political disputes (Bąk et al., 2007; MRR, 2009).

Additionally, there exist a number of historical (macro) regions whose boundaries differ from those of administrative territories. These regions reflect the events of the past two centuries, when Poland lost its independence[5] and was partitioned by the Russians, Austrians and Prussians. After regaining independence in 1918, an enormous effort was made to unify the territory of the Polish state, particularly with regard to legislation[6] and economic development. This effort was continued after 1945 when the state borders of Poland were determined by decision of the superpowers (Potsdam 1945), which led to the loss of lands located to the east of the so-called Curzon line and the incorporation of the lands located to the east of the Lusatian Nysa and Oder Rivers. However, despite the fact that more than 60 years have passed since the end of World War II, these differences are still quite noticeable (Hryniewicz, 2000; Gorzelak and Jałowiecki, 1997), reflected in the economic and socio-cultural differences between the eastern territories (former Russian and Austrian partitions) and the western territories of Poland (Machaj, 2005). Eastern Poland is less developed in terms of infrastructure, the transport network and economic behaviours (MRR, 2007; Bartkowski, 2003), institutional efficiency of self-government administration with respect to the socio-cultural sphere[7] (MRR, 2009; Swianiewicz et al., 2000), as well as social mobilization (Gorzelak and Jałowiecki, 1997).

Such differences were also observed in the CBCED project, which analysed, among other aspects, governance and policies related to entrepreneurship and cross-border cooperation. The material gathered revealed that despite similar activity of the self-government authorities in both regions studied, the institutional efficiency of the authorities of Biała Podlaska, which was evaluated, for example, on the basis of the intensity of use of the local offer by local entrepreneurs, was lower.

In Biała Podlaska only a marginal number of respondents used any entrepreneurship assistance and no respondent tapped into support designated for the development of cross-border cooperation. Moreover, a number of interviewees claimed that assistance of this kind was not provided in the region and that they had never heard of it. On the other hand, they pointed to the lack of cooperation with the local authorities in the field of exchange of knowledge and reported a sense of isolation in the face of these problems and changes, particularly with respect to legal regulations. This resulted in rancour among businesspeople and a negative disposition towards self-government institutions: 'Here we have to get along on our own. There is no help from the administration. We are left alone with our problems (the embargo)' (Biała Podlaska E3). 'There is a problem. We get no information from the authorities. We must find out everything by ourselves. I think that we are being manipulated' (Biała Podlaska E12).

Zgorzelec presented a different case, as a large proportion of the companies interviewed took advantage of some assistance and successfully cooperated with the local authorities. The problems which entrepreneurs faced in this case primarily resulted from legal regulations concerning the labour market, the fiscal burden and environmental protection, but solving these problems was beyond the competences of local authorities. Similar differences occurred with respect to social mobilization, which was evaluated, for example, on the basis of membership in business organizations and business networks. In Biała Podlaska, only a few of the companies interviewed were members of any associations and their opinion of these organizations was rather poor (Box 10.2). On the other hand, in Zgorzelec over half of the companies surveyed were members of some business organizations, or cooperated with other companies.

BOX 10.2   BIAŁA PODLASKA AND ZGORZELEC: DIFFERENCES IN SOCIAL MOBILIZATION

Biała Podlaska: 'I am a member of the Chamber of Commerce. I do not see any advantages apart from current regional information which I get through the Internet.' (Biała Podlaska Enterprise 7)

Zgorzelec: 'The company is a member of the MTD cluster [Grupa Polska Metal Tworzywo Drewno – the Polish Metal Plastic Wood Group]. This cluster was created by the Zgorzelec County. There are about 50 companies in the cluster, they are beneficiaries of the EQUAL project. This cluster involves small and large businesses. Right now it is in its organizational stage. In the past, the cluster had organized trips abroad to trade fairs and exhibitions. Our cluster has established contact with its

German counterpart, the TIM 22 cluster, which will be supporting us. I don't have any more information on this subject, as I
don't always participate in meetings organized by the cluster.'
(Zgorzelec Enterprise 1)

On the basis of these differences, diverging territorial governance structures and practices have been developed, 'constituted by the social institutions and knowledges constructed by people in the course of the
production of place' (Lewis et al., 2002, p. 444; see also Menahem and
Stein, 2008; Ezzamel and Reed, 2008; Demil and Lecocq, 2006; Bovaird,
2005; Silva, 2004; Leiblein, 2003; Leibovitz, 2003; OECD, 2002; Olberding, 2002; Barzelay, 2001; Valler et al., 2000; Pierre, 1999; Stoker, 1998).
These structures and practices might be attributed to two different kinds of
logic of domestic policy change and learning:[8] the 'logic of consequentialism', that was characteristic of Biała Podlaska and the 'logic of appropriateness' that was characteristic of Zgorzelec:

> The 'logic of consequentialism' points to the role of redistribution of resources
> and conceives of existing formal institutions as crucial mediating factors that
> affect domestic actors' capacity for action and hence policy and institutional
> change. This process has been conceptualized as 'single-loop learning'. (Euro-
> pean Commission, 2007, p. 27)

The other logic 'focuses on the process of social learning as a fundamental
mechanism of domestic change and identifies networks [...] and informal
institutions [...] as "thick" mediating mechanisms' (European Commission,
2007, p. 27).

As a result, in the case study regions one arrives at different constellations
of persons/organizations involved in shaping and developing cross-border
cooperation, including the decision-making process, the manner of making
decisions, the extent to which real social needs are taken into account, the
manner of implementation of measures, and so on (Binder et al., 2007;
Mokre and Puntscher-Riekmann, 2007; Bache and Flinders, 2004; Valler et
al., 2000).

DIFFERENCES IN CROSS-BORDER GOVERNANCE STRUCTURES AND PRACTICES

The above-mentioned disparities are further compounded by the different
conditions of cross-border cooperation resulting from Poland's membership in the European Union[9] and the introduction of visas and other

formalities which impede crossing at the Polish–Belarusian border. Prior to Poland's accession to the European Union, neither Belarusians nor Polish citizens needed visas to cross the border. This lack of visa requirements created unusually advantageous conditions for communication and the movement of people. This was also to some extent true of trade exchange between the regions lying on either side of the border, although a lack of well-developed infrastructure as well as different bureaucratic regulations did hinder this exchange. After Poland's accession to the EU in 2004, the Polish–Belarusian border became an external border of the EU (hard border). However, even before that, on 1 October 2003, visas were introduced for Polish and Belarusian citizens following EU requirements. The introduction of visas created significant difficulties for trade as well as for tourist and cultural exchange between Poland and Belarus (Box 10.3).

BOX 10.3   EASTERN BORDER AS A BARRIER TO CROSS-BORDER COOPERATION

According to our informants, 'big time politics' exacerbates the already bad situation at border crossings: 'The border is the barrier. Uncertainty about the possibility of crossing it is tiresome. Many people give up the opportunity to visit Belarus as they do not know how they will be treated at the border and how long it will take to cross it. This is a big discomfort in cross-border contacts' (Key informant, Biała Podlaska Municipality). Additionally, 'the border hampers initiating cooperation. Anybody who goes there for the first time will think ten times before he does it again [...] Along with the integration with EU we neglect our neighbours, which is not normal. For too long already has the border been something sick and inhuman, and when people are out of touch with each other, they tend to believe stereotypes much more easily.' (Key informant, Communal Office of Terespol)

In addition, substantial political differences influence the nature of Polish and Belarusian commercial relations. Biała Podlaska is not an exception with respect to these differences, as they occur along the entire eastern border. Other regions which cooperate with, for example, Russia also face similar problems. Nevertheless, Belarus is unique in this respect (Box 10.4).

BOX 10.4   SPECIFICITY OF BELARUS AS A
PARTNER FOR CROSS-BORDER
COOPERATION

Entrepreneurs who are cooperating with Belarus and Russia emphasize that the latter country represents considerably more advanced privatization processes and liberalization of trade contacts, while Belarus remains a centrally controlled economy, both with respect to the prevailing type of ownership and the freedom of cross-border and international cooperation (all decisions related to current business activities and commercial contracts are made or agreed at higher-than-regional level). This often impedes equality of relations. Unlike the Polish local authorities, which are quite independent in terms of decision making, their Belarusian counterparts are deprived of this autonomy and all activities they would like to initiate must be consulted at a higher level including the national one: 'In the case of formal contacts, the foreign policies of both countries as well as the domestic policies of Belarus have a huge impact on mutual trust between partners. [...] A negative lesson is organizing meetings, conferences and training courses at the time of elections in neighbouring countries. The election of new authorities and replacement of clerical personnel on the eastern side delayed or even thwarted the realization of projects.' (Key informant, Marshall's Office of Lublin)

A different situation is observed in Zgorzelec located on the western border of Poland (soft border), where political differences and visa requirements have become a thing of the past. The new era of Polish–German institutional cross-border cooperation dates back to the early 1990s, when a contract of cooperation based on partnership between the cities of Zgorzelec in Poland and Görlitz on the German side was signed (1991). The same year, the above-mentioned Europa-Haus Görlitz e.V. was established as a platform of cultural cooperation for both cities. Some cross-border cooperation moves beyond Polish–German relations, involving tripartite collaboration (Poland, Germany and the Czech Republic) and broader international cooperation.[10] All of these contacts support the continuity of Polish–German cross-border cooperation and independence of political changes or personal changes (Box 10.5).

BOX 10.5   WESTERN BORDER AS AN ENABLER FOR CROSS-BORDER COOPERATION

'In our region, institutions cooperate smoothly with one another. After the last elections, it turned out that this cooperation was still possible. Every head of a commune or county and every mayor want to work together for their region. We have the example of the Zgorzelec–Bogatynia Park, which was started in March 2006 and is now being developed by the new authorities. It is a continuation of the work of the previous mayors and heads of counties – this is important, in particular in view of the fact that the cooperation runs smoothly.' (Key informant, Zgorzelec County Office)

Consequently, different models of cross-border governance have emerged: a government model in Biała Podlaska (agreement at the national level supported by expression of interest from the regional authorities) and a self-government model in Zgorzelec (agreements between local authorities) (see Table 10.1).

GOVERNANCE: SCALE, INTENSITY AND CHARACTER OF INSTITUTIONAL CROSS-BORDER COOPERATION

Cross-border cooperation has both political and economic aspects. The first is consistent with the general trend reflected in the European regional policy, which perceives a region as a 'fundamental basis of economic and social life' (Macleod and Jones, 2007, p. 1178) and promotes cross-border cooperation as an instrument used to initiate and broaden integration (ESPON, 2006; Gable, 2005; AGEG, AEBR and ARFE, 2004; Anderson et al., 2003). This trend includes a number of potential forms of institutional cooperation between regional and local authorities (Perkmann, 2003) supported by dedicated EU initiatives. The actual shape of this cooperation, its intensity and effectiveness in creating a friendly environment for economic cooperation depend on regional and cross-border governance structures and practices; this is perfectly demonstrated by the two Polish case study regions. Although during the last 20 years both have embraced institutional cross-border cooperation (Table 10.2), Biała Podlaska has developed a small number of examples of such cooperation compared with Zgorzelec.

Table 10.1   Models of cross-border governance

Biała Podlaska	Zgorzelec
• Hard border of the EU	• Soft border of the EU
• Relatively weak Polish eastern foreign policy	• Good relationships with EU partners
• Essential system differences hampering cross-border cooperation, subject to foreign policy (out of control of regional authorities)	• Democracy on both sides
• Different level of autonomy: unlike Polish local authorities that are quite independent in taking decisions, their Belarusian counterparts are deprived of decision autonomy and all the activities they want to initiate must be consulted at a higher level including the national one	• Similar level of autonomy of regional/local authorities
• More formal, official contacts focused on a limited number of areas with the smallest conflict potential	• Wide spectrum of formal and informal contacts covering all areas of socio-economic life

As a consequence there are the same governance structures, but different governance practices (a government model in the case of Biała Podlaska versus a self-government model in Zgorzelec).

Source: Authors.

Moreover, after 2004 (Poland's accession to the European Union) the development of some of these slowed significantly.

This particularly affected the Bug Euroregion, which was established in 1995 and encompassed the Lublin Province (in which Biała Podlaska is located) as well as the border regions of Belarus (the Brest Province) and Ukraine (the Volhynian County with the capital city of Lutsk). One of the aims of the Euroregion was to make use of the common cultural heritage as well as to work jointly for the promotion of peace between the neighbouring nations.[11] In 1996, the Polish–Belarusian International Coordination Committee for Cross-Border Cooperation was created, although the last meeting of the Committee took place in Minsk in 2004. Another example is the Cooperation Agreement between the Biała Podlaska County and Brest County, signed in March 2000, which was an important step towards large-scale formal cooperation. It concerned cooperation between governmental authorities, local authorities, economic and social organizations as

Table 10.2 Forms of institutional cross-border cooperation

Type of cooperation	Objectives	Field	Type of partner	Features		Guarantor of continuity
				Level of formalization		
				Basis for cooperation	Organization of cooperation	
Cooperation of administrative authorities	Creating and developing legal and institutional structures for cross-border cooperation	Multitude of areas encompassing the whole process of regional development	Foreign counterpart	Long-term framework agreements Individual projects	Complex organizational structures	The institutional factor (continuity of governance and politics, long-term agreements are the basis)
Cooperation of organizations of entrepreneurs	Goals subject to the type of one's business	Uniform areas defined by the type of one's business		Cooperation agreement Individual projects	Temporary structures created to manage particular projects	The individual factor (openness of particular people to cooperation, lack of continuity due to project-based cooperation)
Cooperation of business support institutions				Individual projects		
Cooperation of other institutions				Individual projects		

Source: Authors.

well as educational and cultural organizations in the fields of agriculture, environmental protection, civil defence, education, culture, sport and tourism. The basic objective, as defined in the contract, was cooperation in attracting domestic and foreign investors, and helping local enterprises in initiating and expanding mutual contacts. However, the implementation of this agreement was weighed down by impediments in crossing the border following Poland's accession to the European Union (Box 10.6).

BOX 10.6 BIAŁA PODLASKA: IMPEDIMENTS IN CROSSING THE BORDER

'In order to create a good atmosphere, cross-border cooperation with the city of Brest was initiated. An agreement on the partnership of cities was signed [...]. The bridge on the Bug River was marked as the bridge of peace. There were plenty of delegations and mutual visits. The biggest problem was to cross the border. An idea was conceived to provide a train which would make the entrepreneurs' operations easier. Unfortunately, it failed.' (Key informant, Biała Podlaska Municipality)

Partnership agreements, for example, between Biała Podlaska and the Belarusian cities of Brest and Baranowicze, were slightly more successful.[12] This cooperation is concerned with promoting economic partnership through developing the local economy, exchanging experience in the area of municipal administration, public transportation and water supply, cooperation in the field of culture, education and sport, as well as supporting associations which intend to cooperate (Box 10.7).

BOX 10.7 BIAŁA PODLASKA: PARTNERSHIP AGREEMENTS

'Apart from occasional visits and revisits of officials there is exchange in the field of culture, sport, non-economic activities, and youth exchange. Poland's membership in the EU ensured the possibility to use the PHARE CBC funds designated for cross-border cooperation, and we have carried out one project with Baranowicze. The financial aspect of the European Union intensifies this cooperation and creates new instruments' (Key informant City Office of Biała Podlaska). Other examples involve agreements signed by other counties of the Biała Podlaska Province: 'The county office of Zalesie has signed two agreements: the first one with a school in Baranowicze (junior high school attended by about 1200 pupils) and the other one with the county on the Belarusian side of the border. The agreement was signed in 2006. Its aim was teacher and student exchange' (Key informant, Communal Office of Zalesie). 'The county of Terespol has signed a partnership agreement with Brest. We are partners with the head of the county, Polish consulate and other authorities. We maintain good relations on a regular basis. There is a proposal for a new Euroregion – Przebuże. Representatives in Minsk, Kiev, Brussels and the Polish ambassador are helping us with this project' (Key informant, Communal Office of Terespol). 'On the 1st of July, 2006, an agreement was signed on the development of cooperation between Brest and the border cities of Biała Podlaska, Włodawa, Międzyrzecze Podlaskie, and Terespol, as well as between the county of Terespol and the county of Biała Podlaska.' (Key informant, Belarusian Consulate in Biała Podlaska)

Organizations of entrepreneurs, business support organizations and other institutions have also been involved in successful cooperation. For instance, in 2000, a Cooperation Declaration was signed by the Biała Podlaska County and the Belarusian Association of Entrepreneurs and Employers in Minsk. In that agreement, entrepreneurs were represented by the Biała Podlaska Chamber of Commerce. As a result, meetings of entrepreneurs from the Biała Podlaska County and the Brest County representing different kinds of businesses are held in the Biała Podlaska County (Box 10.8).

BOX 10.8   BIAŁA PODLASKA: CROSS-BORDER
          COOPERATION OF BUSINESS
          ORGANIZATIONS

An agreement was signed by the Biała Podlaska Association for Regional Development and the Association of Private Entrepreneurs 'Sodejstwie' – an organization of entrepreneurs from the city of Brest: 'In our cooperation with the "Sodejstwie" association, within the framework of joint projects, we are trying to match entrepreneurs both directly – through seminars, conferences and business meetings, and indirectly – through the publishing of booklets presenting the products and services of Polish and Belarusian entrepreneurs' (Key informant, Biała Podlaska Association for Regional Development and Head of the Commune of Wisznice). In contrast, in the case of the Guild of Craftsmen and Entrepreneurs, 'there is no contact with the Guild in Belarus' (Key informant, Guild of Crafts and Entrepreneurs). Instead, contacts with craft organizations from Germany and France are evolving.

The case of Zgorzelec was (and still is) quite different. Cross-border cooperation between the local authorities has been ongoing for many years, based on long-term international agreements (Box 10.9).

BOX 10.9   ZGORZELEC: CROSS-BORDER COOPERATION BETWEEN THE LOCAL AUTHORITIES

The Zgorzelec County Office 'has been involved in cross-border cooperation for many years now on the basis of the concluded agreements. The Zgorzelec County also cooperates with the neighbouring Lower Silesian–Upper Lusatian County, with which it holds working meetings of the county councils (so far two have taken place). Their objective is to determine joint directions of development and carry out projects motivated by mutual interests. This cooperation has resulted in a quadrilateral agreement (September 2003) concerning the cooperation of the City of Görlitz, the Lower Silesian–Upper Lusatian County, the City of Zgorzelec, and the Zgorzelec County (prior to that time there had been separate agreements between the cities and the counties), which established the Regional Coordination Commission.' (Key informant, Zgorzelec County Office)

This has given rise to some organizational structures (for example, the Regional Coordination Commission and the Polish–German Institute for Coordination of Cross-Border Issues) that guarantee smooth, high quality cooperation. Such structures are being developed both at the level of cooperating communes and counties, as well as at the level of cooperating regions (Box 10.10).

BOX 10.10   ZGORZELEC: CROSS-BORDER ORGANIZATIONAL STRUCTURES

'The Marshal's Office participates in the meetings of the Lower Silesian–Saxon working group, which plans, coordinates, and implements joint undertakings. In the meetings, they review their cooperation to date and determine future tasks. There are also joint meetings of the Education and Sports Commissions of the Saxon Landtag and the Commissions of the Lower Silesian Local Assembly (Parliament). In one of such meetings, in April 2006, they signed a joint declaration concerning cooperation between the Saxon Ministry of Education and the Social Department of the Marshal's Office of the Lower Silesian Province. The Lower Silesian Province, just like in previous years, will participate in two commissions: the Polish–Czech Intergovernmental Commission for Cross-Border Cooperation and the Polish–German Intergovernmental Commission for Interregional and Cross-Border Cooperation. It will also participate in the Polish–Ukrainian Coordination Council for Intergovernmental Cooperation. Those Commissions develop a very broad joint agenda of activities related to cooperation in the fields of tourism, transport, infrastructure, economic cooperation, and others – generally speaking in all possible areas of cooperation. Every year, the Commissions select a number of priority activities. [...] Generally speaking, cooperation at the institutional level is uninterrupted, close, regular, and formal. It is formal due to agreements, and close due to joint working committees and interregional programmes.' (Key informant, Marshall's Office).

One of the most interesting initiatives is the European city Görlitz-Zgorzelec, which is intended to be transformed into a single bilingual, multicultural city with new opportunities related to economic and cultural cooperation. Activities at the level of municipal policies are meant to create a common urban profile and a common cultural centre, common educational institutions, common higher education, common youth culture, and a network of cross-border business relations. Another example is Programme Enlarge-net (Box 10.11).

BOX 10.11   ZGORZELEC: PROGRAMME ENLARGE–NET

'Program Enlarge-net was a trinational concept of spatial development of the border regions of Lower Silesia, the northern part of the Czech Republic, and Saxony. Enlarge-net was established at the end of October 2002 on the initiative of the city of Dresden, the capital of the federal state of Saxony, as an EU pilot programme. The Germans conducted the project, which involved both Poles and Czechs. The objective of the programme was to create a common area consisting of Saxony, Lower Silesia, and three neighbouring Czech areas. It was also meant to solve economic, transportation, and social problems. After over four years of cooperation, the conclusion was that the programme had started too early. It turned out that none of the participating countries was mature enough to create a reasonably uniform area which would have a Czech–Polish–German government, one official language, one currency, and one transportation system, where tourism could flourish. The project ended in 2006.' (Key informant, Zgorzelec Municipality)

Similar intensive cooperation is typical of organizations of entrepreneurs and other regional institutions. For instance, the Federation of Employers of Western Poland established such a cooperation as early as 1993. The Guild of Various Crafts and Small Entrepreneurship in Zgorzelec took advantage of such cooperation long before Poland became a member of the European Union in order to be better prepared for the membership. However, in contrast to the cooperation of administrative authorities, the cooperation of other organizations, conducted independently or in collaboration with other local/regional organizations, is limited to the narrow areas of interest of these organizations.

Nevertheless, the cooperation has led to a number of interesting projects. They include: the Lusatian Buildings Country (cultural heritage); Our Heritage – Walking across Upper Lusatia and a Tourist Guide to the Zgorzelec County (tourism); Academic Coordination Centre in the Neisse–Nisa–Nysa Euroregion (scientific cooperation). Other examples include Polish–German Business Days, which already have a long tradition and attract businesspeople, council representatives as well as economic organizations from Poland, Germany and the Czech Republic (entrepreneurship development). Projects are also concerned with the quality of professional education and employment on both sides of the Nysa (learning and education); a common linguistic training programme for medical staff from Zgorzelec and Görlitz concerning direct contact with patients (medical services) and the IRC Neisse Cluster (Information Relay Centres from the Czech Republic, Saxony, and Western Poland, including the Opole, Lower Silesian, Greater Poland, Lubusz, and West Pomerania provinces). Although no system solutions have been developed on the basis of those projects, some of them have led to creating cross-border structures, in particular related to higher education. Examples include: a joint venture by the Zittau/Görlitz University and universities from Wrocław and Liberec called the Neisse University specializing in post-graduate engineering and management studies; an international college 'Collegium Pontes' created by the Sachsen Institute of Cultural Infrastructure in Görlitz, the University of Wrocław, and Charles University in Prague; and the International Summer School of Arts of the Saxon Institute of Cultural Infrastructure.

Consequently, Zgorzelec has created much more favourable conditions than Biała Podlaska in terms of the development of comprehensive enterprise cross-border cooperation, especially in the case of SMEs (local authorities involved in cross-border cooperation fulfil the function of liaisons; and they initiate and stimulate cooperation development, as well as helping entrepreneurs with finding business partners), reflected in first cross-border cluster initiatives. An interesting example is an initiative informally known as 'The Textile Euroregion' which is being pursued in the textile and clothes industries in the area of the German states (Länder) of Brandenburg and Saxony, the Czech Republic and Poland. The major aim of this cooperation is to strengthen the economic bonds of the border regions by integrating the textile and clothing industries. The Zgorzelec County Office also carries out some interesting activities stimulating cluster development, labelled 'New opportunities for cross-border labour market and economy of the Euroregion of the Neisse–Nisa–Nysa'. This project aims at fostering competitiveness and innovation and stimulating cross-border cooperation through creating a stable cooperation network involving companies and institutions in the metal, wood and plastic sectors. Other fields representing some potential for the development of clusters are tourism and the motor industry.

In contrast, even though Biała Podlaska's local and provincial authorities and business support organizations are involved in cross-border cooperation, this does not lead to any tangible actions apart from courtesy visits or exchanges of experience. The main difficulty in the development of cross-border cooperation is the consequences of the post-accession sealing of the border and the tense relations between Poland and Belarus at the national level, which has largely weighed down on cooperation between SMEs in the region. This makes it difficult to transform the present potential, particularly in the field of tourism, into vibrant, rapidly developing cross-border clusters.

CONCLUSIONS

The aim of this chapter was to outline the diversity of governance structures and practices in Poland and present their impact on the scale, intensity, nature and effects of cross-border cooperation. The results presented indicate a degree of diversification in governance structures and practices in Poland in response to the diversity of political and socio-cultural contexts in which cross-border cooperation is conducted. The political context focuses on the implications of Poland's membership in the European Union (hard versus soft borders) and the dissimilarity versus similarity of the political systems which form the principal framework conditions for cross-border cooperation in both case study regions.

As a result, two different models of cross-border governance have emerged, reflecting different contexts for cross-border cooperation: governmental governance in the case of Biała Podlaska and self-governmental governance in the case of Zgorzelec. The socio-cultural context includes differences in the institutional efficiency of self-government administration with respect to the socio-cultural sphere as well as social mobilization and consolidation of disparate mechanisms of development of regional governance. In Biała Podlaska, this is primarily based on the logic of consequentialism, whilst in Zgorzelec it is closer to the logic of appropriateness (Figure 10.1).

Consequently, Biała Podlaska and Zgorzelec are situated at opposite poles in terms of the likelihood of transforming state borders into assets, opening the way for the cross-border regions to become successful centres of growth (ESPON and Interact, 2007).

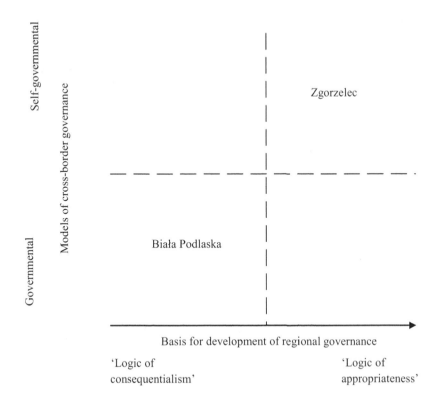

*Figure 10.1   Models of territorial governance for cross-border
cooperation*

NOTES

1. The non-local represents everything that local relations do not include, and which allows local companies and organizations to 'tap into different technical and institutional resources, and to "stay tuned"' (Lagendijk and Oinas, 2005, p. 13).
2. 'Challenges and Prospects of Cross-border Cooperation in the Context of EU Enlargement', 6 Framework Programme, contract no. 029038.
3. Moreover, city offices, province offices, communes and business organizations enter into separate agreements with East European partners. More information on the website: http://www.msz.gov.pl/apps/apps/?portlet=bpt/list.
4. For more information see: http://free.art.pl/euroopera, http://www.euroregion-nysa.pl, http://www.equal.noweszanse.pl, http://www.powiat.zgorzelec.pl, http://www.bip. powiat. zgorzelec.pl, http://www.zgorzelec.com.
5. The last partition of Poland took place in 1795.
6. As three legal systems were in force when Poland regained independence.

7. Integration of local societies, social ties, political culture, self-governance, activity and local democracy.
8. For a comprehensive discussion of studies on learning processes see Welter et al. (Chapter 3 in this volume).
9. This problem is discussed in greater detail in Venesaar and Pihlak (Chapter 2 in this volume).
10. For more information see: http://free.art.pl/euroopera, http://www.euroregion-nysa.pl, http://www.equal.noweszanse.pl, http://www.powiat.zgorzelec.pl, http://www.bip. powiat.zgorzelec.pl, http://www.zgorzelec.com.
11. For more information see: http://www.euroregionbug.pl.
12. For more information see: http://www.bialapodlaska.pl.

REFERENCES

AGEG, AEBR, ARFE (2004), 'European charter for border and cross-border regions: new version', available at: http://www.aebr.net/publikationen/pdfs/ Charta_Final_071004.gb.pdf, accessed 2 April 2007.

Anderson, J., L. O'Dowd and T.M. Wilson (eds) (2003), *New Borders for a Changing Europe–Cross-border Cooperation and Governance*, London: Frank Cass Publishers.

Athey, G., M. Nathan and C. Webber (2007), 'What role do cities play in innovation, and to what extent do we need city-based innovation policies and approaches?', NESTA Working Paper 01, available at: www.nesta.org.uk/assets/pdf/cities_ and_innovation_working_paper_NESTA.pdf, accessed 29 June 2007.

Bache, I. and M. Flinders (2004), 'Multi-level governance and the study of the British state', *Public Policy and Administration*, **19**(1), 31–51.

Bąk, A., R. Chmielewski, M. Krasowska, M. Piotrowska and A. Szymborska (2007), *Raport o rozwoju i polityce regionalnej*, Warsaw: Ministerstwo Rozwoju Regionalnego.

Bartkowski, J. (2003), *Tradycja i polityka. Wpływ tradycji kulturowych polskich regionów na współczesne zachowania społeczne i polityczne*, Warsaw: Wydawnictwo Akademickie Żak.

Barzelay, M. (2001), *The New Public Management: Improving Research and Policy Dialogue*, Oxford, Berkeley and Los Angeles: University of California Press.

Binder, J.K., P. Slits, R. Stoquart, J. Mullen and C.B. Schubert (2007), 'Towards an EU approach to democratic local governance, decentralization and territorial development', available at: http://ec.europa.eu/development/icenter/repository/ Consultation7_background-paper_2008-04-21_EN.pdf, accessed 12 July 2009.

Bovaird, T. (2005), 'Public governance: balancing stakeholder power in a network society', *International Review of Administrative Science*, **71**(2), 217–28.

Capello, R. and P. Nijkamp (eds) (2009), *Handbook of Regional Growth and Development Theories*, Cheltenham, UK and Northampton, MA, USA: Edward Elgar.

Capello, R., R. Camagni, B. Chizzolini and U. Fratesi (2008), *Modelling Regional Scenarios for the Enlarged Europe: European Competitiveness and Global Strategies*, Berlin: Springer.

Capello, R., A. Caragliu and P. Nijkamp (2009), 'Territorial capital and regional growth: increasing returns in cognitive knowledge use', available at: http://www.tinbergen.nl/discussionpapers/09059.pdf, accessed 20 September 2009.

Danson, M.W. (2003), 'Territorial innovation models: a critical survey', *Regional Studies*, **37**(3), 289–302.

Davoudi, S., N. Evans, F. Governa and M. Santangelo (2008), 'Territorial governance in the making: approaches, methodologies, practices', *Boletin de la A.G.E.N.*, **46**, 33–52.

de Vries, J. and H. Priemus (2003), 'Megacorridors in north-west Europe: issues for transnational spatial governance', *Journal of Transport Geography*, **11**, 225–33.

Demil, B. and X. Lecocq (2006), 'Neither market nor hierarchy nor network: the emergence of bazaar governance', *Organization Studies*, **27**(10), 1447–66.

ESPON (2006), 'Territory matters for competitiveness and cohesion', ESPON Synthesis report III, available at: http://www.espon.eu/mmp/online/website/content/publications/98/1229/file_2471/final-synthesis-reportiii_web.pdf, accessed 3 December 2006.

ESPON and Interact (2007), 'Cross-border cooperation: cross-thematic study of INTERREG and ESPON activities', available at: http://www.espon.eu/mmp/online/website/content/interact/1316/80/file_2792/Cross-Border_Cooperation_web.pdf, accessed 9 November 2008.

European Commission (2007), 'EU enlargement and multi-level governance in European regional and environment policies: patterns of learning, adaptation and Europeanization among cohesion countries (Greece, Ireland, Portugal) and lessons for new members (Hungary, Poland)', ADAPT final report, Luxemburg: European Communities.

Ezzamel, M. and M. Reed (2008), 'Governance: a code of multiple colours', *Human Relations*, **61**(5), 597–615.

Gable, J. (2005), 'Governance and cross-border cooperation', available at: http://www.aebr.net/publikationen/pdfs/governancevortragjoensuu.gb.pdf, accessed 3 July 2007.

Gorzelak, G. and B. Jałowiecki (eds) (1997), *Koniunktura gospodarcza i mobilizacja społeczna w gminach '96*, Warsaw: Uniwersytet Warszawski. Europejski Instytut Rozwoju Regionalnego i Lokalnego.

Gualini, E. (2006), 'The rescaling of governance in Europe: new spatial and institutional rationales', *European Planning Studies*, **14**(7), 881–904.

Héritier, A. (ed.) (2002), *Common Goods: Reinventing European and International Governance*, Lanham, MD: Rowman and Littlefield Publishers.

Hryniewicz, J.T. (2000), 'Endo- i egzogenne czynniki rozwoju gospodarczego gmin i regionów', *Studia Regionalne i Lokalne*, **2**(2), 53–77.

Ki, J.-H. (2001), 'The role of two agglomeration economies in the production of innovation: a comparison between localization economies and urbanization economies', *Enterprise and Innovation Management Studies*, **2**(2), 103–17.

Lagendijk, A. and P. Oinas (2005), 'Proximity, external relations and local economic development', in A. Lagendijk and P. Oinas (eds), *Proximity, Distance and Diversity: Issues on Economic Interaction and Local Development*, Aldershot, UK and Burlington, VT: Ashgate, pp. 3–22.

Leiblein, M.J. (2003), 'The choice of organizational governance form and performance: predictions from transaction cost, resource-based, and real options theories', *Journal of Management*, **29**(6), 937–61.

Leibovitz, J. (2003), 'Institutional barriers to associative city-region governance: the politics of institution-building and economic governance in "Canada's Technology Triangle"', *Urban Studies*, **40**(13), 2613–42.

Lewis, N., W. Moran, P. Perrier-Cornet and J. Barker (2002), 'Territoriality, enterprise and réglementation in industry governance', *Progress in Human Geography*, **26**(4), 433–62.

Machaj, I. (2005), *Społeczno-kulturowe konteksty tożsamości mieszkańców wschodniego i zachodniego pogranicza Polski*, Warsaw: Wydawnictwo Naukowe Scholar.

Macleod, G. and M. Jones (2007), 'Territorial, scalar, networked, connected: in what sense a "regional world"?', *Regional Studies*, **41**(9), 1177–91.

Mehde, V. (2006), 'Governance, administrative science, and the paradoxes of new public management', *Public Policy and Administration*, **21**(4), 60–81.

Menahem, G. and R. Stein (2008), 'Between new governance and hollow state: examining varieties of social service provision networks in Israeli municipalities', available at: http://www.allacademic.com/meta/p_mla_apa_research_citation/2/7/9/3/6/p279363_index.html, accessed 30 March 2009.

Mokre, M. and S. Puntscher-Riekmann (2007), 'From good governance to democratic governance? A policy review of the first wave of European governance research', Policy Review Series no. 2, Luxembourg: European Communities.

MRR (2007), 'Program Operacyjny Rozwój Polski Wschodniej 2007–2013', Ministerstwo Rozwoju Regionalnego, available at: http://www.polskawschodnia.gov.pl/Dokumenty/Lists/Dokumentyprogramowe/Attachments/87/PO_RPW_17072009.pdf, accessed 22 August 2009.

MRR (2009), 'Rozwój regionalny w Polsce. Raport 2009', Warsaw: Ministerstwo Rozwoju Regionalnego.

Newman, D. (2000), 'Changing patterns of regional governance in the EU', *Urban Studies*, **37**(5–6), 895–908.

OECD (2001), *Territorial Outlook. Territorial Economy*, Paris: OECD Publishing.

OECD (2002), *Distributed Public Governance: Agencies, Authorities and Other Government Bodies*, Paris: OECD Publishing.

Olberding, J.C. (2002), 'Diving into the "third-waves" of regional governance and economic development strategies: a study of regional partnership for economic development in US metropolitan areas', *Economic Development Quarterly*, **16**(3), 251–72.

Perkmann, M. (2003), 'Construction of new territorial scales: a framework and case study of the EUREGIO cross-border region', *European Urban and Regional Studies*, **10**(2), 153–71.

Pierre, J. (1999), 'Models of urban governance: the institutional dimension of urban politics', *Urban Affairs Review*, **34**(3), 372–96.

Popescu, G. (2008), 'The conflicting logics of cross-border reterritorialization: geopolitics of Euroregions in Eastern Europe', *Political Geography*, **27**, 418–38.

Silva, C.N. (2004), 'Public–private partnership and urban governance: towards a new concept of local government', in M. Barlow and D. Wastl-Walter (eds), *New*

Challenges in Local and Regional Administration, Aldershot, UK and Burlington, VT: Ashgate, pp. 73–84.

Sotarauta, M. (2004), 'Strategy development in learning cities. From classical rhetoric towards dynamic capabilities', SENTE Working Papers no. 8/2004, Tampere: University of Tampere.

Stoker, G. (1998), 'Public–private partnership and urban governance', in P. Jon (ed.), *Partnership in Urban Governance. European and American Experience*, London: Macmillan, pp. 34–51.

Swianiewicz, P., W. Ziemianowicz and M. Mackiewicz (2000), *Sprawność instytucjonalna administracji samorządowej w Polsce: zróżnicowanie regionalne*, Gdansk: Instytut Badań nad Gospodarką Rynkową.

Swyngedouw, E. (2004), 'Globalization or "glocalization"? Networks, territories and rescaling', *Cambridge Review of International Affairs*, **17**(1), 25–48.

Valler, D., A. Wood and P. North (2000), 'Local governance and local business interests: a critical review', *Progress in Human Geography*, **24**(3), 409–28.

Yang, C. (2006), 'The geopolitics of cross-boundary governance in the Greater Pearl River Delta, China: a case study of the proposed Hong Kong–Zhuhai–Macao Bridge', *Political Geography*, **25**, 817–35.

11. Public policy and cross-border entrepreneurship in EU border regions: an enabling or constraining influence?

David Smallbone and Mirela Xheneti

INTRODUCTION

Cross-border entrepreneurship (CBE) refers to forms of entrepreneurial activity that cross international borders and which usually involve some form of cooperation. It offers potential benefits for regions as well as for individual enterprises. For entrepreneurs, it offers an opportunity to access new markets and sources of supply, as well as capital, labour and technology. Cross-border entrepreneurship may contribute to positive externalities on both sides of the border for regions that are typically peripheral to the core of economic activity in their national territories. In this context, cross-border entrepreneurship may be viewed as a potential asset for regional development that policy makers can actively promote.

A wide range of different types of entrepreneurial activity can take place across international borders, from informal petty trading activity at one extreme to formalized joint ventures and strategic alliances between enterprises at the other. At a global level, the increasing internationalization of production systems inevitably leads to the development of cross-border operations, in forms that include subcontracting, joint ventures and franchise arrangements (Weaver, 2000). Whilst some forms may represent long-term cooperation, others may have a limited life, according to the circumstances which led to their creation. Moreover, whilst some links may be between two SMEs, others may involve some form of cooperation arrangement between SMEs and larger companies, whilst some of the simpler forms may involve individual entrepreneurs rather than businesses.

Creating a policy environment to enable and facilitate productive forms of cross-border entrepreneurship may be viewed as a necessary part of the regional development strategies for these border regions, although this is likely to be more difficult to achieve in situations where the border is a 'hard' external border of the EU where border controls represent a potential barrier to movement. In the case of the EU, enlargement has focused policy attention on the encouragement of cross-border cooperation as a means of reducing the increasing disparities between central and peripheral regions in Europe, some of which are associated with the process of enlargement itself. Although cross-border cooperation may be viewed as an asset for regional development, offering potential economic benefits, the hetero-geneity of border regions (including those with hard and soft borders) and the different levels of economic development, institutional settings and levels of regional entrepreneurship affect the nature and extent of inter-action across borders. It is important that this heterogeneity is taken into account when designing policies to assist in the development of these regions.

Taking these features of cross-border cooperation into account, the aim of this chapter is to assess the role of public policy in the development of cross-border entrepreneurship (CBE), identifying both enabling and con-straining influences. Whilst previous research on cross-border cooperation has tended to focus on institutional cooperation and the policy implications of promoting this type of activity, in this chapter we focus particularly on cross-border entrepreneurial activities. The approach taken adopts a broadly based view of what constitutes policy relevant to entrepreneurship development in general and CBE in particular. Our analysis includes the influence of policies specifically aimed at CBE but also wider policy influences. In this regard, the chapter considers cross-border institutional cooperation in so far as it involves entrepreneurs, together with public policies and actions affecting the environment for cross-border entre-preneurial activity. This chapter uses a combination of primary data from the CBCED project (interviews with key informants and entrepreneurs) and secondary data sources to identify: (a) the policies in place relevant to entrepreneurship development and cross-border cooperation; and (b) the awareness and experience of entrepreneurs with regard to these policies and a wider set of public policies and state actions that affect the business environment for entrepreneurial activity.

The key informants interviewed were chosen from a wide range of organizations, including local/regional authorities, chambers of commerce and industry, regional/local development agencies, universities, NGOs to provide an informed view on entrepreneurship in the region, regional/local development and CBC. Enterprises were selected based on the criteria of current/previous involvement in CBC. Interviews were semi-structured to ensure consistency across the 12 CSRs. The interviews were undertaken by the relevant local teams participating in the CBCED project. The data from the interviews was translated into English and entered in the qualitative software NVIVO for analysis. For this chapter, the analysis of qualitative data was based on predefined and emerging themes, combining inductive and deductive logic in the data analysis.

In the first section, a conceptual framework for assessing policies for cross-border entrepreneurship is proposed. The second section is focused on an analysis of the data from the case study regions, presenting a typology of border regions based on the policy framework for entrepreneurship development in border regions.

POLICIES AND GOVERNANCE FOR CROSS-BORDER ENTREPRENEURSHIP: A CONCEPTUAL FRAMEWORK

The process of EU enlargement is redrawing the political map of Europe. The status of many border regions is changing, as some highly external borders become soft if the neighbouring region is part of a new member state. In some cases, regions that were previously at the periphery of the EU's internal market are now closer to its economic core as spatial relationships change as a result of the enlargement process. These changes have potential implications for CBE, which may be stimulated by opportunities to access foreign markets. However, there are sectoral variations in these effects, which in the case of logistics may result in positive externalities across the entire cross-border region (Hijzen et al., 2008; Niebuhr and Stiller, 2004).

However, in the case of external borders of the EU this presents entrepreneurs and businesses with new sources of threats, as well as opportunities, which in turn have implications for regional development. For firms in the border regions, low domestic purchasing power can limit the scale and scope of domestic markets, encouraging those with growth ambitions to look abroad to identify new market opportunities. In such circumstances, subcontracting and other forms of collaborative arrangements with foreign firms offer certain advantages, compared with more independent strategies for penetrating foreign markets, since they can reduce market entry costs and barriers, with lower associated business risks.

One of the factors influencing the scope for cross-border economic activity in a border region is the trade policy which governs interaction across the region's borders. In this regard, the parameters have been changed as a result of EU enlargement, since EU membership means free trade with other member countries, and acceptance of common trade policy with regard to non-member countries. EU membership is accompanied by the adoption of the directives of the Single Internal Market that regulate the free movement of goods and services, the free movement of the population, and also the removal of barriers to doing business in the EU. This typically results in increased incentives to trade across the border because of reduced border impediments and higher market potential.

At the same time, supply-side inelasticities (for example labour immobility) and qualitative differences in the nature of demand (for example consumer tastes), can limit the stimulus to cross-border trade, suggesting that trade policies are not the only influence on the nature and pace of market integration. In the case of the EU's external borders, special emphasis has been given to the harmonization of technical standards, labour policies, competition and other regulatory policies (Vagac et al., 2001). However, these issues are more evident in countries that do not have harmonization of laws, standards, licensing and other regulations that concern trade, because, as discussed previously, many countries with external EU borders are intensifying their efforts on regulatory cooperation or harmonization. For example, Ukraine has often been involved in disputes with other EU members for incorrect implementation of the Agreements on Partnership and Cooperation with the EU, by applying higher excise tax rates to imported products than domestic products.

In some less developed countries, a lack of regulatory harmonization is often associated with rules being arbitrarily applied by customs officials and other public administrators in order to gain personal benefits. Bartlett (2009), for example, has observed that in the case of Macedonia, the institution of tariff quotas (according to which a limited amount of imports are allowed to enter the country duty free or with much reduced tariffs) is a recipe for the institutionalization of corruption, since both the selection of companies and the quota proportions are decided by public administrators. Similar problems have been reported in other Western Balkan countries such as Albania, Kosovo and Serbia. Although countries might commit themselves to regulatory cooperation, harmonization or mutual recognition agreements, the main obstacles to its achievement lie in the understanding of legal and market requirements. As a result, a special role is expected from institutions in facilitating information flows about these issues and, more specifically, institutional exchanges and cooperation on the specific requirements for specific sectors or product categories.

In this respect, institutional cooperation can be instrumental in facilitating cross-border partnerships between enterprises, contributing to enhanced competitiveness for participating regions. At the same time, the heterogeneity of border regions, in terms of relative levels of economic development, formal and social institutional structures, linguistics and ethnicity can all influence economic processes long after the demise of formal and physical barriers (Perkmann, 2005; 2003; Dimitrov et al., 2003; Huber, 2003; Paas, 2003), with potential implications for policy.

Whilst EU enlargement has influenced the opportunities/constraints on cross-border entrepreneurship, its development will be very much dependent on: (1) the wider social, economic, political and institutional context in these countries, as well as (2) policies which can directly affect cross-border entrepreneurship. We discuss each of them briefly in turn.

Policies with Indirect Effects on Cross-Border Entrepreneurship

SMEs interested in developing cross-border cooperation are affected by the wider policy environment, as well as by policies that are specifically targeted at supporting this type of enterprise–enterprise cooperation. In this context a wide range of government policies and actions at both the national and sub-national levels have a potential role to play. The policy environment may foster entrepreneurship by removing (unnecessary) obstacles to enterprise creation and establishing a facilitating environment for private business development (Smallbone and Welter, 2001), or it may discourage it if the opposite policy stance is taken. In terms of the range of policy areas which can impact on entrepreneurship, Smallbone and Welter (2001) identified six ways in which (national) government can affect the nature and pace of SME development. Whilst referring specifically to transition economies, the list is equally applicable to more mature market economies:

1. Macroeconomic policy, since the macroeconomic environment affects the willingness and ability of entrepreneurs (and potential entrepreneurs) to invest.
2. The costs of legislative compliance, which can fall disproportionately heavily on smaller enterprises.
3. Taxation policies, which includes the total tax burden but also the frequency with which changes are made to it and the methods used for collection.
4. The influence of government on the development of a variety of market institutions.
5. The influence of the government on the value placed on enterprise and entrepreneurship in society, which is affected by the curriculum and methods of teaching in the education system (at all levels), but also by the stance of government towards business and property ownership and the behaviour of politicians and government officials in their dealings with private firms.
6. Direct intervention, designed to assist small businesses to overcome size-related disadvantages.

Another relevant aspect of the wider policy environment is the effectiveness of the delivery methods used to implement SME support programmes. In order to effectively deliver policy measures targeted at encouraging and facilitating cross-border cooperation, effective business support agencies and networks in border regions are a prerequisite. Evidence from mature market economies demonstrates that the markets for information, advice, training and consultancy often do not work well as far as small firms are concerned (particularly start-ups) and market failure is a commonly used rationale for intervention. In many of the new member states in the EU, the market for business services is still in the early stages of development, which means that the support infrastructure is often not in place to promote and deliver CBC support or, for that matter, more generic business support policies effectively.

Policies Directly Affecting Cross-Border Entrepreneurship

Policies that are specifically targeted at encouraging and promoting cross-border enterprise-based cooperation typically focus on addressing the needs of firms interested in finding and working with foreign partners, in terms of information, creating a forum where contact with potential partners may be facilitated, and helping with any legal or regulatory issues that may apply in the cross-border market. From a public policy perspective, the aim should be to facilitate the development of mutually beneficial cooperative arrangements, appropriate to the needs of participating firms and their regions. This is an important emphasis because some forms of enterprise partnership can involve highly dependent and/or exploitative relationships.

In a situation of scarce public resources, there is a case for targeting interventions on growth-orientated firms that are seeking either to enter, or to increase, their penetration of foreign markets; and/or seeking to increasingly internationalize their supply base; and/or seeking to access new sources of capital, technology or know-how, whilst lacking the internal resources to achieve this independently. The case of Central and Eastern European countries has shown that firms in these countries have usually pursued a reactive strategy towards internationalization, with a majority cooperating with international firms from developed countries investing there, illustrated by the case of inward investing automotive firms in the Czech Republic and Slovakia. Although there are potential learning benefits for local SME suppliers, associated with such a strategy there are also risks to be managed, as these firms typically end up at the lower end of the supply chain (OECD, 2005). In this regard, international experience shows that business linkages and forms of cooperation have been widely used as a mechanism for small firms to remain competitive in the face of increasing globalization. In less developed and transition economies, supply linkages offer a possible route to accessing international markets, as well as potential access to finance, technology and specialized knowledge. For SMEs in more developed economies, cross-border entrepreneurship offers new market opportunities and/or lower cost production.

One of the key factors influencing the possibility for enterprises to develop cross-border cooperation and/or wider internationalization is access to information. General information on the potential benefits and risks of internationalization and/or business partnerships is necessary to raise awareness of the opportunities presented by different forms of CBC and to facilitate the informed decisions of entrepreneurs. At a general level, information provided through support agencies may include information concerning the regulatory and/or trade regimes of the destination countries. The most immediate and widespread technique used to stimulate SME partnerships is simply to bring potential SME partners together, by fostering business-to-business contacts. Information failures often mean that potentially good SME partners have no knowledge of each other's activities and potentials. One example of a scheme designed to address these issues is the UNIDO's long-running SPX programme, which facilitates contact between SMEs in emerging markets and those operating in mature market economies, where subcontracted components are a routine feature.

Programmes to improve the flow of information available to SMEs can also be found within EU countries. In Estonia, for example, Aktiva is the main online business information portal for both start-ups and established businesses, aiming to increase the availability of information to entrepreneurs/potential entrepreneurs in the country. It is a G2B gateway to information and services necessary for business activities and development. The website is designed as an easy-to-navigate directory of useful information and includes links supplied by a number of public authorities and NGOs. By 2005, 43 per cent of SMEs in Estonia already knew about it (COM, 2006). Although Aktiva is targeted at Estonian SMEs (and only available in Estonian and Russian), the format and concept is potentially transferable to the CBC context. This could contribute to enhancing information flows and act as a window of business opportunities for local enterprises. The concept could be developed further to involve the posting of lists of enterprises looking for foreign partners with their particular requirements, but it could also include a chat-room facility for initial exchanges of information between potential partners. This might be best facilitated through prominent 'regional' bodies, in order to increase its profile and potential coverage.

The development and effective implementation of policies to encourage and facilitate cross-border entrepreneurship is a challenging task, particularly in cases where regions are part of transition economies in which entrepreneurship development overall is modest and market-oriented institutional development limited. In the next sections we investigate empirically the policies affecting entrepreneurship and SME development in the case study regions, together with any active policies for the encouragement and support of cross-border entrepreneurship.

EMPIRICAL EVIDENCE ON POLICY INFLUENCES ON CROSS-BORDER ENTREPRENEURSHIP IN CBCED CASE STUDY REGIONS

The data analysis reveals that some policy issues are of concern across all CSRs. These are mainly associated with the peripheral position of these regions, both geographically and economically. One common theme running through the interviews with entrepreneurs and key informants in the CSRs is the difficulty of operating in peripheral border regions and an associated need for governments to offer special incentives to upgrade their equipment, technology, create new job positions and remain competitive. In some cases, particularly in the Greek and Bulgarian border regions, respondents emphasized the difficulties of operating a small business in a less developed region, suggesting that governments should support regional development by providing financial support for businesses. In other cases, the expressed need was for help in accessing financial support available within their regions, often associated with EU programmes; some requested help in completing funding application procedures, which they perceived as lengthy and bureaucratic. The disadvantages of being located in a peripheral location are also related to major difficulties which firms reported in finding adequate labour, because these regions are typically experiencing economic stagnation and population decline, with outmigration rates being particularly high among young people.

Labour shortages were consistently reported across the CSRs, although in some cases labour quality was emphasized, for example when enterprises had introduced new technology or equipment for which specialized skills are required. When solutions were offered, the expressed need was for improved vocational training. The regional business environment may also have implications for CBE. For example, inadequate infrastructure can constrain the exploitation of CBC potential in various sectors. In tourism, for example, it can result in potential cross-border assets being unexploited.

In some CSRs, entrepreneurs emphasized a need to improve regional marketing in order to attract inward investment. This draws attention to the need to adopt a strategic approach to regional development if the multiplier effects of inward investment are to be maximized through supply chain development. In south-east Estonia, for example, entrepreneurs feel that they are left alone to advertise their region, with enterprises operating in tourism the most affected by this. Other enterprises perceived a strong potential for cross-border cooperation, but needed help in finding the right business partners, suppliers and/or customers on the other side of the border. In some cases, the expressed need related specifically to support for participation in trade fairs and exhibitions, where firms can advertise their products and meet interested cooperation partners, such as in the case of one of the Estonian respondents:

> At the beginning, these fairs were probably quite necessary for our company – also a good way of promoting our products. In Russia I think such fairs are even more efficient than in some other countries, because they bring together so many people from all over Russia who all share an interest towards Finnish products. Visiting and finding all these clients would without such an event be impossible, so in theory if the fair is well organized it is a wonderful way to present your products to an interested audience without spending too much money or time in the promotion. (South Karelia Enterprise 14)

Based on our broad view of what constitutes policy for CBE, three types of regions were identified empirically: (1) regions where public policy is constraining rather than enabling; (2) regions where public policy is largely enabling; and (3) regions where public policy is potentially enabling. We discuss each in turn.

Public Policy is Constraining rather than Enabling

Regions in this group are 'hard', external border regions of the EU where the cross-border partner region is in Russia (South Karelia in Finland; Ida Viru and South East Estonia); Belarus (Biała Podlaska in Poland); or Macedonia (Florina in Greece and Kyustendil in Bulgaria). In such cases, the negative effects are associated with the hard border restrictions and a variety of institutional deficiencies (some specific to cross-border activity, while others are more generally associated with the environment for entrepreneurship), which act as a disincentive for CBE, as outlined below.

Political relations between national governments
Political relationships between national governments can have important implications for CBE, because of their impact on the ease or difficulty

involved in moving goods and/or people across borders. This particularly applies in the case of hard borders, because of the effect of political tension on customs and visa procedures. Such influences are less important in the case of soft borders, although historical relations between countries can affect the stance that governments take towards the active promotion of CBC. Entrepreneurs in both Estonia and Finland perceive Russia as a problematic partner, because of continual changes in its policies and/or regulations, which increases the unpredictability involved in cooperating with enterprises across the border. This affects the extent to which entrepreneurs can rely on cross-border business as a source of revenue and/or resources, which is reflected in the words of one of the Finnish entrepreneurs interviewed:

> The most important thing that I have learnt from doing business across the border is that it is best not to make too extensive plans based on previous agreements – what is agreed today, may not be a valid agreement the next day. There is always a certain amount of unpredictability when doing business with Russian officials and partners. (South Karelia Enterprise 8)

On the other hand, Estonian entrepreneurs recognize that it is beneficial for both parties to cooperate. Those that have long-term partners or personal contacts in Russia try to adapt themselves to this situation.

> Especially in the territories bordering South-Estonia one can sense the negative influence of Russian propaganda for Estonia (e.g. not to buy Estonian goods, sell more expensively to them, etc.). However, those with good personal contacts and long-term cooperation in Russia cope very well and have no remarkable problems. (South East Estonia Household 10)

Political relations between countries can be a major barrier to CBE because, unlike some other barriers, entrepreneurs feel unable to exert any influence over it:

> Some projects have come to a halt as Russian investors don't want to invest just due to the political situation. It's necessary to work for improving the bilateral relations between the countries as otherwise CBC may come to a halt, because the prices in Russia increase all the time and the risk is very big. These factors may become critical, when it's not worth any more to take so big risks. (Ida Viru Enterprise 10)

Political problems have also affected the environment for CBE in the Florina/Pella CSR on the border of Greece and Macedonia, reflected in a long-standing dispute about the name of Macedonia. The Greek embargo at the beginning of the 1990s acted as a negative influence on trade development in this region. Tensions about the name still exist and have also contributed to a reluctant attitude towards CBE on the part of many entrepreneurs. The dispute has practical implications for bringing goods in and out of the country, since invoices which include the name 'Macedonia' are not accepted in Greece, and invoices that refer to FYRoM are unacceptable in Macedonia. At the same time, these political problems do not prevent entrepreneurs from seeking cross-border business opportunities, which is illustrated by the following quote:

> The most important barrier of course is the 'naming issue'. Exporting from the FYRoM to Greece is extremely difficult even though they can offer us some cheap and high quality products, such as peppers, grapes for wine and granites, but the local traders cannot import them as long as 'Macedonia' is written on the invoices. These traders would like to solve this issue and to tell you the truth they don't care about the name; all they want to do is business and profits. We are the only ones in the world calling that country as the FYRoM. (Florina Enterprise 18)

Business owners in the CSRs bordering Russia and Macedonia urge their governments to find ways to resolve the political tensions between countries because they are jeopardizing the development of their business activities. Two specific issues have been identified from the interviews with entrepreneurs: first, governments are distant from the concerns of entrepreneurs in border regions and secondly, entrepreneurs seeking business opportunities across the border place economic factors above history and politics.

Visa regimes
The visa regime can also have a direct influence on the ease or difficulty of CBE. Reported difficulties mainly refer to extended bureaucratic procedures. Examples reported included cases where cooperation partners were unable to attend a meeting on the other side of the border due to delays in issuing visas. Such examples were reported in Florina Enterprise 13; Enterprise 15; Kyustendil Enterprise 5; Enterprise 6; Enterprise 16 and South Karelia Enterprise 1; Enterprise 12, Enterprise 21. Visas can also be expensive (Ida Viru Enterprise 2; Kyustendil Enterprise 1; Enterprise 5; Enterprise 19; South Karelia Enterprise 8; South East Estonia Enterprise 14). In addition, sometimes entrepreneurs are only granted limited entry visas, which means more trips to an embassy, with more associated expenses. These barriers were also widely mentioned in Kyustendil because of the new requirements for Macedonians, following Bulgaria's entry to the

EU. The new visa regime has negatively affected many Bulgarian entrepreneurs that have (potential) partners in Macedonia, despite the Zone 50 initiative, which had recently allowed citizens within the 50 kilometre zone to benefit from one year multiple entry visas.

> EU enlargement has negative effect because of the visa regime. It may be said that 'Bulgaria integrates with EU but it becomes estranged from her Balkan neighbours'. The intensity of cross-border activity has dropped off. According to expectation this activity will be stopped during the next one to two years. (Kyustendil Household 5)

In the Estonian and Finnish border regions with Russia, the problem in obtaining visas was also perceived as a negative influence on CBC, particularly by enterprises operating in tour services and/or accommodation provision. Such enterprises report difficulties because visas are not only expensive and subject to frequent price changes, but the risk of not getting a visa on time can have a direct impact on their businesses. These problems are best illustrated in the words of an entrepreneur from South Karelia:

> What has really hindered our business is the current practice with visas: when the travel agencies book a room with us, there is always a risk that the person will not receive a visa and this is of course a problem for everyone. (South Karelia Enterprise 21)

However, in practice, few businesses interviewed stopped their cross-border activities because of these problems. They usually tried to find ways to circumvent visa-related problems as illustrated below:

> I have a Bulgarian passport, so I don't have visa problem. I have it two years. It is easier to go to Greece with Bulgarian passport. I have it only because of business. (Florina Household 18, Macedonian household)

> Till now, I used to get multi-visa, meaning one year-limitless entries-visa. Some years ago, I used to work for a Greek company here, MIHOS, for eight years. Recently I wasn't able to get visa. This created lots of problems to my business. Now, I think I am able to get a Bulgarian passport. This will be very good for my job, as Bulgaria is in the EU. It is very easy, you just have to go to the Bulgarian Embassy and sign a paper where you say 'I feel Bulgarian'. (Florina Household 21, Macedonian household)

> In order to solve this problem and for some other personal benefits he is currently taking the necessary actions to procure himself a Bulgarian citizenship. (Kyustendil Household 2, Macedonian household)

Those business owners that had stopped CBC tended to be either those trading in, or transporting, perishable goods that are adversely affected by long waiting hours at the border, or businesses that found it hard to deal with the corruption of custom officers. Nevertheless, we can conclude that the intensity of CBC would be likely to be higher if such constraints were absent. These are all issues under the domain of central governments that cannot be solved at the local level.

Customs procedures
In the hard external border regions of the EU, entrepreneurs share negative experiences with customs procedures. Entrepreneurs operating in the CSRs bordering Belarus, Russia and Macedonia commonly reported that the interpretation and implementation of regulations is often dependent on the customs officers' mood.

> The border is the barrier. Uncertainty about the possibility of its crossing is tiring. Many people give up the opportunity to visit Belarus as they do not know how they will be treated at the border and how long it will take to cross it. This is a big concern in cross-border contact. (Key informant, Biała Podlaska)

The discretionary use of power by customs officers is associated with high reported levels of corruption, appearing ubiquitous in the borders of the CSRs bordering Russia, Macedonia and Belarus. However, interviews with respondents suggest some cultural differences in attitudes towards this, with entrepreneurs in Finland and Germany appearing to be the most uncomfortable when faced with a need to offer bribes:

> The customs (Russian) is in a league of its own when it comes to corruption – they always expect bribes, and it is almost impossible to get anything done without making some sort of payments to the right officials… . Prior to this they had kindly informed us that by visiting them and making certain payments to the persons handling this matter would get things moving, but we have refused this request. (South Karelia Enterprise 18)

Another closely related issue refers to the highly bureaucratic procedures at the (hard) borders. These are influenced by the rapid changes in laws and regulations, by the lack of information available and a lack of clear responsibilities as to who is going to implement what. Since these situations are the norm rather than the exception in Russia, many problems are created at the borders since entrepreneurs are typically not informed about changes in legislation. As one Finnish entrepreneur states:

> The Russian customs are not very good at informing people about the changes in the tariffs and e.g. changes in the codes for our products. And what is quite problematic is that they do not even distribute the information among the customs officials, and often the new regulations and practices are backdated, so we should have adopted the new practices a month before we even heard of these changes. So suddenly we are indebted to the customs, and none of our trucks are allowed to cross the border until we have paid our 'debts'. The customs is such an institution that it is absolutely impossible for us to predict their activities and there is no way of preparing ourselves for the changes to come. (South Karelia Enterprise 14)

Long border delays as a result of a lack of capacity on the part of customs officials to process goods quickly are also problematic, especially at the Estonian–Russian border. They have been further intensified following a decision by the Russian government to check every Estonian lorry crossing the border. Since this decision was not accompanied by any increase in the number of custom officers, it led to long waiting hours and frustration amongst those that travel to Russia. This situation has been exacerbated by the political relations between the two neighbouring countries.

> At some point crossing the border was problematic, the transport firms didn't want to go, and the queues were long. Last week I talked to a truck driver. He goes to St. Petersburg, making a weekly cycle; in Estonia they upload for 40 minutes, but in Russia they download for 3 days, and then there is unknown number of days on the border. So there are problems with crossing the border. (South East Estonia Enterprise 8)

Despite the need to be at the border for long hours with poor facilities, entrepreneurs also face the risk of compromising their reliability as partners because they cannot fulfil delivery obligations with their partners on the other side of the border. Tour operators face the additional risk of not being able to offer value for money to their customers. For example, a company that organizes tours to Vyborg (in Russia) from South Karelia states:

> The border formalities can be very slow at times. We have estimated that even when the service is at its best, we have to reserve one hour for the border formalities in Vyborg. This optimal situation leaves the tourists with three hours to spend in Vyborg and that is enough. But unfortunately at times our passengers end up spending up to four hours in the customs and then they have to come back to the boat without visiting Vyborg! They pay 30 euros for the Russian visa and what do they get in return? They get to sit on the boat, sit on the bus and spend four hours in the Russian customs. (South Karelia Enterprise 8)

The obvious solution in such cases would seem to be the opening of new border crossing points as many entrepreneurs, especially in Estonia or in

Greece border regions, urge. The negative effects of national policies and actions have often jeopardized the positive outcomes that individual institutional cross-border initiatives may have produced. For example, in border regions in Estonia entrepreneurs have received assistance in the past under EU-funded programmes, such as SAPARD, currently INTERREG, under the European Regional Development Fund and Cohesion Fund, as the following quotation illustrates:

> The firm has received investment support, firstly through SAPARD programme (pre-accession measure) and later from EU structural assistance. It was very positive and came at a right point of time as it allowed investing in necessary things like cooling systems, warehouses and hygiene. It's a pity that there is no more such support for manufacturing industry. (South East Estonia Enterprise 7)

At the same time, government is not a determining influence on entrepreneurship development, since the drive, commitment and ability of some entrepreneurs to identify and exploit business opportunities leads to profitable outcomes, although these may be more costly to exploit than they need to be.

Public Policy is Largely Enabling

These CSRs are regions with 'soft' borders with another EU member state, such as Tornio in Finland (with Sweden); Gorlitz in Germany (with Poland); Hochfranken in Germany (with the Czech Republic); and in Greece, Serres (with Bulgaria) where a well-developed business support infrastructure is demonstrating some engagement with entrepreneurs and offering support to their cross-border activities. The Finnish and German regions appear to have the best developed business support infrastructure at the local level, with a number of established organizations that support business development. The two Finnish regions, Hochfranken in Germany and Serres in Greece reported the highest use of generic business support. Enterprises in the Greek regions appear to have benefited from the provisions of the Development Law (2004), which subsidizes business development in the less-developed areas of Greece, with grants offered for investment in equipment and/or in the creation of new workplaces. Applications under this law have also created demand for external support from enterprises related to the preparation of all the necessary documents. Whilst this law does not directly support cross-border activities, by assisting firms to become more competitive, it can indirectly affect decisions to undertake, or further develop cross-border activities.

These regions include the best examples of support organizations focusing on cross-border activities, such as the Cross-Border Chamber and Information Centre in Tornio–Haparanda. This organization supports interaction between the Swedish and Finnish Chambers of Commerce in promoting networking between enterprises to help them expand their markets and increase cross-border entrepreneurial activities. It also provides information to promote contacts, cooperation, trade and the benefits of knowledge exchange. In the Görlitz–Zgorzelec cross-border region, cooperation between chambers of commerce on both sides of the border includes helping members find appropriate business contacts and obtaining accurate information on the legislative issues faced when doing business on the other side of the border. However, the reported use of such support by enterprises was low in all CSRs, with only Görlitz containing more than a handful of firms receiving such support (and this was specifically focused on raising awareness). This requires chambers of commerce to keep in regular contact with each other about practical aspects of doing business in their respective territories. These events have concentrated first, on providing information about the regulations that firms would need to comply with across the border; and secondly, on helping to make contacts with businesses on the other side of the border and/or with consulting companies offering more specific help. The latter typically included assistance to firms in participating in business fairs, where contact with businesses operating in the same or complementary activities can be made, as well as help in obtaining information related to doing business in the neighbouring country.

Public Policy is Potentially Enabling

Regions in this group have soft borders but involve new members of the EU and countries with a weakly developed business support infrastructure. Countries that have recently joined the EU have experienced changes in the regulatory environment as a result of accession to the EU, resulting from a need to harmonize national with EU legislation. These changes have often been accompanied by increased levels of bureaucracy in public institutions. In some cases, entrepreneurs emphasize the bureaucracy and corruption in foreign institutions; in other cases, in institutions in their own country. In their endeavours to get all the necessary documentation for their cross-border activities, entrepreneurs can spend several months waiting for all procedures to be completed and obtaining all permits and licences.

> People have to be 'very friendly' to Czech institutions 'then there will be no problems'. However, the processing of the documents for the activities in the

Czech Republic took nine months at the consulate in Dresden (Germany) and was very complex, as I had to appear always in person. (Hochfranken Enterprise 17)

Polish authorities constitute another obstacle on the institutional level, which are partly even more bureaucratic than German ones. (Görlitz Enterprise 2)

A tax consultant's name recognition plays an important role with institutions and authorities in the Czech Republic. The latter are extremely laboured, so that the tax consultant even visited the authority in person in order to accelerate the proceedings. It is nearly futile for a German to deal with the authorities. (Hochfranken Enterprise 12)

Whilst border controls are no longer a major barrier to increasing CBE in these regions, the business support infrastructure is insufficiently developed to offer entrepreneurs effective support for it. The burden that customs procedures can place on cross-border activities is evident in the accounts of those entrepreneurs that have experienced a change in the status of their border (that is, from soft to hard or vice versa). In CSRs where borders had changed from hard to soft, entrepreneurs referred to the enabling influence of the smoothing of customs procedures (such as the removal of double tariffs and VAT) on cross-border business activity. This applied in the case of Zgorzelec in Poland (bordering Germany) and Petrich in Bulgaria (bordering Greece).

The nature and extent of the existing business support infrastructure varies between CSRs although there are common features. Business support institutions include chambers of commerce, together with other business associations and business support centres providing different types and levels of support. The funding base of these organizations also varies, with implications for the nature and extent of the support provided, as well as for their sustainability. Some rely mainly on membership fees; some are in receipt of core funding from public sources (such as those that are part of national business support networks), whilst in others the funding is project based. This particularly applies in some of the poorer CSRs, such as Serres (Greece) and those in new EU member states, where EU funding has been used to support organizations and initiatives on a project basis. Some of the support provided is generic; some is more specialized (for example business incubators); some is available to all firms; whilst other support is targeted at specific types of enterprises or those with specific behavioural characteristics (for example innovation centres). When entrepreneurs in the Bulgarian CSRs were asked about their use of business support, they commonly referred to EU-funded programmes, such as SAPARD, PHARE or INTERREG. For example, in the border region of Petrich in Bulgaria, the

PHARE and SAPARD programmes (which are both pre-accession measures) were mentioned in relation to financing investment in technology,
equipment and business development in general. At the same time, in some
regions, entrepreneurs report a policy implementation gap:

> various measures are taken on national level for support of SMEs, but most of
> them are only 'on paper' and do not work in practice. Small firms are unprivi-
> leged in comparison to the bigger ones regarding access to information for
> existing programmes and projects for business support. Besides resources from
> EU projects do not reach the small firms because of lack of free mediums of
> circulation necessary for co-financing. (Petrich Enterprise 19)

Some of the variation between CSRs reflects differences between countries
with respect to the development of SME or entrepreneurship policies,
whereas in other cases, CSRs have less developed business support infrastructures than other parts of the same country. This is particularly the case
in the Bulgarian, Estonian and Polish regions, especially South East Estonia
and Biała Podlaska in Poland. In the Petrich CSR (Bulgaria), the local
chamber of commerce only recently started its operations, and was reported
to be underfinanced and understaffed. In such cases, it is difficult for
chambers of commerce to play an active role in finding opportunities for
CBE which will positively affect business development in the region.

CONCLUSIONS

The chapter set out to assess the current role of public policy in relation to
the development of cross-border entrepreneurship in EU border regions, on
the basis that cross-border cooperation involving enterprises represents a
potential tool for regional development in regions that are typically disadvantaged by their peripherality. The empirical evidence shows that in
many regions, entrepreneurs develop forms of cross-border cooperation
(for example subcontracting, use of relatively cheap labour from the other
side of the border) without policy support and, in some cases, despite
barriers resulting from the wider policy environment. However, in such
circumstances, the extent of such cooperation is limited and its contribution
to regional development typically underfulfilled.

The findings overall support the need to take a broadly based view of
what constitutes policy. Policies to promote CBE are unlikely to be successful unless the wider policy environment for entrepreneurship is positive. As
a consequence, policies to support CBE need to be embedded within wider
regional development programmes promoting entrepreneurship. Whilst
specific policies (such as partner search facilities and 'meet the buyer'

events) can undoubtedly help to promote CBE, their take-up is likely to be affected by the credibility of the organization and its effectiveness in delivering the support to local businesses and its integration with 'mainstream' business support. In this context, it is perhaps not surprising that, in general, public policy with respect to CBE tends to reflect the policy of the state towards the entrepreneurship and economic development more generally.

The reported use of business support targeted at cross-border cooperation by enterprises in CSRs was low in all regions, with only Görlitz containing more than a handful of firms receiving such support. This may be somewhat surprising in view of the fact that all enterprises interviewed were either involved in CBE or had experience of it in the past. However, in practice, this reflects low take-up of generic business support services, with only a few firms in each region reporting some use of it. The exceptions were in the two Finnish regions, Hochfranken in Germany, and Serres in Greece.

Improved information provision appears also to be a priority, particularly with respect to raising awareness about the potential benefits of cross-border cooperation. This is especially important for border regions in the new EU member countries where there is a need for businesses to be acquainted with EU programmes and other forms of support that are available. Another issue relates to the continuity and sustainability of support provided, which can be a problem when reliance is placed on short-term project funding.

Reported labour shortages emphasize the need to improve the educational and economic infrastructure in these peripheral regions, as part of a strategy of retaining more young people. Complementary measures in the short term might include agreements between local authorities to facilitate labour movement across the border. Improved vocational training is another priority to provide the workforce with the skills and competences demanded by the regions' enterprises. Other issues identified included a lack of investment in the region, low purchasing power and a strong perception of being peripheral. This emphasizes the need for a comprehensive and integrated approach to regional development policy to enable entrepreneurship to increase its contribution to the development of these peripheral regions.

Interventions designed to promote CBE as a regional development tool can be frustrated by changes in border regulations and/or procedures which increase the time and cost involved in cross-border activities. This may be viewed as a specific example of a wider policy issue concerning the effects of government regulations on business behaviour and performance, emphasizing that the costs of compliance can fall disproportionately on small businesses. As far as CBE is concerned, the regulatory framework includes customs procedures and visa regimes, which can both be affected by political relations between national governments, as well as by the behaviour of officials at a local level. Although the study included some entrepreneurs who have decided to discontinue cross-border business activities as a result, for others it is an aspect of their external environment they are forced to adapt to, perhaps because of limited alternative opportunities. It would be helpful if cross-border projects that seek to promote cross-border business activity could include representatives of border authorities as part of an attempt to remove unnecessary barriers to cross-border movement of goods and people. Improving the transport and communications infrastructure can also be a prerequisite for facilitating the development of productive cross-border enterprise activity.

REFERENCES

Bartlett, W. (2009), 'Regional integration and free-trade agreements in the Balkans: opportunities, obstacles, and policy issues', *Economic Change and Restructuring*, **42**(1), 25–46.

COM (2006), *European Charter for Small Enterprises: 2006 Good Practice Selection*, Brussels: Commision of the European Communities.

Dimitrov, M., G. Petrakos, S. Totev and M. Tsiapa (2003), 'Cross-border cooperation in south-eastern Europe: the enterprises' point of view', *Eastern European Economics*, **41**(6), 5–25.

Hijzen, A., H. Gorg and M. Manchin (2008), 'Cross-border mergers and acquisitions and the role of trade costs', *European Economic Review*, **52**(5), 849–66.

Huber, P.B. (2003), 'On the determinants of cross-border cooperation of Austrian firms with Central and Eastern European partners', *Regional Studies*, **37**(9), 947–55.

Niebuhr, A. and S. Stiller (2004), 'Integration effects in border regions – a survey of economic theory and empirical studies', *Review of Regional Research*, **24**, 3–21.

OECD (2005), *Building Competitive Regions: Strategies and Governance*, Paris: OECD.

Paas, T. (2003), 'Regional integration and international trade in the context of EU eastward enlargement', Hamburg Institute of International Economics Discussion Paper, Hamburg: Institute of International Economics.

Perkmann, M. (2003) 'Cross-border regions in Europe: significance and drivers of regional cross-border cooperation', *European Urban and Regional Planning Studies*, **10**(2), 153–71.

Perkmann, M. (2005), 'Cross-border cooperation as policy entrepreneurship: explaining the variable success of European cross-border regions', CSGR Working Paper no. 166/05, Warwick.

Smallbone, D. and F. Welter (2001), 'The distinctiveness of entrepreneurship in transition economies', *Small Business Economics*, **16**(4), 249–62.

UNCTAD (2006), 'Developing business linkages', Trade and Development Board, Commission on Enterprise, Business Facilitation and Development, Geneva: UNCTAD.

Vagac, L., V. Palenik, V. Kvetan and K. Krivanska (2001), 'Trade effects of EU integration: the case of the Slovak Republic', PHARE ACE Research Project P97-8134-R: Enlarging the EU: The Trade Balance Effects.

Weaver, M. (2000) 'Strategic alliances as vehicles for international growth', in D. Sexton and A. Lundström (eds), *Handbook of Entrepreneurship*, Oxford and Malden, MA: Blackwell, pp. 387–407.

Index

Abbreviations used in the index:
CBC – cross-border cooperation
CBE – cross-border entrepreneurship